DEAD OR ALIVE

THE CHOICE IS YOURS

THE DEFINITIVE SELF-PROTECTION HANDBOOK

GEOFF THOMPSON

summersdale

Reprinted 2005, 2006, 2008

Summersdale Publishers
46 West Street
Chichester
West Sussex
PO19 1RP
UK
www.summersdale.com
www.geoffthompson.com

Printed and bound in Great Britain.

ISBN 978 1 84024 279 9

Photos by John Leape

IMPORTANT NOTE:
The author and the publishers cannot accept any responsibility for and prosecutions or proceedings brought or instituted against any person or body as a result of the use or misuse of any techniques described in this book or any loss, injury or damage caused thereby.

Also by Geoff Thompson:

Watch My Back
Red Mist
The Elephant and the Twig
The Great Escape
A Book for the Seriously Stressed
Fear – The Friend of Exceptional People
The Throws & Take-downs of Judo
The Throws & Take-downs of Sombo
The Throws & Take-downs of Free-Style Wrestling
The Throws & Take-downs of Greco-Roman Wrestling
Animal Day
The Art of Fighting Without Fighting
The Fence
The Pavement Arena
Real Head, Knees and Elbows
Real Grappling
Real Kicking
Real Punching
Three Second Fighter
Weight Training for the Martial Artist
Pins: the Bedrock
The Escapes
Chokes and Strangles
Fighting from your Back
Fighting from your Knees
Arm Bars and Joint Locks

About the Author

Geoff Thompson claims that his biological birthdate is 1960, though his hair-line goes right back to the First World War.

He has worked as a floor sweeper, chemical worker, pizza maker, road digger, hod carrier, martial-arts instructor, bricklayer, picture seller, delivery driver and nightclub bouncer before giving up 'proper work' in 1992 to write full time.

He is now a bestselling author, BAFTA-nominated screenwriter, magazine columnist, playwright and novelist.

He lives in Coventry with his wife Sharon, and holds a 6th dan in Japanese karate, 1st dan in Judo and was voted the number one self-defence author in the world by *Black Belt Magazine* USA.

FOR MY WIFE SHARON, AS ALWAYS,
WITH ALL MY LOVE.
TO MUM AND DAD, I LOVE YOU VERY MUCH.
THANKS FOR 44 YEARS OF TOTAL SUPPORT
AND ENCOURAGEMENT.

'Thus, those that win one hundred triumphs in one hundred conflicts,
Do not have supreme skill.
Those who have supreme skill,
Use strategy to bend others without coming to conflict.
The ideal strategy, therefore, is to thwart a plan.
The next best is to thwart a negotiation.
The next best is to thwart a strategy.
The inferior politic is to attack a fortified area.
Attacking a fortified area is an art of last resort;
Those skilled in executing a strategy,
Bend the strategy of others without conflict;
Uproot the fortifications of others with out attacking;
Absorb the organisations of others without prolonged operations.'

Sun Tzu
The Art of War

Contents

Author Introduction

Dead or Alive has been a very successful book for me. Over the years I have received favorable and consistent sales and excellent feedback. It first came out in 1996 (where did all that time go?) and the publishers thought that it might be a good time to update the book – new cover, new author foreword and any amendments to material that may have dated. 'No problem,' I said. 'I'm right onto it.'

I expected that after reading through the (near) 90,000 words there would be a lot of work involved; after all, a lot can change in eight years. I was wrong. I was pleased (and also disappointed) to see that there was very little that needed to change and absolutely nothing to update, just a bit of polishing and some new illustrations. Pleased because (being frank) it was less work for me (and being very busy that is always a bonus) and disappointed because, well, things should have changed, they should need updating. Shouldn't they? They should have gotten better at the very least. I was doubly disappointed that they hadn't. In fact, looking at the current crime statistics, they have gotten worse instead of better. This book – probably the only one of its kind in the world today – is more needed now than it was in 1996 when I first released it. I don't know why I was surprised by the increase of societal violence; it is after all plastered all over the papers and on the news every day of the week. It is totally normal now to read about armed robberies, killings, rapes and gang attacks in the very next street to your own.

It would appear that what is happening globally is being reflected locally. There is real and immediate danger out there and we need to be aware of it, we need to make our loved ones and friends and neighbours aware of it.

There is a crude urgency in the writing style of this book that I have deliberately not changed in the new edition. When I wrote it way back then I was still very much living and breathing self-protection. I was passionate, perhaps over-zealous in the delivery. Even though I am eight years more practised as a writer and perhaps better able to deliver the same words more objectively, I decided not to. I like the urgency. I think that the zealous undercurrent is entirely appropriate in a subject so life and death.

So here it is. Dead or alive. Your choice. The information in this book is as hot as it is current and – if employed – it might prove life saving.

Geoff Thompson 2004

Introduction

To find a book about real self-protection is a rare event for me. The emphasis is on real. Over the years I have seen a succession of self-defence books written by people whose only experience of violent conflict has patently been in the arena of their own safe imagination. They write, evidently, from a perspective of never having been there themselves, and garnish unreal scenarios with unworkable physical techniques.

Good self-protection is first and foremost about avoiding violent situations, but should the worst arise it is equally about coping with instant fear and shock. The best techniques in the world are of little value if a victim, through fear, is frozen into immobility. A writer on self-protection who is unable to portray these feelings and emotions so as to imbue people with a true sense about what conflict will do to them on an emotional level has not been there and his teachings are, as a consequence, meaningless.

Geoff Thompson does not fall into this category. Having successfully survived hundreds of violent confrontations in the front line of security work he knows and conveys these emotions in print to allow you, the reader, to experience safely the reality of violent conflict. The physical teachings, whilst important, are secondary. In this book you will read about fear control, adrenalin switches and the psychology of conflict. You will read about awareness and the avoidance of threat and, uniquely, you will read interviews with muggers to hear how they ply their trade of violence. From the other side of the coin there are interviews with the victims of such violence, but most importantly you will be hearing from a man who has not only been there, but who can portray with honesty the whole range of fear and emotions that need to be kept in control to survive confrontations.

Don't expect a magic photo sequence of techniques which you can adopt as the grail of self-protection; expect to find the harsh reality of violence and how to keep control of oneself and one's emotions to be able to function on a physical level.

I commend this book to anyone who is genuinely concerned about their own self-protection.

Peter Consterdine

8th Dan Karate, ex Great Britain and England Karate International Joint Chief Instructor British Combat Association (the principal British self-defence organisation) Professional Bodyguard and Security Advisor. Author of The Modern Bodyguard.

Prologue

Whenever I hear the words 'self-defence' my alarm bells start ringing and I think back to the Bruce Lee era when there were so many unqualified, so-called martial artists opening bogus clubs all over the country. 'Come and do a six week course and learn to defend yourself.'

The realities, of course, are very different. How very refreshing it was to receive such a realistic and effective approach to self-defence written by Geoff Thompson, a Shotokan Karate third dan. His first-hand experiences in working at nightclubs have enabled him to adapt his Karate skills to more realistic self-defence situations.

His philosophy is that if you can walk away from a situation you should do so, but if you are cornered you should be prepared, in all aspects, to defend yourself, and being prepared is being well-practised!

This book will give you every aspect of self-defence that you will need, what you have to do now is put them into practice. This is the best self-defence book that I have ever read and I am sure that it will be a great help to you in the future.

Neil Adams MBE
Former World Judo Champion and Olympic silver medallist

Foreword

What can you say about a man born 44 years ago in Coventry, England, who leaves school with no academic qualifications worth a light, then hits the streets to become a doorman – the bouncer?

What does one say about this man who has since written nine bestselling books, is an internationally recognised authority on the subject of self-protection; contributes to just about every worthwhile journal on the subject, and is now becoming a household name on television?

The answers are simple. Geoff Thompson knows exactly what he is talking about because he's been there. He has lived with violence.

Dead or Alive, therefore, has to be the definitive work on self-protection for all of us. Like it or not, violence is with us to stay, and it could strike you down now.

As someone who works with the most extreme form of violence on a daily basis (and you cannot beat a serial killer or mass-murderer on that score) I have, not unlike many of my colleagues, always searched for the reasons behind homicidal violence; and by God, isn't society spoon-fed such a mish-mash of excuses in defence of the offender who commits a violent crime? Alcohol abuse; potty-training abuse; genetic disorders; social abuse; the catch-all of a bump on the head as a child; along with just about every half-baked excuse that an inventive psychiatrist, social worker or lawyer can invent. So we must ask ourselves: are we not living in a world where lead balls bounce, elephants fly and fairies reign supreme?

And, have we somehow forgotten that our streets are infested with human scum who actually enjoy smashing their bullying fists into the faces of our children, wives and the elderly?

If one has a problem with any of this we should cast our eyes across to America which is undoubtedly the most violent society in this modern world. If they have not learned a single lesson on how to prevent, control and eradicate much of that behaviour, then we might assume that they would have some authority in place to professionally advise how to protect against what is recognised as a social epidemic of truly monstrous proportions. They kill British tourists there, you know.

So what can you say about Geoff Thompson, who is about to go down big in the States?

Let's not kid ourselves; we don't live in a Utopian world where the idea of a crime-free society is even a slight prospect for the future, and as this spinning planet becomes ever more populated, crime will undoubtedly increase, and there can be no cure. So don't let's kid ourselves on something different.

Dead or Alive, gives us a choice, and it was an honour for me to be asked to write the foreword to this amazing, if not disturbing, book. Read it, and if nothing else you might see the precursors of human aggression and violence. It could help protect you, or a loved one, from assault, robbery, sexual assault and murder. Just

11

flip through the pages and say, 'It won't happen to me'. Well, the choice is yours.

What draws me to this book is Geoff's natural talent in understanding the behavioural characteristics of an offender prior to an attack – the body language as it were. He could certainly teach an anthropologist a thing or two. Lectures from these academics are all very well, but when the only form of antisocial behaviour inflicted upon them has been a book thrown at them by a mischievous student, knowing why a monkey scratches under its arm pits is of little benefit when coming face to face with a distant cousin, the skinhead, who has the desire to remodel one's face.

Taken into a more serious context, we should all know about 'eye contact', 'love signals' and body language when it boils down to courtship and sex, but we don't have a clue about body-talk when it precedes violence in whatever form it may arrive.

It has now been established within the modus operandi of hundreds of violent offenders, specifically serial killers, that they don't simply begin their criminal careers by killing. In the overwhelming majority of cases, these social misfits graduate from petty theft to minor sexual assaults on to rape, then sexual homicide. This type kills for some type of profit, that being his selfish desire for sex, and in many cases murder will surely follow. It is where in that criminal's career he draws your number from his hat that counts. That lottery could give you a punch on the nose or a hole in the ground. The choice is his, not yours.

Looking back with the great gift of hindsight tucked neatly in to my pocket, I have studied many of my own subjects, and after speaking with law enforcement officers and psychologists throughout the western world, there is no doubt that the victims of these malefactors could have done so much more to protect themselves from the wolf in sheep's clothing. I am not suggesting that if they had read this book they may not have been robbed, raped or killed. I am saying if they had been more aware, say 'streetwise', they might be alive today.

Perhaps the most fascinating aspect of Geoff's work can be better illustrated when comparing this book to what might be called the bible on sexual homicide written by the FBI. It is not a widely recognised text for the public at large, and I immediately saw parallels between *Dead or Alive* and the FBI's study of violent criminal behaviour; specifically, confrontation.

When one considers that the FBI has ultimate experience and the world's foremost authorities on hand to compile such a book, and Geoff didn't know it existed until I gave him my copy, then I'd say they could find a good friend in Mr. Thompson, because he's written this book using common sense and personal experience allied with a tremendous insight which puts much current and empirical thinking in the shade.

However, before I pin too many stars to Geoff's chest, I have to tell you I am not saying that every man or woman would have the mental ability or wherewithal to stab a finger in the eye of a potential rapist. I'd even be somewhat hard pushed to knee someone in what is commonly called the 'wedding tackle'. But we all should have the savvy to close the car window or cross the street when we smell trouble in the air. If you can't sense a confrontation of sorts, then when a ring-covered, tattooed set of knuckles comes travelling in your direction at the speed of sound, don't blame anyone else but yourself – perhaps the thug as well – for missing the obvious. He wasn't crossing the road with a bicycle chain in his hand to ask for a helping hand, well, was he?

So, I am very happy to endorse Geoff Thompson, this book, and all of his work. My only secret fear is that he leaves his valuable expertise at that; for society will be worse off if he does. We all have much to learn from the mind of this former bouncer. Of that I am sure.

And, I suppose, it falls to me with some form of thanks, and tongue in cheek, to recognise the roundabout way the few offenders have assisted Geoff with his research for this book. The muggers, rapists and killers will also retrospectively commend the text, and American killers will agree to almost anything prior to 15 seconds of 2,500 volts.

Ever mindful of being accused of scaremongering, I say BUY THIS BOOK. Don't wait to read it in the doctor's waiting room or at the hospital, and mortuaries don't provide for bedtime reading.

Christopher Berry-Dee
Bestselling author of Ladykiller *and* A Question Of Evidence.
Criminologist; Associate Producer; Television Presenter.

Chapter One

Avoidance and Awareness

'Learn from nature: how often do you see the mouse playing by the hawk's nest?'

Sensei Harry Cook

'Therefore, when the time and place of the challenge is known,
One can meet the challenge from a thousand miles away.
But when the time and place of the challenge is not known,
One cannot protect all flanks;
If through measuring the strategies of others,
We find their numbers exceed our own,
Does this indicate triumph or defeat?
It is said: "Triumph can be measured."'

Sun Tzu

Welcome to *Dead or Alive*. Throughout the next 200-odd pages I hope to enlighten and educate the uninitiated and demonstrate the many personal survival imperatives which are needed in a society that is fast becoming an infestation of gratuitous violence. For the record this is not yet another hypothetical manual of inappropriate quick fixes that might leave you deader than disco. I'll leave that to the academics. The information herein is derived from a lifetime's study where mental self-dissection was necessary to root out all of my own weaknesses before I could gain promotion and elevation to the highest planes of understanding and survival. Now, after many dangerous years of search and research, spending thousands of nights standing on cold nightclub doors and tangling with life's gratuitously violent minority, I stand on the plateau of understanding, enlightened. Shocked beyond measure, but enlightened. I have studied the psyche of violent people first-hand, talked (and fought) with hundreds of professional street fighters, muggers and robbers, at times dropping to their primeval levels just to survive. Now, as I pull away from the obesely criminal, I draw my conclusions upon them and upon violence. From these deductions are born a better understanding of how to counter such people in the face of a violent or potentially violent assault.

A fire prevention video teaches you how to prevent fires with the use of deterrents and alarms, and how to escape a fire with the minimum of fuss. What it doesn't try to do is make you into a fireman. So it is with this book. I do not want to teach you how to be a professional street fighter, rather how to avoid being face to face with someone who will enjoy smashing your bones to dust. Prevention, via awareness, is far more palatable than the often unlikely cure of a physical response.

It's not my intention to try and tell you, the reader, whether or not you should engage in a physical encounter should you find yourself the victim of criminal assault; that is not my right. What I should like to do is offer up the options so that you might weigh the odds and choose for yourself.

If a mugger snatches your purse or wallet containing twenty pounds, your idea of self-defence may be to let him have it; twenty pounds is hardly worth dying for after all. However, if the same attacker forces you into a dark alley and wants to add rape to his booty, you may not be so happy to capitulate. He may even want to kill you – it's not unknown. No one can tell you in cases like this that you MUST or MUST NOT fight back, only you can decide. So, dead or alive? The choice is yours.

I'm tired of watching the same predictable run of safe bet 'self-defence' advisors on the TV and in popular magazines demonstrating tame release techniques that would not break wind and advising the uninitiated on what can or cannot be employed, in defence and in the eyes of the law; frightened of overstepping the moral and legal boundaries that might have a bored MP or an elitist senior police officer writing to *The Times* in protest.

I will dare to break this negative and often dishonest cycle with *Dead or Alive*. How? By being honest – even if I do break a few unwritten rules en route.

I'm fed up with being asked onto TV and chat shows as a defence expert and then being told in the green-room what I can and cannot say on air. They don't really want a defence expert, they want a puppet. There is little point in offering counsel when my advice is censored and scripted by a 'windy' television editor or producer.

What you read in this book is how it is, ugly and in your face. I'm not saying that it's what you want to hear, it may not be (good advice rarely is), but it will be the truth and those that listen will be better prepared for their perception.

You may have hoped for a 'picture book'; if you did I fear you may already be disappointed and probably sadly deluded. This is a book of knowledge, not pictures, but in the world of *real*, knowledge is power.

Where this book will differ from the many that you might read in its genre is in its empiricism: the techniques, attack rituals etc. have all been developed in real life scenarios. The interviews with attackers, muggers, rapists and killers are all authentic and there for one reason and one reason alone – understanding the attacker will help you to avoid him, and in the extreme case, deal with him. If you want to know how a mugger chooses a victim, this being the first step in his attack ritual, don't go and ask a psychologist or a policeman – ask a mugger. Obviously very few people are capable of doing this so I have done it for you.

AVOIDANCE AND AWARENESS

Whenever I talk about the need for self-protection, invariably someone will say 'you're scaremongering'. People will undoubtedly say the same about this book, and yet every day of the week we see adverts, emblazoned across our TV screens and newspapers, graphically reconstructing horrific car crashes that warn us not to drink and drive. We are also exposed to the horrors and consequences of drug abuse, showing the mourning parents of a juvenile O.D. victim, that advise us to 'say no to drugs'. Even the dangers of faulty gas appliances are given more credence, via horrific TV advertisements, than the frightening increase in violence against the person.

It is not my aim in this book to scaremonger – only to educate.

Way back as far as 1995 – and in London alone – over 50,000 people fell victim to violent attack, compared with an estimated national total of 16,000 casualties resulting from road crashes in which at least one driver or rider was over the legal alcohol limit. And it isn't getting any better – but you probably don't need me to tell you that. It is after all covered every day in the newspaper and bulletins.

I make no apologies if this book shocks – I hope it does, because maybe then people will take note and better prepare themselves for the pandemic increase in unsolicited violent attack.

It can happen to you and, if you're not vigilant, it *will* happen to you.

Please don't be disappointed that this book's foremost objective is NOT the physical response. When teaching children road safety the imperative is not how to deal with the trauma of being knocked over, we know that this is often too late. Rather, we teach our children how to avoid being hit by a car.

To the majority, being attacked IS like being hit by a car – so the prerogative of self-protection has to be flight over fight.

That is not to say that the physical response should not be addressed; avoidance may not always be an option and we all make mistakes – even monkeys fall out of trees. In the appropriate chapters I shall cover things physical and throughout this text you will find a myriad of techniques that cover most conceivable angles of attack.

Most people are not and never will be physically or mentally equipped to cope with violent conflict; the expected, immediate response of this majority is terror and capitulation.

The best tools I can offer the reader are honesty, insight and realism to be used in the 'fight for flight'.

Most potential confrontations are avoidable if you use the tool of awareness, follow the prescribed rules and use your common sense. Most of those that are not avoidable, if dealt with positively, are controllable. For the minority that are out of the purlieus of your control, you will, no doubt, have to fight for your life. It is then that every scrap of knowledge you can take from this book, other empirical books, and actual self-protection classes will undoubtedly help to weigh the odds in your favour.

For those that think acquiescence may be a safer option, recent surveys have shown that capitulating to an assailant, or pleading, 'Do what you want, but please don't hurt me' (especially in rape scenarios) will not and do not guarantee victim safety. Capitulating victims also, in most cases, suffer far more than other victims with negative emotional aftermath.

Most books of this genre seem to be garnished with hypothetical step-by-step Karate-type illustrations showing the reader 'what to do when attacked', with easy to learn wrist locks and release techniques that totally lack credence; these being demonstrated, emotionlessly, by shop window mannequins. No mention is made of the victim's state of mind in such a scenario, of the extreme trauma involved in a confrontational situation. In many cases we are being taught to swim by people who have never gotten wet themselves.

All seem to be working on the premise that the victim has already been grabbed/ throttled/punched etc., totally ignoring those pivotal seconds, minutes, often even hours before contact.

If you have to become physical the concept of defence is very often unsound, unless you are facing a very inferior attacker – which is not the norm. Pre-emption is the order of the day, your best means of defence is attack and, whilst the law may not thank me for telling you this, it's the truth. Very often the views of those in law enforcement will change according to whether they are talking on the record or off. I have taught many police officers in my time who came to me for instruction because what they are taught on an official level simply does not work against non-compliant people.

Of course once you have been attacked and pre-emption is no longer an option, most of the techniques that are the perfunctory by-products of such defence books and courses are as unworkable as they are unrealistic. If you are not already incapacitated you will be fighting, tooth and nail, for your life.

Awareness allows a pre-emptive response (avoidance, escape, dissuasion or attack), the victim recognising menace before the 'monster metamorphosis'. This allows him/her to deal with it before it deals with them.

What I should like to do is shock you, the reader, within the safety of these pages, thus developing a sharp, preventive enlightenment. As Ed Howe said, 'A good shock is often better than good advice.'

A book filled simply with physical techniques may only heighten vulnerability, giving the reader a false sense of security. One young lady said to me after completing a six-week self-defence course (and I quote)

'I baby sit for a friend twice a week. In the evening, afterwards, I take the short cut home and walk across the local park. It always scares me. Now that I have done a self-defence course I feel a lot safer when I take the shortcut across the park.'

If she had have been taught properly she would no longer be taking the short cut through the park.

TARGET HARDENING

The key phrase in contemporary self-protection is target hardening. By making yourself a hard target you lessen your chances of being chosen as a potential victim.

I once interviewed a group of burglars and I asked them for their prime requisite when selecting a house to rob. They said, 'We always look for properties that are not protected.' The houses that sported an alarm box, dog pictures in the window, window locks, etc. were very often bypassed by the average robber.

'Why bother bursting your balls on a dwelling with all that protection when there are rakes of houses around the corner with fuck all, just asking to be robbed. These people kill us, they fucking gripe about having their houses robbed yet they leave us an invite at the door. They just make it easy for us.'

Many of the burglars rob the same house three or more times because the owners do nothing to stop them.

Self-protection works in a similar vein. If you make yourself a hard target by following the rules of awareness you too will be bypassed for an easier target. If you don't make yourself aware, you will be chosen again and again.

The Four 'D's

There are four techniques often used by attackers, especially muggers and rapists, in preparing victims for attack. Although these are nearly always overlooked by self-defence writers, the four 'D's – *dialogue, deception, distraction* and *destruction* – are the most important element of self-protection to be aware of.

DIALOGUE

Dialogue designed to disarm and distract the targeted victim is the professional attacker's most common priming technique. An attacker will approach a potential victim in a non-threatening way and begin a conversation. Often, he will ask a question about directions, ask if you have the time, a light, or any spare change. His objective is to make you think about his question, so that you do not notice the weapon he is drawing or his accomplice coming round behind you. It only takes a second of distraction for you to get into deep trouble. Understanding this will make you more aware and keep you alert, which is the most important part of target hardening.

DECEPTION

An attacker uses deception to make himself appear harmless. Dialogue and appearance are the most common methods used to deceive victims, to make them let down their guard. Do not expect dangerous people to stand out in a crowd.

Attacks may start with politeness, even with an ingratiating approach. Deception is the attacker's greatest asset. Every attack I have ever documented that was not a blind-side attack (the ones that happen when you do not use awareness) came through deception, the attacker using this as a window of opportunity.

DISTRACTION

Distraction is a part of deception and usually comes through dialogue. The attacker may ask his victim a question and then initiate attack while the victim is thinking about the answer. This distraction also switches off any instinctive, spontaneous physical response the victim may have. A man with twenty years of physical training in a fighting art can be stripped of his ability by this simple ploy. I have witnessed many trained fighters, who are monsters in the controlled arena, get beaten by a guy with only an ounce of their physical ability. How? They were distracted before the attack. Rob, a hardened street fighter and nightclub doorman, always told potential opponents that he didn't want to fight before he attacked them. Their first thought when recovering consciousness would be: 'I'm sure he said he didn't want to fight!'

If the distraction is submissive, 'I don't want any trouble, can we talk about it?' it will also take your assailant down from a state of fight or flight to one of low awareness, because your submissiveness tells him that the danger is over and he can relax into self-congratulation.

Brain engagement, via disarming/distracting dialogue, gives the victim a blind second. This is when the assailant strikes. The distraction is also used by the experienced attacker to take down any protective fences that may have been constructed by the victim (the 'fence' is dealt with in detail in a later chapter).

DESTRUCTION

This is the final product of expert priming. Few people survive the first physical blow and most are out of the game before they even realise that they are in it.

Even trained martial artists often get suckered by the four 'D's because these do not appear on their training curriculum. They do not understand the enemy they are facing. The attacker uses the techniques of deception and distraction to prime a victim that is only trained in 'physical response'.

Adrenal dump

If a situation does become live your body will usually experience a huge injection of adrenalin, known as *adrenal dump*. While adrenalin can add speed and strength to the body's responses and also dull pain, the adrenal dump causes sensations very similar to those of fear. Consequently many people freeze under its influence. If you can't control the person on the inside then it is safe to say that you cannot control the person on the outside (the attacker).

Colour Codes of Awareness

Probably the finest preventive method is the utilisation of colour codes (also called 'coding up'), a concept devised by Jeff Cooper, an American combat pistol instructor, to help recognise, evaluate and subsequently avoid potential threat. The codes are a yardstick measuring rising threat and, if adhered to, they make most situations avoidable.

Cooper designed the codes of awareness to allow people a 360 degree environmental awareness. What I would like to add to this, with respect to the great man, is also awareness of attack ritual, physical reality and of bodily reactions to confrontation – after all awareness is a many-splendoured thing.

The codes of awareness consist of four colours, in ascending order of your awareness: white, yellow, orange and red.

CODE WHITE

This is the state of oblivion to danger, of being 'switched off'. A person in code white is unaware of an environment, its inhabitants and their ritual of attack. Code white is the victim state that all attackers look for.

CODE YELLOW

Known as 'switched on', this is a state of threat awareness in which perception allows 360 degree peripheral awareness of such environmental danger areas as secluded doorways or dark alleys, and the person understands such psychological hazards as adrenal dump and attack rituals.

Initially, code yellow is similar to commentary driving, where you talk through and describe, as you drive, everything around you. Similarly, as you walk, run a subconscious commentary of everything happening in your surroundings. Ultimately, with practice, you will maintain a subconscious constant awareness without the commentary. It is not a state of paranoia but of heightened observance.

CODE ORANGE

This is the state of threat evaluation. Orange represents rising threat, allowing evaluation if circumstances deteriorate. For instance, you may notice a couple of suspicious-looking men over the road from you; if they begin to cross in your direction and you feel there is a possible threat, code orange will allow assessment and evaluation of the situation.

CODE RED

The final state is that of threat avoidance – also called 'fight or flight'. The situation is evaluated in code orange. If there is a threat, prepare to fight or run. Never stand and fight if there is a possibility of 'flight'.

If no threat presents itself, drop back to orange and yellow; never lose your awareness and drop to white. Many people have been beaten in real situations because they have lost their *zanshin* (awareness). Stay switched on.

**COOPER'S COLOUR CODES
A YARDSTICK TO MEASURETHREAT**

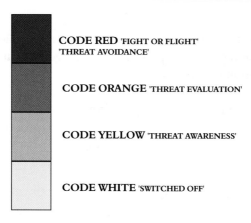

CODE RED 'FIGHT OR FLIGHT'
'THREAT AVOIDANCE'

CODE ORANGE 'THREAT EVALUATION'

CODE YELLOW 'THREAT AWARENESS'

CODE WHITE 'SWITCHED OFF'

Of course, this whole colour-coding system works on the premise that you are in code yellow in the first place: you cannot evaluate a situation that you have not noticed developing, nor can you prepare for fight or flight if you have not seen and evaluated a danger. In code white, you are only likely to know about a dangerous situation when it is too late. The same applies with the following rules; you need to be in code yellow (switched on) to make any use of them at all. So in all cases, 'code up'.

In the home

Whilst I do not wish to spoil your quality time in the home, I do feel it necessary to advise the reader on a few home truths to avoid the unthinkable: an attack in the home.

• Fit your house with good door and window locks. This includes a door safety chain. Do not leave accessible windows open, night or day. The harder you make it for an intruder to enter your home, the more likely he is to move on.

• Make sure you lock outside doors and change the locks if previous tenants still have their old keys.

• If your home is up for sale, never show a prospective buyer around on your own. Many unfortunates have fallen victim to rape and murder by men posing as prospective house buyers. Don't be rushed into showing someone around your house, no matter how much you want to sell it.

• As simple as it might sound, always draw the curtains after dark. Otherwise you are on display to criminals looking for a way in.

• Whenever returning to an empty house, be extra careful. Look out for signs of forced entry. Obviously, if you notice any, don't go into the house but get away quickly and quietly and phone the police. The same goes for anything or anyone suspicious: always phone the police immediately.

• Install a porch light and/or spy hole at your front door. This will allow you to see who you are dealing with before opening the door – remember deception is the leading technique of a professional attacker, he may call at your house under the guise of any number of things. Always be a little suspicious of unexpected visitors.

• Never admit anyone in to your home, i.e. service men, without first checking their credentials. If you are still unsure, take their ID number and phone their headquarters for verification. Since attackers sometimes pose as officials to gain entry, you should also check their ID and that they are who and what they say they are. If you have even the smallest doubt in your mind don't let them into your house; if they are official they shouldn't mind a bit.

• House alarms are a great deterrent. Many of the burglars that I interviewed said that they never bothered to enter a house with an alarm as it was too much hassle. This is not to say that an alarm is the answer to all your prayers. It's not. If someone really wants to get into your house, I mean *really* wants to, then nothing barring a shotgun in their face is going to stop them – but an alarm does help. If installing an alarm system is too expensive, put up empty alarm boxes on your outside walls to deter would-be criminals and, even if you haven't got a dog, put up a sign to say that you have.

• Keep gates/outhouses locked when not in use.

• If criminals want to nick your belongings make them work very hard for it and remember: the longer it takes them to get in and the more noise they have to make to do it, the more chance there is of them being caught red-handed.

In the car
Many attacks start when victims are getting in or out of cars, or when cars break down. There are also a lot of attacks on motorists when they are stationary.

• First things first: join a reputable motoring association like the AA, RAC or National Breakdown. It's a false economy not to have membership and many people have been attacked when stuck out in the sticks, or even on a busy motorway, because they have had no means of breakdown support.

• Before you set out on a journey, make sure your car is fuelled and serviced. Plan your route and let people know where you are going and how long you expect to be gone.

• Entering and exiting your car is a very vulnerable time. When approaching your car, stay coded up, especially after dark. Have the car keys ready in your hand.

• The very second that you sit in your car, before you do anything else – before you put the keys in the ignition, straighten your skirt, put the seat belt on, or anything else – LOCK THE DOORS. John David Guise Cannan, the British serial killer and rapist, attacked many of his victims just as they were putting the keys into the ignition. He would wait until they felt safe within their vehicle, then he'd yank open the driver's door, threaten them, usually with a knife, and order them into the passenger seat before climbing in, driving off and raping and murdering them – usually in the privacy of his own home.

If you're thinking that you'd just jump out of that car and run away, think again. Many women have fallen victim to the likes of Cannan and been frozen by fear into immobility. One woman was abducted in her own car, by a man and in broad daylight, without a weapon. Her attacker even had the audacity to stop and fill the car up at a petrol station. He left the woman alone in the unlocked car while he went to pay, telling her that if she tried to escape he would hunt her down and kill her. This was in broad daylight with many people walking by, but the poor victim was too frightened to speak, let alone run.

• If you can afford it, have an emergency mobile phone in the car. If not, consider having a fake mobile phone, which you can pretend to call the police on. Make sure you have loose change for a payphone in an emergency.

• Never pick up hitch-hikers. I hate to say this because I feel sorry for the people that are genuinely trying to travel on a budget, but to pick up a hitch-hiker of any description is to place yourself in grave danger.

• If you have to keep valuables in the car keep them out of sight, in the boot or glove compartment. Many car robberies are done by the opportunist criminal.

• Park in well-lit areas. What may seem safe, light and populated by day, may not be when returning at night, so park by a streetlight. Unlit car parks should be avoided where and whenever possible. If not they should be treated with great caution as they are playgrounds for thieves and crooks. As Harry Cook says, 'don't play by the hawk's nest.'

• Use a steering lock, preferably a good heavy-duty one that will make sure your car stays where you want it to, and that could be used as a weapon if required.

• Keep a large torch in your glove compartment; a 'Maglite' is recommended. This can also double as a weapon; if possible, practise using it as an attacking tool.

• When parking your car try to reverse in to a space, it will make for a quicker getaway 'if and when'.

• If you have to speak to someone from the car, only wind the window down a couple of inches. Many of the American serial killers attacked people who were driving with their doors unlocked and/or their windows wide open. Of course, in a free society we should not have to take these drastic measures and of course we should be free to leave whatever we want unlocked, unsecured in any way. On one of the radio show interviews I did on self-protection for women a young (naive) feminist woman, also a guest on the show, complained that 'women should not have to be careful about where they walk and who they talk to and what they wear and how far they take a man before they say "no"'. She was actually in an official position at one of the local universities and she, incredibly, advised young women that they should 'do anything you want and don't worry about attack and rape. Why should we have to be careful,' she told them, 'just because we are women?'

She was offended when I told her that she didn't have the maturity to hold such a position of authority, that she was a walking victim and that she was also placing the women in her charge in a victim state by offering them bad advice. Did I say offended? I meant absolutely outraged; I think if she could have got away with it she might have attacked me.

The people we are talking about, those in society that attack for fun or profit do not give a monkey's fuck about what is right or wrong. They have no morals and would take great pleasure in brutally raping a girl just like this young woman; they have already decided to break the law and are on the very dark side of wrong, so when you break the rules because you 'have that right' they are as happy as Larry. You've done all their hard work for them by offering yourself on the proverbial plate. A lot of attacks, certainly rape, are actuated by the opportunist criminal, so when you flout the rules you are giving them the opportunity they desire.

I also believe that this young lady thought that she might be able to handle a would-be rapist, teach the blighter a lesson he wouldn't forget. Think again. For someone this unprepared, this much in a victim state, the first she is likely to know of the attack situation is a broken nose, gushing blood, severe shock and a brutal rape that would change the course of her young life. Some never recover from this heinous crime. This is your life that we are talking about so, please, be at least a little more realistic about how you take care of it.

Break-downs

• A basic knowledge of car mechanics, wheel changing, etc., will help if your car breaks down, and you will not be tempted to accept the help of a complete stranger who could be an attacker. Many women have fallen victim to this ploy and have been raped/gang raped and/or killed as a consequence. Harsh but true.

• If you are with a motoring association, contact them, from your mobile if you have one, and then stay with the car until they arrive. Lock the door and windows.

• If you are offered help from any one unofficial, courteously decline all assistance except asking them to call the AA/RAC/police for you if you haven't managed to do so yourself already.

• If you break down on the motorway, park as close to the emergency telephone box as possible and call the breakdown services. Again, return to the car and lock the doors and windows.

• If you break down in an urban area, go to a shop or garage to call for assistance.

• In the countryside, park the car and walk to the nearest phone or the closest residence and ask them to phone for you. If you are female, don't enter the residence unless another female is present – even then be on your guard.

Car Abductions

• If you are kidnapped in your own car remember that, although you will be terrified, you still have control because you are driving the car. The attacker will often use false promises (do as I say and I won't hurt you, do as I say or I will hurt you) to force victim compliance. This cannot be relied upon – you must take charge. If the attacker is not wearing a seat belt it would be easy to project him through the windscreen by stamping your foot on the brakes.

Another option is to crash the car whilst it is traveling at a relatively slow speed. This is best effected in a public area, though not one that will endanger other people. Crashing, or just bumping, your car will give you the opportunity to escape while your attacker is wondering what happened. If you know the area, drive at speed to the nearest police station, or if you see a policeman, stop the car next to him.

If you do decide to crash the car try to hit something that has a little give, like a bush or another car.

In cases of abduction it is always wise to make your escape attempt as early as possible, the longer you take, the harder it becomes. If you have a game plan already worked out for such scenarios – they are happening more and more these days after all – it will help. The further away from populated areas you are taken the worse it is going to be – get away while there are people around. It has to be said that being pro-active in these cases does take a lot of courage; you have to be very brave and take the initiative.

Taxi Drivers

This is a difficult job. Every day the taxi driver is forced, by trade, to pick up strangers.

I know a few taxi drivers and I don't want to teach them how to suck eggs, but my advice is be choosy about who rides in your cab. Listen to your instincts; if the client doesn't feel right, don't pick him up.

• If you find yourself with a dangerous passenger, drive him to the local police station. I gave this advice to a taxi driver once in a TV phone-in on self-defence, and he replied, 'it's not that easy.' Of course it's not, it's very hard, it's frightening. Every aspect of protecting yourself is hard. If it was easy to defend yourself, attackers wouldn't attack and self-protection teachers would be out of work. You have to be gutsy and just do it, as the Nike adverts say. An attacker is unlikely to want to attack the driver of the car whilst it is in motion because he is as likely to get as hurt in the subsequent crash as the driver. What he will do however is rant and rave and threaten to punch your lights out if you do not comply with his wishes. There have been a few taxi drivers kidnapped in their own cab in my own city, then badly beaten and robbed, one even thrown semi-conscious into a lake in some remote area out of the city. So compliance does not guarantee safety; you're likely to get a beating anyway, and possibly raped if you are a woman. Be decisive and take charge. If the area is populated, jump out of the cab and make a run for it; anything is better than being driven to an unknown location by an unknown entity.

• You also have the advantage of a two-way radio in the cab, don't be frightened to use it.

• Don't chase a fare stealer. If a client runs off without paying you can live with that; I wouldn't advise a chase. Many taxi drivers have been injured, sometimes fatally, in the pursuit of a 'runner'. I would even advise shouting 'MAY DAY,

MAY DAY' or 'POLICE EMERGENCY, POLICE EMERGENCY' down the radio, the guy in the back is hardly likely to know any better and will probably run like a mad thing.

• If you have the choice, drive a black cab with a glass partition between you and the customer.

• At the time of writing this book there have been a spate of taxi rapes where young women have been picked up by bogus taxi drivers, driven to a secluded spot and attacked, raped, and even killed. So, on that subject, never take a taxi unless it is from a bonafide company. Women should insist on a female driver if it makes them feel safer.

• If a friend or taxi driver drops you off at night, ask them to wait until you are in the house safely.

On foot

• If you take the dog for a walk, or go jogging on a regular basis, vary times and routes so that a potential attacker can never place you to a certain place at a certain time. Never walk or jog in remote areas alone.

• If you wear expensive jewellery, try to keep it covered until you reach your destination. Again the opportunist criminal may only attack if he sees the chance of taking an expensive bracelet, watch or necklace.

If you think that someone may be following you, go to the nearest place where there will be people around, and inform the police. Basically the more people there are around you, the less likely an attacker is to try and attack you. Besides pain, the thing that frightens muggers/attackers the most is being caught; the more witnesses there are the more likely he is to be caught and so the less likely he is to attack. If he does still attack, you have more chance of someone coming to your assistance.

There are always exceptions to the rules, of course; some attackers are not playing with a full deck and will attack you no matter what the circumstance. All the same you are still better off in a crowd than alone.

• Never take the short cut home if doing so involves going into or through sparsely-populated or badly-lit areas. These places are notorious for harbouring the criminal fraternity. I know that this is an old cliche, but if you put your hand into the fire then you are going to get burned – better to arrive late than not to arrive at all. And if you are late, why take the short cut anyway: you are already late and the short cut is unlikely to change that. We had a young woman in Coventry take a short cut from her boyfriend's to her mother's across some barren land, maybe only two hundred yards long. Five years later they still haven't found the poor girl, dead or alive.

• If your bag is snatched, don't give chase unless you know what you are doing. One girl in the Midlands recently chased a thief who stole her bag, but when she caught up with him at a local park he beat her up and brutally raped her. You hear stories about the woman who chased the robber and bashed him with her umbrella, and this might even have happened once or twice. In the real world, forget it. Your health, your life, is worth more than the contents of your handbag. If you are trying to catch a guy that has just stolen from you, the chances are he is an habitual thief with lots of previous and he won't take kindly to you trying to actuate a citizen's arrest. He is very unlikely to say 'OK Guv, it's a fair cop' and escort you to the station: that kind of crook disappeared with Dixon of Dock Green. What he is likely to do is hit you, with anything at hand, to stop you from apprehending him because capture will probably mean remand and then prison. If 'doing' you means escaping the big house then he'll do you without blinking an eyelid. You may die in pursuit of twenty quid and your credit cards – let him have them.

Also, if you are not very careful you could end up like the dog that chases fire engines, when he finally catches it he doesn't know what to do. I could chase a robber that stole my wallet and give him a good hiding, but then I'm a well built male with thirty-plus years of fighting experience under my belt – when I catch him I will know what to do. Unfortunately, most people will not, so let it go and learn from the experience.

The Black Dog

A friend rang me up the other day, an experienced martial artist, and told me how he had been mugged in broad daylight the previous day by two skinheads with Stanleys (Stanley knives – razor-sharp craft knives). He was with his wife and baby daughter at the time of the assault and his attackers had threatened to cut his child if he did not hand over his wallet. He gave them his money. Now he was beating himself up because he had not fought back. He wasn't sleeping at night because of what Sir Winston Churchill called the Black Dog. The Black Dog is the dark side of the inner opponent, the ego, that taunts you after an incident, any incident, where you perhaps did less (in your own estimation) in your own defence than you thought manly. Many people go through their whole lives allowing the Black Dog to haunt their dreams and steal their sleep. Don't have any of it, in circumstances like these flight is the right option.

But with every action that we take in life there is a consequence; if you pick up one end of a stick then you pick up the other, as they say. Part of making any decision in life is the consequence of that decision. One of the best ways of dealing with the Black Dog is anticipating his arrival in the aftermath and then denying him any control by constantly affirming to yourself that you made the right decision in the circumstances, or, if the decision turned out to be wrong, that you can handle the consequences of your mistakes. While I would certainly have been pretty pissed off too, self-protection, as I told my friend, is not about defending one's ego, it is about defending one's life or the lives of loved ones. I know he made the right choice, and faced with the same options, I'd be giving those muggers my wad, and in a hurry. If my pride was dented, my child would have been intact. I'm not saying that I am against people that fight back, in fact I admire them, very much so; what I am saying is that I would not risk the life of my child just to keep my manhood intact. If, however, the attackers demanded more than my wallet, let's say that they also wanted to rape my wife (after all I'd already given them the wallet with out much of a fuss) then that would have been an altogether different matter. I would have been forced into a situation where, no matter what I did, one of my loved ones was going to get hurt, so I would take the initiative and hurt those threatening them first.

So if you do acquiesce, don't add insult to injury by beating yourself up after the fact, you did good to get out unhurt, and if others escaped unhurt then pat yourself on the back and kick the Black Dog up the arse – I'd sacrifice my ego and eat a little humble pie in exchange for the safety of others. Any day of the week.

In town

• On public transport try to sit in full view of other travellers and/or public transport staff and try not to get pulled into public order offences that are nothing to do with you (mind your own business) – if some low-life wants to smoke in a no-smoking area, let the transport security deal with it: that's their job, and they are trained to do it a lot better than you. Often we feel it is our absolute duty to tell some garrulous youth that he should be doing this and should not be doing that, but it's not our duty and unless you want a piece of them, stay out of it. Displaced aggression is probably behind many unsolicited attacks in society; make the decision not to trigger it or you are likely to become the focus for his displacement. I'm not trying to justify the actions of reprobates, I have no sympathy with these attackers, but I do understand their mentality and how it is going to affect you if you step, uninvited, into their world. If you feel you must have your say at least be ready for the consequences of your actions – remember, if you pick up one end of the stick you pick up the other too.

For example, there was a case reported in which a motorist stopped on a busy road to let an elderly pedestrian cross, but when the old guy didn't thank the motorist for his kindness, he got out of his car and buried a crow bar into the old man's head, fracturing his skull. 'That'll teach you not to say thank you, you bastard,' he was heard to say as the man lay in an ever-increasing pool of his own blood. Displaced aggression – watch out for it, it's a doozy. The rule of thumb is mind your own business or suffer the consequences. Leave it to the professionals.

The critics out there will already be bleating about a distinct lack of public spirit in the last paragraph, so I must temper my statement by underlining the fact that I am only offering the options and not making decisions for you. If you feel the need to get involved in a fracas about some guy smoking in a non-smoking area of the train/restaurant, etc., etc., then that's your prerogative: go ahead. All I'm saying is be prepared for the consequences of your actions.

This is not to say, either, that you should not help others who may be in distress, but even then you should be very wary. And if you do act, do not expect help or sympathy from the police in the aftermath because you are very unlikely to get it. This might sound a little cynical to many but, believe me, I have a lot of experience of how these things can go drastically wrong. Phoning the police may be a better alternative than trying to tackle a guy you've noticed trying to steal a car. Recently a friend of mine intervened in an argument between a young lady and her rather irate boyfriend. For his troubles he had his right bicep severed to the bone (he was attacked by the boyfriend and the woman he was trying to help), leaving him with a permanent disability. To add to his woe the police took him to court and charged him with assault on the irate boyfriend. He endured a year of physical and mental discomfort before the case came before a court and he was finally cleared. I admired him for trying to help the lady but he walked into a situation blind. So look before you leap.

• Always keep in company whenever possible, as you are far less likely to be attacked whilst with a group of people. Attackers mostly prey on the lone victim. Like the cheetah hunting the antelope the hunter preys on those that are detached from the herd.

• When you have to walk alone down a dark or empty street, stick to the edge of the path, away from secluded doorways and entries. These are favourite haunts for attackers. The harder you make it for someone to attack you, the more likely he is to 'select' another, more vulnerable victim.

• Avoid areas, nightclubs, pubs, etc. that have a reputation for violence. To frequent these places is to court trouble. You'd practically have to be a recluse to not know the rough bars in your own city, so avoid them; let the rough inhabit the rough bars, you stick to places where violence after a beer isn't as perfunctory as a mint after dinner.

The danger often occurs when you are in a city that you are not familiar with, perhaps on holiday or visiting friends. If you are not sure ask someone. In most cities and towns the people are almost perversely proud of their rough bars and won't hesitate to point them out to you like silver cups in a trophy cupboard: 'Oh yeah, we had five stabbings here last month, one fatal.'

First response is always avoidance: if you don't frequent the shitholes you're less likely to encounter shit.

• Face the traffic when walking, whenever possible. If a driver tries to pick you up or force you into his car, in your escape you will be running in the opposite direction. Make your way quickly to the nearest lighted or inhabited area, and try to get onto the opposite side of the street. This will make it harder for the attacker should he contemplate trying again. Don't change routes if doing so means placing yourself in a more vulnerable position or area.

• Kerb crawlers generally beckon their intended victims to the car. Never move near to the car, be curt and do not engage in any conversation with anyone in the car other than what is necessary. If they ask directions, and you decide to help, do so from a safe distance. Never move close to the car. Shawcross, the American serial killer and mass rapist, often entrapped his victims by beckoning them to his car and then dragging them through the open window. He often drove off with them half-in and half-out of the window, stopping his car some several hundred yards down the road and bundling them into the back seat, usually knocked senseless and defenceless. He'd then drive them to a secluded area to rape and kill them. Whilst we warn our children of the dangers of car abduction we very rarely heed the same advice ourselves.

• Never accept a lift from a stranger, as your vulnerability is greatly heightened when you do so.

In the nightclub or pub

• If you sense menace in a drinking place, leave and go somewhere else, that's the easy and simple solution. Someone once asked me at a seminar on self-defence what he should do if someone stared menacingly at him in the pub and they felt that there may be an attack. 'Put your drink down and go somewhere else,' I said. 'For the price of a pint you've saved yourself a hell of a lot of trouble.'

Again, this is not about defending your ego, it is about possibly defending your life or your liberty and if a pub or club is so threatening that I think I might be attacked 'just for being there' then I sure as hell don't want to drink there any more. There are dozens of drinking holes in every town or city; choose one where you will be sharing the company of people a little less barbarous. Often people feel that they have to fight for their territory. Don't bother if that territory is a spot by the bar at the 'Egg and Chip', because it just isn't worth it. What you also have to remember is that, trained or not, the consequences of fighting, especially when it is for something that does not need fighting for, can be a life-changing event. People have died and others gone to prison for fighting over nothing.

And if you're not a fighter, you are back to chasing fire engines and not knowing what to do when you catch them. If you feel you have to fight for your patch, better make sure you know how to fight first.

On the other hand, you may be a very capable person when it comes to the physical response but is a patch in the pub worth killing another human being for? Although killing the other guy might not be your intention it is the worst-case scenario and it happens in bar fights every night of the week. I don't know about you but when I fight it has to be because I've been pushed into a corner and my antagonist has left me with no other option. So what I ask myself is, 'Is what I am fighting for worth risking my liberty?' If the answer is no then I try and back-pedal as gracefully as the situation will allow; if the answer is yes then I go ahead fully committed with justification as my ally. When I wake up the next day, no matter what the outcome of the affray, I can say to myself 'I only did what I had to do'. It will also help me in court if I can demonstrate that I did not want to fight and that I was left no other option. So, unless you are forced into it, try and avoid a physical encounter. If you can't, then give it everything that you have and then some.

• If you think that there is going to be trouble in a club and getting away may be difficult, if there are doormen working ask for their help, that's what they are paid for. Although many may seem a little unapproachable they will respond if you go to them for help (if they are any good).

If you think you are going to be followed from a pub/club, ask the doormen to let you out of another exit, or to 'watch your back' if you leave via the main exit.

• If the fight kicks off and there are doormen employed – don't get involved. There is no such thing as someone 'just trying to stop a fight.' When the doormen rush in to stop an affray all they will see is flailing bodies that need removing from the club. If yours is one of them you'll be removed and the more you try to argue your case the graver the situation will get for you. By all means inform the doormen of trouble but don't try and do their job for them. When they rush in they will be in code red, they will not have time to discern who is right and who is wrong. (From my experience of dealing with bar fights no one was ever in the wrong, it was always the fault of the other party – we never took sides, everyone involved left the club.)

Some of these rules may seem impractical and people may decide not to act on many of them. That of course is your prerogative. But if you do flout the rules, please be extra aware and expect the consequences.

Chapter Two

Attackers and Attack Rituals: Lessons Learned

'Know the other and know yourself;
One hundred challenges without danger;
Know the other and know not yourself;
One triumph for one defeat;
Know not the other and know not yourself'
Every challenge is certain peril.'

Sun Tzu

If you know why, where and how an attack is likely to happen it stands to reason that this knowledge will help you to avoid such situations, or prepare for them.

In bygone days, nearly all attacks on people were relegated to the hours of darkness and the deepest crevices of seclusion, i.e. down a dark alley at night. So, hypothetically, if you avoided dark secluded places you were pretty damned safe. Not so in today's liberated society where the antagonists have crawled out of the crevices, come off the night shift, and anybody, any time, any place is fair game. Why? There could be a myriad reasons, but these are not really important in the realms of this text because politics may confuse rather than enlighten the situation. What does matter and what you do need to know is how they happen and how to avoid them.

There are, of course, lots of different types of attackers and attacks. Some choose to rob, some choose to rape, whilst others instigate gratuitous violence for no other profit than malice.

Some assailants are cold-blooded in that they meticulously plan their attacks before they set about executing them; many are opportunists who will only commit an offence if a safe situation arises in their everyday lives. All are uniform in one thing. They have little or no regard for human life. Men, women and children are being attacked absolutely indiscriminately often even in highly populated areas where the frightened and seemingly unsympathetic general public hide under the veil of, 'It's nothing to do with me', or 'I don't want to get involved'. So if you do find yourself in a dangerous attack scenario, don't rely on any help from passers-by. More often than not that is exactly what they will do – pass you by.

Last year a friend of mine was leaving a city-centre pub after enjoying a night out with his wife. As they made their way through a busy end-of-evening crowd, they noticed a young lady being attacked outside a busy chip shop by what turned out to be her estranged boyfriend! My friend, not a man trained in any fighting system, tried to help the girl but was viciously attacked by her assailant who pulled out a knife and severed his bicep from the bone and also slashed and stabbed him in several other areas of the body. My friend was left with some terrible injuries. The girl that was initially being attacked turned on my friend's wife and attacked her also. The police were not sympathetic and my friend was dragged through the courts for nearly a year trying to prove that his attempted defence of the woman was not in fact an unprovoked racial attack, as the knifeman and his girlfriend swore in court. The police knew that my friend was in the right but, for whatever reason, did not come to his aid. The knifeman was a known villain with lots of previous. This is only one of the reasons why the general public do not assist in broad daylight attacks, they do not want to stand in court like a common criminal facing a law that, in this day and age, has to be seen as the second enemy.

Incidents between men and women are also seen by passers-by as domestic: 'oh, don't get involved, it's probably just a domestic.' The next day you read in the paper that some young woman was raped in broad daylight and no one came to her aid.

I was faced with a similar dilemma very recently. Picture the scene:

I was walking through the city centre of Coventry on a very busy, sunny afternoon. A heavily tattooed, big violent beast of a man with a face like a caveman's ugly club and knuckles that dragged ape-like along the floor was pushing a middle-aged woman from pillar to post. The woman was crying and her daughter, 14 years old, was sobbing and asking passers by for help – no one seemed to hear her.

You're walking by, she asks you, begs you for help! What are you going to do? In the safety of your house, reading this book, it would be very easy to say, 'Yeah, I'd help her'. But this guy is going to punch the head in of any man or woman that interferes, he's going to hurt you, stamp your head into the pavement – what are you going to do, do you still want to get involved? It's difficult, isn't it?

It did look domestic to me (it was actually, the monster being her estranged boyfriend) and I could understand why people walked by: they had no training in how to deal with a violent man like this. He had already floored one young man who tried to stop him, and it was easier to walk away than it was to stand and get involved. The few men who did venture forward were dragged away by their wives and girlfriends, who were saying, 'It's nothing to do with us, just leave it.'

The first thing you need to know when facing a situation like this is that, in all likelihood, you are going to be attacked by the man the very first time you try and intervene. He is building to a crescendo of anger and will let it 'spill' on anyone that enters his world, if for no other reason than to prove his virility to a woman who has thrown it in to question and is telling him, through her tears, 'Pick on some one your own size, you're not man enough to, are you?' To disprove this damning accusation and reinstate his manhood he will hit the first person that gives him cause to. This is also partly displaced aggression.

So first things first, he is very likely to hit you if you get too close, which is OK if that's your game. If it's not and that clenched fist contains a sharp implement you may pay with your life, so if you go in then go in prepared or not at all. If the opportunity arises you should first call the police and make them aware of the situation. They may take a while to get there which is not going to save her the beating she is about to get, so you still have to do something until they arrive.

If you are worried that it may be purely domestic and that the woman might not want help (in this case there was no question of that, she desperately wanted help from someone, anyone) and that she may turn on you if you interfere, then ask her. Stand at a safe range and ask her if she wants your help, if she tells you to 'fuck off and mind your own business!' then you can be on your merry way with your conscience clear. If she does want help she will tell you so. Your offer of help will also help you determine the state of mind of the man involved. If he threatens you at this stage then take the threat seriously and approach with caution.

What I did when I got involved in this little fracas in Coventry city centre was to start off at a slight distance and try to talk the man down. This allowed me to monitor how aggressive he was (if at any point the man had gotten physical with the woman I'd have run straight in and stopped him). He wasn't having any of it and told me to keep out of it 'or else'. At this point I knew that it was going to get physical.

I closed the gap and continued to try and talk him out of attacking her, all the time maintaining a fence (detailed later) so that he could not attack me unawares. I hoped this would at least distract him from hitting her until the police came and took over – but they never came. After five minutes of trying everything I knew to talk him down I realised that I was fighting a losing battle. I hadn't wanted to get physical because I didn't feel I had that right. I didn't know, and still don't, why they were arguing and didn't want to take sides. All I did know was that I wasn't prepared to let him hit her whilst I was there, so in the end I told the woman and her young daughter to go home and that I would deal with him. I hoped that this might have warned him off but every time they tried to walk away he stood in front of them and grabbed the woman across the face and told her that he was going to batter her. I realised that he wasn't going to let them go so the next time he lunged for her I whacked him in the head with a little punch that knocked him flying backwards.

The lady and her daughter, taking the initiative, ran in the opposite direction and, I believe, broke the record for the minute mile. Now the fight was mine and I told the fellow in front of me so. But for some reason he was no longer keen on fighting and wanted to shake my hand and buy me a drink. I didn't want to touch, let alone shake, his hand, and neither did I care to share a drink with him. I told him this and he took it well. I wandered off and had a coffee with Sharon.

Generally the attacker of today is a cowardly person who either fights from the podium of alcohol/drugs or attacks from behind, possibly with the crutch of a weapon or accomplice/s, or both.

Excepting possibly the rapist, who often works on the basis that he believes himself physically superior to his victim, most attackers work with the aid of one or more accomplice. They are looking for victims, those that are in code white and/or detached from the herd. Alone or with a team, these people, due to their proverbial yellow streaks, will not cross your path if you practise target hardening. If they do and you fight back ferociously with well-aimed and precise attacks, they will often abort, though I have to reiterate: a physical response is the inferior politic. If you do decide to employ physical means, make sure you know your way around the fighting arena or you may just add anger to the attacker's artillery by daring to strike him. If you strike, you need to know that it will inflict damage enough for you to effect an escape.

THE RITUAL OF VIOLENCE

Most attacks are preceded by stalking and dialogue entrapments. Most attackers use dialogue as their leading technique, but I find that many instructors of self-defence are so concerned about the physical tricks that they forget those vital seconds leading up to assault. It is those people that handle the pre-fight most effectively that tend to win when a situation becomes live. In fact, if you are switched on to the attacker's ritual, you will not usually even be selected as a victim.

This is absolutely the most important factor in real situations and yet it is one area nearly always overlooked by other defence gurus.

One aspect of the ritual is the aforementioned four 'D's. This involves body language as well as the spoken word. Such dialogue is often called *the interview*. I'll explain more about this in the relevant paragraph.

If you can spot the ritual, you can stop the crime.

STREET SPEAK

The language of the street also needs deciphering. Much of the attacker's dialogue is used by him, innately, as a trigger for violence and to engage a potential victim's brain before assault. Positive interpretation of this speak will unveil signs of imminent attack – literally giving you a countdown.

The ritual alters according to the category of attack, as does the dialogue. The genre of attack can vary from gratuitous assault to serial rape/murder.

I have to make the point before I go on that none of what you are reading here is or will be of any relevance if the victim is switched off. Deceptive dialogue and cunning entrapments are hardly necessary if the victim is walking across a field at night or down a dark alley in a sparsely populated area. When this is the case – it very often is – most assaults will be physical and violent almost immediately. The ritual is only used in a bid to trick an intended victim or heighten their vulnerability. If the victim has already done the priming for them by placing themselves in a victim state, then they'll be attacked without any warning. To notice rituals and entrapments you have to be switched on and have your eyes wide open: otherwise, suffer the fate of those before you.

If the intent is robbery or rape the dialogue is often disarming or incidental: 'Have you got a light, please?' or 'can you give me directions to Smith Street please, I'm a little lost?' The attacker is looking to switch the victim off before attack. In the case of the gratuitous assault where the intent is attack for attack's sake, the dialogue is more likely to be aggressive, 'What are you looking at?'

In either case the dialogue is employed to gain and distract attention before attack.

Generally speaking, the greater the crime, the greater the deception. At the bottom end of the scale the gratuitous attacker will engage his intended victim with aggressive dialogue ('I'm gonna batter you, you bastard!'). At the top of the scale the rapist/murderer will prime his victim with anything from a gentlemanly request for directions, to sending his intended victims champagne, flowers and a dinner invitation. This happened in the case of killer John Cannan, who usually did this to women he had spotted in the street and followed or just met: they were the ultimate primers for rape and murder. The more cunning attackers drop into the thespian role with Oscar-winning perfection.

GRATUITOUS ASSAULT

This mindless form of violence, increasingly common, often starts with as little as eye contact. In a volatile situation, eye contact is construed as a subliminal challenge to fight. Many of the fights I witnessed in my time as a nightclub doorman began with the 'eye contact challenge'.

You don't have to do anything wrong to be the victim of this kind of attacker, you just have to be there.

And please don't make the mistake of so many before you by looking for the logic in the attack. There will be no logic and to look for it will only add confusion and indecision, and in those seconds of indecision you will have been robbed and beaten – there is no logic.

Most assaults of this nature, if it helps you to know, are in my opinion due to displaced aggression. If you, whoever you are, trigger that aggression, you will become the object of it. Whatever is pissing these people off in their sad lives, whoever is trampling on their roses, pissing on their parade, you will become the object of that pent-up aggression because you spilled their beer, cut them up in the car, looked at their girlfriend or simply because you were there. That attack is very often brutal, sometimes fatal.

Being in code yellow will allow you to detect and subsequently avoid these philistines and these incidents in the primary stages.

In the bar or the street you can often spot the gratuitous attacker. He'll have a bad attitude, probably propping up the bar or stalking the dance floor, his elbows pushed out from his sides as though carrying buckets of water. He'll have the customary curled upper lip and will probably be very rude to anyone that moves within a few feet of him. If he's walking down the street he'll do so with an over-confident, arrogant bounce. If he's with others he'll probably be very loud, garrulous and erratic in his movements. He may also be mean and moody with a very aggressive gait. Again, as in the nightclub, he'll be stalking, looking for eye contact. If you are in code yellow, you can spot these signs from a mile off.

There are two kinds of eye contact that may escalate into violence.

Often, when you make eye contact with someone and it becomes increasingly obvious that you do not know each other, the ego clicks in and goes to work. The initial accidental eye contact becomes a fully-fledged staring contest. The eyes, being a sensitive organ, cannot hold a stare for too long with out the occurrence of soreness, watering or blinking. Not wanting to blink first, this possibly being construed as a 'back down', the one with the sorest eyes throws a verbal challenge ('You fucking looking at me?') to hide the fact that he needs to blink. If the verbal challenge is returned ('Yeah, I am looking at you. What you gonna do about it?') then the fight, after a few formalities, is probably on.

THE EYE-CONTACT CHALLENGER

This is the man who is looking for a fight, the first person to hold eye contact with him will become his victim.

These are his ritualistic steps:

1) EYE CONTACT

You may catch the eye of someone across a crowded room or a street. The look lingers.

2) THE QUESTION

'Who are you looking at? Want a fucking picture?'

3) THE APPROACH

A physical approach follows.

4) QUESTION REITERATION

'I said, do you want a fucking picture?' The reiteration, with added vehemence.

5) ACTUAL CHALLENGE

'Do you wanna 'go', then?'

6) SINGLE SYLLABLE CHALLENGE

Often the assailant may attack at actual challenge. If he doesn't, and as a precursor to violence, he will often drop into single syllables that act as subliminal action triggers to his attack. Words like 'yeah', 'and' or 'so' are often employed just before attack. The single syllable is a sure sign that the interview is nearing an end and the introduction of the physical is imminent.

Running concurrently will be signs of adrenal reaction:

Arm splaying

The attacker's arms will splay in a fit of exclamation. This is, to him, a way of making him appear physically bigger before attack.

Finger beckoning

The attacker will often beckon his victim on with his fingers.

Head nodding

The assailant may sporadically nod his head.

Neck Pecking

He will peck his neck like a cockerel, usually in conjunction with his single syllable challenge. This protects the throat.

Eye bulge

Due to the tunnel vision that accompanies adrenaline surges, the attacker's eyes may appear wide and staring.

Dropped eyebrows

The eyebrows drop before attack to protect the eyes.

Stancing up

He will often turn sideways on and take up a fighting stance. This hides the major organs from attack.

Distance close-down

With every passing second of the altercation, the attacker will advance closer to his victim, his movements and tone becoming more erratic and aggressive the closer he gets to actual attack.

It is worth mentioning that the foregoing is the complete ritual. Occasionally, depending upon the victim's response, the attacker may jump steps, for instance from the question to the actual challenge, so an early exit is always advisable.

My Advice

Whilst it may bash your ego a little, my advice is sound if you do not want to engage in a physical encounter. Most people do not want to fight and yet still find themselves engaging in arguments that will certainly lead to violence and that could have been left. A man walking down the street alone will think nothing of ignoring a group of barracking men across the road; put the same man in the same situation and add a female companion and the same young man will be ready to argue and fight the world to defend his manhood, even though his lady is begging him not to get involved. These insults mean nothing and should be ignored. Lads, the ladies are not impressed when you walk into a fight that you could have walked out of. I have been involved in many hundreds of fights and can categorically state that it is the stronger man that can walk away. So please, walk away. The time to fight is when you are given no other choice. If I have a fight I want it to be for a better reason than 'the guy was staring at me'. If I end up in court on a manslaughter charge I don't want the judge to be saying to me, 'you killed this man because he spilled your beer, Mr Thompson?'

Violence is a serious game; don't walk into it with any romantic ideas of how it is going to be. It is always ugly and always frightening. I have never stood in front of a man that I wanted to fight, never had perfect conditions, never thought 'yeah, I'm ready for this.' Every fight for me has been more like, 'I don't want to be here, I don't need this, is this going to be the one that gets me killed or jailed?'

Having said all that and meant it, if it is going to kick off and you are sure and there is no other way, don't hesitate. Be first, never allow anyone the opportunity to attack you first. If you can't walk away and you have the honest belief that you are going to be attacked, attack first and then get away. The police may not give you this advice, even though it is well within the law, because they feel that to sanction it is to invite it in. They won't tell you this either because they don't want some murder suspect turning up on the front cover of the national newspapers saying 'I only did what PC Dick told me to.'

The police are often frightened of the consequences of being honest, perhaps believing that the general populace do not have the intelligence to handle being able, lawfully, to attack first. One PC, he shall remain nameless (actually I have had several reports of this happening at police-run courses for nightclub doormen), told one of my friends on a doorman training course that he could not legally attack first. Instead he should wait to be attacked and then counter attack – with reasonable force of course – if he wanted to stay within the law. Now forgive me if I overreact here, but that is not just bad advice, it's a downright lie. The law allows pre-emption as long as it fits with the circumstances; that is that you have an honest belief that you are about to be attacked so you attack first. I will deal with this in more detail in a later chapter.

In the case of the cursory glancer I advise that you do not hold eye contact and if you are sure that it is just a cursory glance and not a challenging stare (it will usually be very obvious) just smile, perhaps say hello and then break the eye contact, this will probably leave him thinking 'I must know him, where do I know him from?' The ritual is then broken at the very first stage. If he does ask you what you are looking at, just apologise and say that you thought he looked familiar, and if he asks you if you want trouble say no. This will usually end the confrontation because he will feel as though he has won and wander off. This will be hard if you are a male with an ego to feed but a lot easier if you are a confident person that does not need to hurt people to prove masculinity. Ladies very rarely have a problem with submissiveness because it is not usually in their nature to be the protector unless they have been brought up with a weak male role model. If this is the case a woman may have developed male characteristics to balance the loss in her habitat, one of those being the ego. If you are still approached put up a 'fence' (to be detailed) and prepare for a physical encounter.

THE EYE CONTACT CHALLENGER

Firstly, if you sense a rowdy individual, walk tall and hold yourself confidently, and even if you do not feel dauntless, act it. After all, 'when ignorance is mutual, confidence is king.' Confident people are very rarely chosen as victims for attack. Whenever possible avoid eye contact where you sense aggression, but do not bow your head, this can be seen as a sign of weakness and may draw the attacker in for the kill. The challenger's ritual can be crushed before it starts by simply avoiding eye contact. If you are switched on you will have noticed him from a mile off and avoidance will not be a problem. This may take some discipline; it is often hard not to stare, you often feel almost drawn to something that you should not look at. If you do not make eye contact then you have avoided a situation.

If eye contact has already occurred, break the engagement immediately and separate yourself from the aggressor by as great a distance as possible, as soon as possible. If this proves fruitless and aggressive verbal follows, do not retaliate, just walk away, as a verbal counter could act as a catalyst. If you do not or cannot decamp at this stage and are approached, prepare for fight or flight. Only fight if there is no other option open to you.

Retaliation to the verbal challenge, however justified, will be seen by your aggressor as an acceptance to fight. From my experience, if you do not make a hasty exit at *actual challenge*, especially if you do verbally counter, more threats and a possible attack will result. A non counter and immediate exit on the part of the victim usually results in the challenger aborting, perceiving the response, or lack of it, to be an embryonic victory. Therefore if a verbal challenge is thrown do not counter.

If you can't get away and are approached then you must prepare yourself for fight or flight.

If you are in a pub and you sense trouble it is my advice to leave the pub and find another that is less threatening.

An ounce of prevention is better than a pound of cure.

At and before eye contact you should have been in code yellow. This will have given you awareness, not only of the potential situation, but also of the 'ritual'.

Like a cancer, confrontation should be caught and thus treated as early as possible; the longer you leave it, the graver it will become.

Treat a small malignancy rather than a full-grown tumour.

If a verbal challenge is thrown, you should rise with the threat to code orange where a potency assessment may be made. If an approach follows, you will/should automatically rise to code red, this being 'fight or flight'. The approach may be across the bar of a public house, the street or, in a traffic incident, it may be someone getting out of their car and approaching your vehicle.

At this stage you should have already utilised your 'flight' option and be a hundred yards down the road. Where 'flight' may not be plausible you may take advantage of the aforementioned four 'D's; if it works for your attacker then it can work for you. As the famous Japanese strategist Miyomoto Musashi said in his *Book of Five Rings*, 'What is true for one is true for a thousand and what is true for a thousand is true for ten thousand.' In other words, if it works against you it can also work for you.

Recap

First response:
Avoidance.

Second response:
Escape.

Third response:
The first verbal challenge when followed by an approach will usually be reiterated. This is when your four 'D's will come in to play. When the attacker reiterates his verbal challenge you will enter dialogue, telling him firmly that you don't want trouble and to keep away from you. This may be repeated several times before moving to –

Fourth response:
Physical confrontation.

If he is still aggressive and forward moving, it is likely that he intends to become physical – both are precursors to attack. If at this point escape is still not a viable option utilise the fourth response. Use deception and distraction: 'Look mate, I don't want any trouble, can't we talk about this?' By telling him that you don't want trouble you will disarm and thus deceive him. By asking him, 'Can't we talk about this?' you are intimating that you wish to elongate the conversation, because a question demands an answer. By engaging his brain as a possible precursor to pre-empting him (attack or escape), your question will also act as an action trigger to your own pre-emption. The deception used can be any of your design, as can your action trigger. Anything you can do or say to distract/deceive the attacker is good, even if it is abstract. You may ask the attacker, 'Is your mum's name Elsie?' The fact that this is peripheral to your circumstances only adds to the effect; you not only procure brain engagement, you add to their total bemusement. This engagement/bemusement will buy you one free shot.

Your fourth D is *destruction*. Your first choice should always be to run and your last choice to destroy, using a pre-emptive attack that should be fired immediately after asking the engaging question (whatever that may be).

Fifth response:
Non-confrontational verbal. If the attacker retaliates to your attack with greater violence, try to re-engage him in conversation, bringing him down from his rage.

Sixth response:
Escalated physical attack. If his attack still ensues use anything and everything to incapacitate the attacker for long enough to effect escape.

PHYSICALLY SPEAKING
If you decide that a physical response is your choice action, as soon as you are approached take up a small forty-five degree stance (Pic.1) by moving your right (or left) leg inconspicuously behind you and splaying your arms (fence), as though in exclamation. This is done simultaneously with your replying dialogue. As you will see in the illustrations, the fence allows you to control the distance between you and the attacker, disabling any attempts he may make at grabbing/striking you. Though it may be on a subconscious level your fence will act as a barrier between you and him. Try not to touch the assailant with your hands unless you are forced to, as the touch may fuel the fire and possibly result in your wrists being grabbed.

If he keeps forcing forward, you are in danger and an

Pic. 1

attack is certainly imminent, so make your decision with haste. Indecision begets defeat. For the duration of dialogue it is imperative to maintain distance control until you are ready to run or strike. When you strike make it a telling blow to a vulnerable area (see relative chapter), explode into the opponent with every fibre of your being, then run!! Many defence gurus advocate a second strike, a finisher. If there is a choice in the matter, don't do it. The few seconds you buy with your first strike could easily be lost if you linger for even a second. With some of the people I interviewed, and certainly in many of the incidents I have witnessed, this attempted and unnecessary *coup de grâce* resulted in the victim being grabbed, and subsequently defeated.

This is from my case histories:

'I punched my attacker in the face and he yelled in pain. When I tried to hit him again, like I'd been taught, he grabbed hold of me and pulled me to the floor and head-butted me, breaking my nose. I should have just run when I had the chance.'

There is also the danger of your attacker's accomplices (if he has any) coming to his aid if you do not take advantage and beat a hasty retreat. So unless a second strike is absolutely necessary, the rule of thumb is 'hit and run'.

For appropriate attacking techniques and fence work, please refer to the relevant chapters on the physical response.

If the attacker has a weapon, and does not respond to the victim's verbal dissuasion, it is always wise to employ added verbal distractions before engaging in a physical response.

The disarming approach: the professional attacker

The professional attacks for profit and covets compliance. He does not want to fight. To make his job easier he employs guile as opposed to force, this coming via deception. As with all predators, he seeks people in a victim state, or code white. He is, most often, very different from the archetypal, celluloid attacker that we have been programmed to expect, as you will see from the case histories.

I think this is best described by Christopher Berry-Dee (Chris has interviewed many of the world's most notorious serial rapists and killers and has kindly allowed me to use relevant extracts from those insightful tapes) and Robin Odell in their true crime book *Ladykiller*:

'Such predators are difficult to detect because their behaviour is masked with protective cunning. They merge into society and appear to all intents and purposes normal and well adjusted. Yet they are loners, restlessly roaming from place to place in search of opportunities to fulfil their lusts.'

DEAD OR ALIVE

This is the case with the most disarming of predators. They rarely look like potential attackers. The archetypal stocking-faced robber with a cosh and a swag bag is far removed from the real world villain who is more likely to be dressed in a smart suit and tie. John Cannan was such a killer. These are his own words:

'I bought my ladies roses and champagne. I always wore a suit and drove my black BMW. Christ, why should a successful man like me – I look like Sascha Distelle – kill anyone?'

Cannan is now serving life in prison for the murder of Shirley Banks, and numerous other rapes.

Then there was Michael Benniman Sams, a brutal killer, yet the most unlikely man in the world to commit such heinous crimes as he only had one leg. In his own words:

'Who'd have thought a one-legged man could hurt anyone – not even Teena would have ... she's my wife. Julie [Julie Dart, brutally murdered by Sams] thought I was harmless, took pity on me ... then I smashed her head in with a hammer.'

Sams is also serving life in prison for the murder of Julie Dart, and the kidnapping of Stephanie Slater, plus other kidnapping and extortion offences.

The opportunities these professionals seek are those formerly described. Often the attacker may not even be looking for a victim, but if an opportunity falls into their lap, they will act.

Again, intentions vary. The muggers interviewed in the chapter on case histories intended to rob, the rapists intended to rape, often killing their victims as an afterthought or by mistake, the killers intended to kill. The more serious the crime and experienced the criminal, the more deceptive the priming; the attacker adopting a cunning veil to beguile his intended victims.

I shall deal with them individually, still bearing in mind that all use deception, as a leading technique, in varying degrees.

I know that I may have already said this but it bears repeating: if the victim is in code white, deception often becomes an unnecessary tool, the 'blind-side attack' prevailing. In this instance the first the victim knows of the incursion is the physical attack itself – by then it is often too late.

As with most attacks the mugger follows a ritual and understanding this is the pre-requisite to avoidance.

The Mugger

'There was this geezer and his missus, outside a telephone box. Their car had the bonnet up, the woman went in to the 'phone box. We walked up to the 'phone box and pretended to queue for the phone. The geezer looked like he had money, good clothes, smart car. I gave J [his accomplice] the signal by winking at him; I then asked the geezer the time and we both pulled out our knives. When he looked up we told him to hand over his wallet.'

As far as I can work out there are four different kinds of mugger:

1) The snatch and run mugger, who literally rips your handbag/briefcase from your shoulder/hand and runs away at speed, or even drives away on a bike.

2) The blind-side mugger who suddenly appears out of an entry without any apparent warning.

3) The defiant mugger who attacks without ritual or fear of the law or consequences, usually because you have walked into his patch or have inadvertently crossed his path and he wants what you have got (whatever that might be).

4) The professional mugger who plans his attacks and uses deception as a way in.

Environmental awareness is the best way to avoid the first three, but a thorough understanding of attack ritual is the only real way of avoiding the fourth.

These are the ritualistic steps of the latter. If you can spot the ritual in the early stages you can avoid attack – you are not a victim.

VICTIM SELECTION

'Choosing a victim isn't hard. People are just asking to be robbed. I came out of Pizza Hut the other night, about 10.30 p.m., there was this girl walking down the side of the duel carriageway, on her own. She must have only been, what, 17, at the very most. She might as well have had a sign across her chest saying "Attack me!" Then they moan when someone does attack them. And the lads are as bad. They haven't got a fucking clue. We used to thumb a lift from town, after the nightclub. Some fucking idiot would pick us up, three of us, then wonder what he'd done wrong when we mugged him for all he's got. I reckon 'alf the fuckers aren't all there. I mean, don't they read the papers? Don't they know how we [muggers] work?'

CASE HISTORIES

The ideal victim is in code white, mentally and/or environmentally, those daydreaming or detached from the herd. Selection often occurs in sparsely populated locations; the mugger wanting as little fuss as possible in the execution of his attack. He favours the quiet park/street/entry etc. This does not mean that people are safe in highly populated areas like shopping malls, busy streets etc. Very often the mugger stalks such places for victims, after selection following them to a safe attack zone like the car park of a mall. It is thought that Stephanie Slater, murdered by Cannan, was stalked in just such a way. Cannan spotted her in the store of a shopping mall and followed her to the car park, which was his trade mark, pouncing as she got into her car.

VICTIM STALKING

'Once we've chosen a victim we follow them, cross the road, walk past them maybe two or three times. We wait for them to walk in to a side street or park, anywhere quiet. Some of them must be thick not to notice what's going on.'

CASE HISTORIES

A stalking of the chosen victim, for priming, and awareness assessment, will occur. If necessary the victim will be followed in the hope that he/she will heighten their vulnerability mentally or environmentally by walking into a park, down a quiet street etc. If the victim is followed from a shopping mall the attacker often waits for him/her to put the shopping in the boot of the car or even strikes as he/she enters the car. It is at such times that even normally vigilant people drop their guard, and though it may only be for a second, that is all the attacker needs.

When you have your hands full of shopping and are perhaps trying to get the kids into the car you may not notice that you are being followed. Often the attacker covers the whole of a car park without being noticed and his attack is then so swift that even other people in the car park do not notice what has happened. When you are off-loading the shopping and getting into the car, be very aware; as soon as you are in the car bang the locks on immediately.

EXPLORATORY APPROACH

'We walk up to them and ask the time – this distracts them. If they look like they know what we're gonna do, or if they look a bit tough or answer with a rough voice then we just walk off.'

CASE HISTORIES

The exploratory approach will often be coupled with disarming dialogue, (the four 'D's) used to prime the victim for attack. It is also used as a secondary awareness assessment – the attacker wants to see if you are switched on and wants to make sure he is safe before he attacks.

If at this point, or at any point after victim stalking, the victim appears switched off, the mugger may initiate his attack/threatened attack without further priming.

Unless the attacker is a real pro he will show signs of adrenal reaction in the exploratory approach that you will sense, so listen to your instincts.

Assessment

NEGATIVE ASSESSMENT

If the mugger feels that the chosen victim is switched on to the attempt and his secondary assessment is negative, he will often abort and find a more vulnerable victim.

POSITIVE ASSESSMENT

'....this distracts them [asking the time] while we pull out our knives. When they look up we say, "Give us your fucking money!" They usually look blank. Both of us shout at them, "Get your fucking wallet out", and put the knives closer to their face.'

CASE HISTORIES

If the mugger feels that the chosen victim is switched off, he may initiate the attack/threatened attack whilst the victim is engaged in answering his disarming question (this may be anything from asking directions to asking the time). Often the disarming question will switch off those that are switched on. An experienced attacker will use deception to take down any defensive fences that his intended victims may have put up.

THREATENED ATTACK

'This was taking too long [the attack], I thought to myself. I said, "I'm going to give you to the count of three [to hand over his wallet], or else", and pushed the knife closer to his throat. He handed over his wallet and ran off. If he'd refused to give us the wallet by three, we'd have just run away.'

CASE HISTORIES

I found this very interesting as many of the muggers that I interviewed used the threatened attack (as opposed to the actual attack) to prime their victims because, they said, if they got caught and they had used violence in the course of the attack, the sentence they got would be longer. They frightened their victims into supplication, rather than beat them into supplication.

The mugger will often threaten the victim with attack to frighten them into supplication, frequently underlining the threat with a weapon or an accomplice, or both.

The threats will be aggressive and menacing; this effecting adrenal dump in the victim, quickly escalating to the freeze syndrome (the reasoning process mistakes adrenalin for fear, often freezing victims into immobility). The threats are repeated with escalating aggression causing the victim to experience multiple adrenal release, grossly heightening the supposed feeling of fear and adding to the freeze. The threats, of course, are married with demands for money/credit cards etc.

THE FALSE PROMISE
Often the mugger threatens to hurt the victim if they are not compliant, or not to hurt the victim in exchange for compliance. The promise cannot be relied on.

ACTUAL ATTACK

'Sometimes, if they're a bit brave, I'll give them a dig, then they're mine. I've 'ad blokes who really look like they're gonna go for it, you give them a bit of pain and the fight falls out of them. They become just like babies.'

CASE HISTORIES
Some muggers may use a physical attack, creating compliance via disablement; others initiate an attack to disable the victim, before robbing them.

Sometimes the attack will be minimal, used only to add to freeze, other times the attack will be frenzied and severe. Any chance of a physical defence, other than actually attacking back with the same degree of ferocity (or greater) of ferocity, is unlikely to be effective. The concepts of blocking an assailant's blows or using hypothetical release techniques are not sound; if the situation has got this far only the very strong will survive.

BODY LANGUAGE
Running concurrently with attack ritual will be signs of adrenal reaction (the attacker will be scared too). This attack body language, if spotted, can help you to recognise potential menace. It has to be said, though, that many of the very experienced attackers may have learned to hide adrenal reaction, and only an expert eye will see imminent attack.

1) Erratic eye movement
The attacker, or his accomplice, concerned about being caught mid act, will constantly be checking for police/general public involvement; whilst he is speaking to you his eyes will be darting in other directions. If the attacker keeps looking past and around you as he speaks, this is not a good sign.

2) Adrenal reaction

Unless the attacker is seasoned he will be showing signs of adrenalin. His face will appear pale and his eyes wide from adrenalin induced tunnel vision; he will be stern and unsmiling and he may also fidget in an attempt to hide adrenal shake (the body will shiver as though cold) and his voice may have a nervous quiver.

3) Hand concealment

If the attacker is carrying a weapon, the bearing hand may be hidden, either in his pocket or behind his back. If one or both of his hands is concealed, beware. Some attackers do not hide their hands; rather they turn the palm or palms away from the chosen victim on approach, or keep the offending hand close to their leg to conceal the weapon.

Other attackers will keep their hands on full display, extracting a weapon from its hiding place as they approach, or immediately after asking an engaging question.

My friend was killed in just such a way. His attacker approached with his right palm turned into his right thigh so that his knife was hidden. He got very close to my friend and asked a question to distract him, then plunged the hidden knife into his heart. That single stab wound killed him.

So look out for concealment. If you can't see the attacker's hand or hands, or if the palm is turned in or even if the attacker has his hand in his pocket, you have to ask yourself why. It is very likely because he is concealing a

Knife concealed at side of attacker's leg

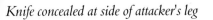

weapon. Cannan used to carry an old carrier bag in which he kept a number of killing implements. When he asked his intended victim a question, again as a distraction, he would reach into his bag and take out his weapon.

If the approach is by more than one person they will all usually display the same physical traits.

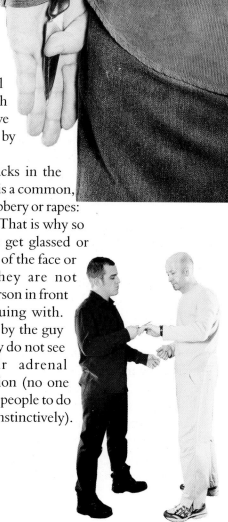

PINCER MOVEMENT

If more than one assailant is involved it is usual for one of the attackers to deploy the victim with distracting dialogue, whilst the other(s) move to your offside. Whilst the victim is distracted by the questioner, his accomplice(s) attack.

This was one of the most common attacks in the nightclub when I worked as a doorman and is a common, though, unbelievably, innate, ploy of gang robbery or rapes: the pincer movement. That is why so many people seem to get glassed or stabbed in the side of the face or neck because they are not attacked by the person in front that they are arguing with. They are attacked by the guy at the side that they do not see because of their adrenal induced tunnel vision (no one seems to teach these people to do this; they just do it instinctively).

The Rapist/Killer

Some of the extracts in this chapter are a little shocking and so I apologise if I cause any offence. I think that it is very important that you, whoever you are, understand how these terrible people operate and how little they care for human life and emotion. If you think that these people are not out there then think again: at the time of writing this book the West Midlands police have openly admitted that they believe there are five serial killers on the loose who are responsible for dozens of brutal killings. They have just started a manhunt involving some 200 police officers to catch these people. It is also widely believed that there are over 200 serial killers at large in the world today.

So read the following information as it is all true, none of it is made up, and use the knowledge to protect yourself from indiscriminate attack. If you want to know what a rapist looks for in a victim and how he is going to react to certain stimuli, ask a rapist, especially one that is locked up for the rest of his days and is no longer a threat. He'll tell you and revel in it, and whilst you might hate him, he'll give you, us, the information that we need to protect ourselves from others of that ilk. Chris Berry-Dee sums it up nicely in this extract from *Ladykiller*:

'Ladies. Consider the scenario: you are about to leave a crowd of friends after a summer's day picnic, when you notice a good looking man, attempting to load a pile of groceries in to his car. He is struggling in his work because he has obviously broken one arm – it's in a sling. And imagine, as you pass him, that he asks you could you help him out – just for a second.'

If you decide to become the good Samaritan, also consider this. Theodore Robert Bundy killed at least 34 young women, using entrapment skills such as this. As soon as his intended victim was in his space, Bundy turned in to a murderous entity with a switch that is abnormal by any human standards. He beat them unconscious, then took them away to rape and kill at his leisure.

The serial killer and sexual sadist, Michael Bruce Ross, was a former college graduate at Cornell. During the eighties this Connecticut murderer, who worked as an insurance salesman, raped upwards of 25 young women – killing at least 8. When finally arrested, Detective Mike Malchik, veteran of 50 successful homicide investigations, said of Ross, 'He was the most unlikely killer I have ever met.'

Whilst it is slightly peripheral to the main aim of this book, I think it important to illustrate that there are different kinds of rapists; understanding this can only help in your endeavours to detect and thus avoid attack.

Not every rapist is of the stalking variety, some use seduction to initiate rape, others are weak willed men who cannot control their sexual arousal when a girl says no.

THE COMPENSATORY RAPIST

This type of attacker generally has no self-worth and low self-esteem. He rapes to compensate for the fact that he believes no women in her right mind would agree to have sexual intercourse with him. He fantasises that his victim will fall in love with him, and wants her to become sexually aroused during the rape, often even trying to make a date with her after his crime.

THE EXPLOITATIVE RAPIST

For this type of attacker, sexual behaviour is expressed as an impulsive predatory act. His attack is determined more by situation and context than by fantasy, as in the case of the compensatory rapist. He can be best described as a man constantly on the prowl, looking until a safe situation presents itself.

THE DISPLACED RAPIST

For this type of attacker sexual behaviour is an expression of anger and rage. His victims represent, in a displaced fashion, a hated individual in their everyday life who they do not/cannot, for whatever reason, stand up to. All their anger is vented on their victim.

THE SADISTIC RAPIST

Sexual behaviour to the sadistic rapist is an expression of sexual-aggressive (sadistic) fantasy. To him there appears no differentiation between sexual and aggressive feelings. As sexual arousal increases, aggressive feelings increase also, and vice versa. His assault often begins as a seduction, his anger emerging as he becomes sexually aroused, the seduction then becoming a violent rape.

THE DATE RAPIST

Often a perfectly reasonable person until turned down in his sexual advances, his uncontrollable lusts turn to rape when his victim says 'No!' Often, post-rape, the attacker still does not feel that he has actually raped and believes that his victim's resistance was a part of foreplay.

Realistically, the genre of rapist should be of no real concern as we are dealing here with avoidance as opposed to a physical defence. One avoids them all in the same way, by not being there.

It is true to say that different types of rapist will react differently to varying forms of victim response, whether it be verbal, or physical. The displaced rapist may respond positively to verbal dissuasion as this allows him to see the victim as a real person and not the cause of his anger and rage. But the sadistic rapist, exploitative rapist, the date rapist and the compensatory rapist probably will not. Being able to differentiate between one genre of rapist and another, before and during an attack, is highly unlikely; you should therefore treat the previous descriptions as informational knowledge. When it comes to defence, don't be in the situation; if you are and a physical response is imperative, employ the following defence strategies for best effect.

Often the rapist/killer operates through mass deception and practised guile, and is usually the last person in the world you'd suspect; he may be someone that you know, though perhaps only in passing.

'If I were walking along a dark alleyway at night, and heard footsteps behind me, and if I turned round and saw Michael Ross ... I would have been relieved. Michael is just like the guy next door.'

These are the words of a streetwise, hard-nosed American journalist, Karen Clark. She was describing Michael Ross, after an interview with him on Death Row, Osborn Correctional Institute, Somers, Connecticut. Ross, is responsible for upwards of 25 rapes and sexual assaults, aligned with 8 horrific homicides. He is the ultimate killing machine – and sexual sadist. Ross is a wolf in sheep's clothing.

His biggest deception was the way he looked, as opposed to the way he entrapped. Many of the world's most vicious attackers are like this, and no one is above suspicion. A serial killer in west America, a man that killed many young women brutally, and without mercy, turned out to be a local self-defence instructor.

Michael Ross, when asked what women could do to avoid attack said:

'If I were to give women any advice, I'd say, don't trust anyone, period – because you ain't got a clue what's in their heads...'

Whilst I am not trying to suggest that all attacks or attackers are as extreme as this, I would like to put across the following points. Attackers rarely look how we would expect them to, rather they may look like someone's elderly father or younger brother and to all intents and purposes, harmless. Also they will very often use mass deception (the four 'D's) before initiating their attack.

Again, if you are in code white, mentally and/or environmentally, you are/will be an easy target, so the aforementioned deception would be an unnecessary tool. The first you are likely to know of the assault would be the attack itself. Understanding of rituals are useless, if you are not aware. It's like teaching a child the Green Cross Code (a method used for children to cross the road safely); it will not stop that child from being knocked over by a car if the child does not use the information. If you are coded up (in code yellow) you will spot the signs as the attacker goes through his priming ritual and this will allow you to be pre-emptive in your avoidance, escape or attack.

The ritual of the elite attacker is masked by professional cunning, though to the perceptive the ritual will still be noticeable and avoidance will be possible. Make yourself a hard target and you will not be noted for victim selection. Vigilance is the key here, as with all attack scenarios; early detection and prevention is far better than what is often the unlikely cure of a physical response.

'The best defence is vigilance.'

This is what Arthur J. Shawcross (the Monster of the Rivers) said about his victims at interview, 19th September 1994. This account has been substantiated by Captain Lynde M. Johnston – Head of Homicide, Rochester Police Department, New York, and Detective Lenny Borriello, the arresting officer. Shawcross is serving 250 years at the Sullivan Correctional Institute, Fallsburg.

'I've killed 13 women; raped dozens more. I've probably killed 54 in my time ... Sometimes they talk to me and I'd let them live ... others? Well, they were dead the moment I saw them. I'd beat up on them, rape them. Yeah, I've eaten human flesh ... tastes like pork ... I prefer the genitalia, period. But you ask Clara, she's marrying me next year. She trusts me. Remorse? No way, period. They all asked for it, suckers, the whole lot. Well, I look like their fathers, don't I?'

That was one of Shawcross' best primers for attack; he looked like an old guy that wouldn't hurt a fly, like your father. This is a big part of deception and deception is used as a way in, a window.

The rapists' ritualistic steps are a facsimile of those of the mugger, though with added cunning, and though I don't like to repeat myself this stuff needs repeating.

VICTIM SELECTION

'She was playing up to the role, the big beautiful smile and getting into the car, which was kind of tragic, but she had advertised to get blown away.'
Christopher Berry-Dee's interview with serial killer Arthur Shawcross, 1994

The victim is selected similarly to all attack victims, though the rapist may be looking for a specific type of person – blond, brunette, buxom, slight etc. This is a contributing factor that the victim has no control over, so it does not come in to the reckoning. What is important is the fact that the attacker makes his selection from those that are in a victim state, code white, mentally and/or environmentally. If you are in code yellow you will notice the build up of events and be in a position to take preventive measures.

There are also occasions when the victim may be in code yellow mentally but in code white environmentally; that is, she may be switched on to attack ritual, but be in a dangerous and vulnerable place. Other times the victim may be switched on in every sense and the attacker uses guile and deception to switch her off.

Again, these are the words of Michael Ross, taken during a televised interview with Christopher Berry-Dee, 24th September 1994.

'I had fantasies as a youth, then went on to following women home. I got my sexual kicks from that at first. Then I raped – at least a dozen times ... then I killed. Why? Because she knew me from college. They were easy to chat to. They all liked me because I looked so harmless. Most women are stupid – they trust good looking guys like me. I'd say they deserved all they got. I carried one woman's shopping home, then, when we got into her yard, I lifted her baby out of the stroller and smashed its head into a tree. Then I raped and strangled the mother. She lived and that isn't any fault of mine, that was a pure act of God.'

VICTIM STALKING

'A sex attacker who struck in a Southampton park earlier this week may be a dangerous 'stalker' with a vendetta against students.

The mature student, who did not want to be named, described how the smartly dressed man had tried to engage her in conversation before the attack. "He said hello so familiarly that I felt I must know him," she said. "But then he started chatting me up, asking me what I was doing that night, so I just ignored him." At this point the man's behaviour changed and he attacked her.'

The Daily Echo, 1994

The victim is often stalked for awareness assessment and possibly followed in the hope that her vulnerability will be heightened.

EXPLORATORY APPROACH

'He walked past the car. About two or three minutes later she saw the man again walking towards the Sava Centre roundabout. She went back to her book and looked up again when she was aware of someone approaching the car.

'Her driver's side window was open. The man spoke to her. "Excuse me," he said. "Can you tell me where Balfour Drive is ... it's supposed to be around here somewhere ... have you got an A-Z in the car?"'

Ladykiller

If the victim is completely unaware, the first approach will be the attack/threatened attack itself, though more often than not further priming will take place in the guise of the four 'D's. Disarming/incidental dialogue is employed for the duel purposes of secondary awareness assessment and brain engagement. Assessment

NEGATIVE ASSESSMENT

The attacker will make a negative assessment if, on approach, he feels the victim is suspicious of his intentions. In this instant he will either abort, or attempt, via deceptive dialogue, to switch off the victim.

If, however, the victim is environmentally vulnerable – for instance, walking across a field at night with no hope of raising an alarm – the attack may still ensue without further priming or without any priming at all.

POSITIVE ASSESSMENT

If, on approach, the attacker feels his chosen victim is switched off, he may initiate attack/threatened attack whilst the victim is distracted.

THREATENED ATTACK

'I didn't really do anything at first. All my breath had gone out of me when I landed and I could feel this great weight on my back. His hand had left my mouth and I could feel him fumbling with my skirt, but I didn't have the breath to scream. He was on my back and telling me to keep still or he would kill me.'

Unleash the Lioness by Robin Houseman

If the attacker deems the immediate locale safe, he may carry out an assault there and then, often using the threat of attack to frighten the victim into compliance. Uncompliance may result in a controlled attack to underline the threat and then an aggression escalated reiteration of the threat. This is usually enough to frighten most people into complete supplication. Both the threat and the controlled attack cause adrenal dump, or what we call the wow factor, in the victim, whose reasoning process mistakes the feeling of adrenalin for sheer terror. The threat is often used by the attacker as a false promise: 'If you do what I say you won't get hurt!' These promises without exception are, of course, rarely kept. This is especially the case with the rapist and abductor.

ACTUAL ATTACK

'February 1993, Oxford. Following a row with her boyfriend, a twenty seven year old pharmacist was attacked when she walked home alone.

A man grabbed her as she was walking past some railings. Although she managed to get hold of his hair, he had his hands around her throat. The women told the court that she thought she was going to be found dead the next morning, so she conceded to his demands to save her own life.

'He then dragged her in to an alleyway and tied her hands before raping her.'

Unleash the Lioness

This is where the majority of self-defence books begin, with the attack itself and advocating the use of defence strategies that are as impractical as they are unlikely. This is not so much because of the physical concept of blocking an attack, though even the highly skilled would baulk at such a task, but more because the initial attack is very rarely seen by the victim as it is masked by practised and deceptive cunning.

The actual attack is used by the assailant to disable his victim, forcing compliance through injury/unconsciousness or, as already stated, to cause terror compliance by effecting adrenal dump.

ABDUCTION

'I asked one girl directions from my car. She stuck her head in to the electric window. It was a busy street at night. I dragged her 150 yards then smashed her unconscious. Then I took her away and raped and killed her. Slut.'
Arthur J. Shawcross (The Monster of the Rivers) during interview, 19th September 1994

Some rapists initiate attack as their intended victims get into, or out of, vehicles, using the same to effect abduction. In the majority of cases they utilise total surprise or a false promise to ensure compliance. The victim is then taken away from the herd where the attacker enacts the crime.

Often the attacker will use his own or a hired vehicle to trawl for victims, abducting after using the age-old ploy of stopping and asking for directions and then bundling the victim into his car when they least expect it. Many women warn their children of this ploy, and yet paradoxically fall foul of it themselves.

This is how Cannan effected the abduction of Shirley Banks:

'Shirley Banks, a slim vivacious blond, probably turned many men's heads that evening. We know she turned one for sure. That of John Cannan. Although we cannot be certain of his movements, but following his previous pattern of behaviour, he had probably been wandering through the store, driven by an overwhelming desire to seek out a female victim. Then his blue eyes would have settled on Shirley while she innocently browsed through the clothesrails in search of a dress. In an effort to remain inconspicuous in the ladies' department he would seemingly have interested himself with a possible gift for a girlfriend. However his eyes were furtively following Shirley's every move. Now he was stalking his prey, and waiting patiently for the chance to pounce. As she walked to her car he was but a few steps behind her.

'If we follow the pattern of his attempt to abduct Julia Holman, he probably approached his victim with menace, as she entered her car, and got into her car beside her.'

John Cannan was later convicted of the abduction and murder of Shirley Banks. She was last seen alive in a busy shopping mall.

Body Language

The rapist, or certainly the experienced attacker, will show very little outward display of bad intention. The predators, in what is an increasingly violent society, all too often wear sheep's clothing.

ERRATIC EYE MOVEMENT

Very often even the experienced attacker will be unable to mask his fear of being caught mid act so will be constantly checking for police/general public involvement. As he verbally primes his intended victim he may look through, past or around them, checking the safety of his environment.

ADRENAL REACTION

The attacker may show signs of adrenalin reaction that will give him away. His face may appear pale, his eyes staring with the effect of tunnel vision, he may be wearing a false smile that will set your alarm bells ringing. A possible fidget to hide 'adrenal shake' and a nervous quiver in his voice are also telltale signs. This is a man about to attack and rape, so you'll possibly sense an uncomfortable aura. Trust your instincts.

HAND CONCEALMENT

If you cannot see both the attacker's hands, or palms, there is a good chance that he is hiding a weapon. It is unnatural to walk, or stand, with the palms of the hands hidden, so if you can't see the palms there may be a weapon concealed. Others, like John Cannan, will carry a shopping bag or some kind of carrier, in which a weapon may be hidden.

  If there is more than one assailant they may all display the same physical traits.

PINCER MOVEMENT

When more than one assailant is involved, one attacker will deploy the victim with disarming banter, whilst the other/s will attack from the victim's blind-side, attacking during brain engagement.

  Listen to your instincts. Many people, in retrospect, say they sensed menace long before they were attacked, but did not act upon it, putting their perception down to paranoia. The following true story is a good example of acting on instinct.

Asks the time...   *draws knife out of carrier bag*

'On Thursday 29 October 1978, three weeks to the day since Shirley went missing [Shirley Banks, abducted and killed by John Cannan], a man entered a boutique known as Gingers in Leamington Spa. It was about 3.55 p.m. and the owner, 40 year old Carmel Cleary, was arranging clothes on the rails, whilst her manageress, Jane Child, sat at the desk at the front of the shop. They were the only people in the premises which was situated at 20a Regent Street. The man who was wearing black trousers and a grey zip up bomber jacket had a silver grey crash helmet on his head with the visor raised. His jacket was bulging as if there was something bulky in it and a pair of blue grey gloves poked out of the top left-hand pocket.

'The man stood beside one of the clothes rails and said, "I'm looking for some gift ideas." Carmel Cleary walked over to where he was standing and produced some jumpers. He said, "She's a size 38." Carmel drew his attention to one of the garments and explained, "This is a medium, this will fit her."

'"I could tell," she said later, "that he was not interested in the jumpers." The man said he wanted something brighter and walked over to the display rails near the desk. "She's only 24," he said and paused to look at some of the items displayed.

'Sensing that the man did not appear genuine in his enquires, Carmel Cleary moved over to the desk and casually spoke to Jane Child. She asked her to phone Room Service, a nearby shop, on the pretext of settling an account. This was a ploy to bring somebody else in to the shop.

'Suddenly the man was standing next to the two women. He held an orange-handled knife with a serrated blade in his left hand with which he threatened Mrs Cleary. Holding the weapon to her stomach and speaking to Jane Child he said, "Turn out the lights, lock the door and if you scream, I'll knife her." Mrs Cleary picked up the shop keys from the desk and Jane Child walked to the corner of the boutique where the light switches were located. The intruder said, "What are you doing?" and, still brandishing the knife, walked over to her.

'At this point, using great presence of mind, Carmel Cleary dashed across to the front of the shop and ran out in to the street screaming, "Help! Help! There's a man in the shop with a knife." Her desperate screams attracted the immediate attention of Andrew Riley, a builder, who had just entered Regent Street from Portland Street. He ran towards her asking, "What's up?" The shop owner gasped out, "He's got a knife." As they spoke, the man rushed out of Gingers, turned left and ran down in to Portland Street.

'Some minutes later the police apprehended John Cannan, later convicted of the killing of Shirley Banks and suspected of many other abductions and murders. Neither woman in the shop was physically injured.'

The Defence

This covers most genres of attack, assault, mugging, rape etc. and is my advice and mine alone. I can only give you the options and leave you to make your own choice. What I will say though is, whenever possible, stick to the sequence of avoidance, escape and dissuasion before considering a physical response. The latter has to be trained for; it is not enough to just throw a punch and hope for the best. A partially effective blow may do nothing more than piss your attacker off and cause him to be more violent. So train for physical if you think you want to use it. It's no use having a gun in the cupboard if you don't know how to load the bullets. Most of the people that I see around the country just would not be able to deal with a physical response, no disrespect intended but they would be completely ineffective – so get some training under you belt. Many people feel that they are not capable of training for physical combat; to be honest if you have learned to drive a car you can learn to throw a punch.

Your idea of good defence may be to give the attacker what he wants. That choice is yours as some people can live with the aftermath of assault better than others, so no one has the right to tell you what you should and should not do. However, the more dangerous the attack, rape, murder etc. the harder the decision to acquiesce becomes. No one is going to lose too much sleep over a stolen handbag but very few people want to give up their lives without a fight, and even if they are prepared to do that, they are very unlikely to allow an attacker carte blanche on their family.

I can only give you the options and my opinion; you have to decide on your own course of action. The publishers of this book and I can take no responsibility for that choice.

Julia went with three colleagues to the Colonial Bar *at the* Watershed *in central Bristol. She stayed chatting to her friends until 6.50 p.m. when she decided to leave.*

Julia had left her car that morning at Canon's Marsh car park, a short distance from the Watershed. She walked alongside the harbour for a short distance and then used an alleyway to reach Canons Road.

'Using the gap in the fence she entered the open-air car park and strolled towards her blue Ford Fiesta. She took the keys out of her handbag as she approached it, then unlocked the door, slid in to the driver's seat and pulled the door shut.

'As she put her keys in to the ignition, her driver's door was wrenched open and she found herself looking at a man who was a total stranger. He produced what she took to be a handgun with a barrel about six inches long. Bending his head into the car and thrusting the gun against her side, he said, "If you do what I say you won't get hurt". He pushed her as though he wanted her to move across in to the front passenger seat while continuing to point the gun at her.

'With great presence of mind, Julia Holman swung her legs around to the right and kicked out at him, at the same time pushing him off balance with her hands. She also shouted at him and gave out a loud scream. As the man straightened up she slammed the car door shut, started the engine and rapidly drove out of the car park. She noticed, in her rearview mirror, that he casually walked off in the direction of the city.'

The day after Julia's attempted abduction, Thursday 8th October, Shirley Banks disappeared form the centre of Bristol. John Cannan was subsequently convicted of her murder.

The following advice about defence is from a Home Office report in *The Daily Telegraph*, Tuesday 5th March 1991.

'Victims should always resist their attackers with all the force they can muster, says a home office report published yesterday in the psychology of sex offenders. The study found that in half the cases where the attacker used gratuitous or 'excessive' violence the victim had offered little or no resistance.'

As with all attack scenarios prevention is the best defence. If it comes down to a physical response, unless you are highly trained or very instinctive, your chances of success are not good as everything is against you.

Again the key is to be vigilant, practising awareness by being coded up, utilising the concept of target hardening. Catch the criminal in his preparatory stages and break his ritual, simply by being aware of bad intention. You will usually spot menace if you are in code yellow and thus the consequential stalking and approach.

If you are approached keep a safe range between you and your potential attacker, even if the approach appears genuine, and never take your eyes off him. Beware of deception. If the attacker, or suspected attacker, walks away, fine. If not and a threat follows, or you feel that you are about to be threatened, use your lead hand (fence -to be detailed later) to stop him getting any closer to you and draw as much attention to your dilemma as possible. If an attack ensues, shout 'fire!', as opposed to 'rape!' or 'robbery!' Many people will not come to your aid if you are being attacked but will come running when someone shouts fire.

First response: Escape
As with all attack scenarios, your first response should be that of escape.

Second response: Verbal confrontation
If escape is not possible your second response should be a firm verbal confrontation. Tell the attacker to leave you alone. Make a fuss, draw attention to your dilemma. This may need reiterating several times. Shout or scream to attract attention from passers by.

If the attacker remains and no weapon is present, move on to the third response, physical confrontation.

If there is a weapon present, first use verbal dissuasion, engaging the attacker in conversation and setting the scene for escape. If this is fruitless and the offender makes aggressive threats, gestures or physical violence, then move onto the third response.

Third response: Physical confrontation
Make a pre-emptive attack and escape.

Fourth response: Non confrontive verbal
If the aggression abates, but escape is still not an option, the victim should engage the attacker in conversation and set the scene for possible escape.

If the attacker counters third response with greater violence, resume conversation and try to talk the attacker down from his rage.

Fifth Response: Escalated physical confrontation
If the aggression still does not abate and the attack continues the victim should use anything and everything to incapacitate the attacker to avoid further serious assault. The victim should try to use cunning and deception to veil their attack.

ATTACKER WITH A WEAPON

If the attacker is brandishing a weapon it is always wise to use added verbal dissuasion before engaging in a physical response. If the victim decides that a pre-emptive strike is needed, add cunning to veil the attack.

If you can't summon up the courage to be aggressive then feign submissivness and, under its veil, when the attacker seems at his most vulnerable, make a pre-emptive attack. Make sure that the attack is a critical one to the opponent's vulnerable areas – jaw, eyes, throat etc. Hit and run.

Where distance control is not an option and the situation may have escalated to actual attack, fight back with all your might, again screaming and shouting, to draw attention to your dilemma, and attack, using every part of your body as a weapon. If you are holding keys, or anything incidental that may second as a weapon, use that also.

Many rapists will use the false promise to effect victim compliance, especially in abduction cases. It's important that you do not fall for this ploy. Every woman that was ever raped was hurt, if not physically, mentally.

Again, expect fear, control it with the knowledge that it is adrenalin and it is there to help. If the situation has become so dire that the victim has to resort to a physical response, it will require her to convert fear into rage and a sense of helplessness into a battle for survival.

The following is another true story, typical of many: an exemplification of rituals and deception, taken from the book *Ladykiller*:

'Donna and Gerry had recently returned from a holiday in Egypt where they had picked up a gastric infection. As a result they were both tired and an argument ensued over Gerry's decision to retire to bed a little earlier than usual.

'Donna slipped in to bed but could not settle down. The argument smouldered on. Eventually, 30 year old Donna decided to get up. She dressed in a yellow jumper and blue skirt, then went out of the house to calm down. It was a cool night and Donna reflected that she and Gerry had been married for four years and, although their relationship was a good one, they occasionally had tiffs for which their antidote was that one of them went out to "cool off". On this particular occasion, Donna took a book with her and went for a drive in the family's Vauxhall Cavalier. She drove down Langley Hill along the A4 and turned in to Chantry Green off the Sava Centre roundabout. Parking under a street lamp, she turned off the engine and listened to the radio whilst reading her book. She recalled hearing the midnight news on Radio 2 and afterwards heard approaching footsteps.

'Looking in the rear view mirror, Donna noticed a man walking along the footpath on the opposite side of the road. He walked past the car. About two or three minutes later she saw the man again walking towards the Sava centre roundabout. She went back to her book and looked up again when she was aware of some one approaching the car.

'Her driver's side window was open. The man spoke to her. "Excuse me," he said. "Can you tell me where Balfour Drive is?"

'Donna replied, "I'm sorry, I'm afraid I don't ..."

"'It's supposed to be around here somewhere. I've been walking around here for quite a while." They conversed briefly about Balfour Drive with the man looking up and down the road.

"'Have you got an A-Z in the car?" he asked. Donna glanced over her shoulder in to the back of the Cavalier and, as she did so, was aware that he was reaching for the door handle. He opened the door and said, "Don't make a fucking move, or noise, see this knife, if you don't do as you're told, you'll get it in your gut." He was holding a knife with a blade four inches long.

'Donna was terrified, but she had worked in a building society where the staff were advised always to give in to any demand rather than risk violence. She said, "What do you want?" thinking that the man was after money or jewellery.

"'I just want sex," he replied. "Get in the back of the car. Get down on the fucking floor." The man climbed in to the driver's seat of the car and drove them off to an industrial park where he parked the car in partial darkness next to a rubbish skip. This set the scene for a terrifying rape.

'The perpetrator was "handsome and charming" John Cannan.'

This entrapment was used again and again by Cannan, a classical demonstration of the aforementioned 'ritual of violence'. In this case the victim was self-selected: she placed herself, albeit inadvertently, in a victim state by breaking every rule in the book about 'target hardening'. Cannan stalked her by walking past the car a couple of times, in his initial approach he utilised the four 'D's: Dialogue ('can you tell me where Balfour Drive is?'), Deception ('It's supposed to be around here somewhere. I've been walking around for quite a while'; Cannan deceives her into believing that he is genuinely lost), Distraction ('Have you got an A-Z in the car?') and ultimately Destruction (brutal rape). Cannan also used the false promise ('see this knife, if you don't do as you're told, you'll get it in your gut') to force compliance.

It is also demonstrative of code white, mentally and environmentally, and of victim naivety. Cannan was renowned for his trawling of victims. In this case we are not sure if he was trawling, and happened upon Donna, or if it was an opportunist attack that fell right into his lap. Either way his victim was in code white, thus making his job easier.

Many attacks happen after lovers' tiffs; the lady (or the man) storming off, leaving the lady on her own, either out of the house or, when socialising, to make her own way home from the pub/club. This can be a highly vulnerable time for women and should be avoided at all costs. Or for women out with a girlfriend, if she goes off with a man leaving you to make your own way home, be very careful. Ask the pub/club staff if they might call you a taxi, explain your dilemma. Don't end up walking the streets looking for a cab, or worse still, walking home or taking a lift from a stranger.

FOR YOUR INFORMATION

Surveys throughout the world have also shown that attack and rape victims who fought back did not sustain any greater injury than those who succumbed. It is also a well known medical fact that rape victims who fight back against their attackers recover from the mental torture that often follows far more quickly than those that do not. The duration of most attacks is short; the longer the attack lasts the more danger the attacker finds himself in. This is another good reason why I believe fight-back, on the part of the victim, is essential. It complicates matters for the attacker who can ill afford the time delay that victim reticence would cause. The more ferocious your fight back, the more likely he is to abort the assault. The archetypal attacker thrives upon the capitulating victim who is moulded into supplication by sheer terror. Fight back will also draw attention from passers-by, another dangerous complication for the attacker that will again force him to abort.

TELLTALE SIGNS

Code yellow allows the victim to spot the telltale signs that the mugger emits in his selection stage.

Close observation will highlight the assailant's suspicious actions: he will stand out like a sore thumb. His eyes will follow the victim closely and dart away if the look is returned, he will be falsely casual, as though trying to look occupied, with no occupying matter. The fact that he has noticed his intended victim's vigilance will, at this stage, usually be enough to cause early abortion of the intended attack, awareness making the victim a hard target. The victim should let the attacker know by his/her actions that he has been noted. If the victim mingles with other people, goes in to a shop, makes a hasty retreat etc., the attacker will move on, going back into selection mode and look for another victim, preferably someone that is not so aware.

ACQUIESCENCE

Due to the sheer terror evoked by an attack scenario, many people are frozen into immobility and compliance by abject terror, caused by adrenal dump. This forces them to submit for fear of the attacker killing them. The victim might say 'Don't hurt me and I'll do anything that you want.' This may be as a last resort, when all else has failed, to stop the attack. This capitulation is often interpreted by the attacker as participation and can exasperate the intensity of the attack.

This, taken from the book *Sexual Homicide: Patterns and Motives*, is what the Behavioural Sciences Unit of the FBI had to say about acquiescence:

'In general the decision to submit or acquiesce to an attacker is a difficult one, determined as much by the violence of the assault as by the victim's emotional state and specific fears (such as death or rape). Some women will be able to cope much better than others with the knowledge that they submitted.

'Acquiescence can invoke, in some victims, post assault rage and/or guilt, while other victims may be able to accept and feel comfortable with whatever actions they felt were necessary to survive the assault with a minimum of physical and emotional injury. If, after other strategies have failed, acquiescence is deemed to be the optimum response to protect life and reduce physical injury in a given situation, it is important that the victim be comfortable with such a choice and be aware that post assault guilt feelings will probably arise.'

DATE RAPE

Date rape, a relatively new expression imported from America, has already received much coverage in the popular press in this and other countries. It is a very sensitive subject.

What might start out as a special date, or even a platonic offer of a nightcap could end in date rape. So, in addition to the foregoing, and for basic avoidance and survival, be very fussy and sceptical about who you take lifts with or invite into your home. Until you know the person who wants to take you out a little better, stick to places that you know well, better still try to go out in a foursome.

Habits of youth. The first sexual encounter for many men is likely to have been with a girl that needed coaxing into having sex – his first attempts being refused until, after much persistence, 'no', finally becomes, 'oh, go on then'. Token resistance can also be a small part of foreplay. So it is important not to lead a man on without knowing how far you want to go. If you go part way and then stop, the man may see it as a part of the lover's ritualistic foreplay, he may also think that you, like the girls in his youth, just need a little more coaxing.

Alcohol can also play a major part in date rape. Many women drop their guard under its influence and become more amorous than usual, maybe even flirty. With men, alcohol swells the ego and bravado often comes to the forefront. Aggression may also be triggered, even in someone that may usually be timid.

Things are said and done under the influence of alcohol that, in a sober state, would be completely out of character. Be extra careful when having a drink, and think very carefully before inviting someone home for a nightcap, that may turn in to a nightmare.

If you invite someone in for a coffee, be sure to stipulate that coffee is all that is on offer. For many men the offer of coffee is the greatest aphrodisiac in the world, whilst for the young lady it is often, genuinely, just a kind offer of a nightcap and perhaps a chat. If you invite a man for coffee, or accept an invitation from him, you may be at risk. If you offer or accept, be firm so that the offer cannot be misconstrued. Even then, be on your guard – some men listen with their ears closed.

If you do not want sex, it may be better not to make or accept the invitation until you know the person a lot better. Whilst I understand that this may sound ridiculously paranoid, it is the only fail-safe preventive method. If you really like the man, make a date to meet him again. If he likes and respects you he will accept this without demur.

If you are not sure whether or not you want sex say no and wait until you are absolutely certain. Confusion on the part of the lady could lead to a serious misunderstanding later.

Whilst it is the lady's prerogative to change her mind, at any stage, it would be naive to lead him on if you have no intention of having sex. It will also make it easier for the man to make you feel guilty for saying no if he can claim that you led him on earlier.

Sex is no longer a taboo subject. If you are enjoying a man's company, but have no intention of making sex a part of the evening, don't hesitate to tell him so right from the start. Tell him that you like his company and would like to talk, but nothing else. This is working on the premise that you know what you want; sex is often a spontaneous end to a lovely evening. The demand for sex, when unwanted, is a very ugly end to a lovely evening.

You may well go home with a man, intending to have sex with him, and change your mind if he turns out to be less than you desired. If you say no, it must mean no. It must be said emphatically and without hesitation. If a man thinks there is even the slightest chance that you will change your mind he will persist, the more aroused he gets, the more insistent his demands will become.

If he is a regular boyfriend and he threatens to go home in a sulk when you turn him down, let him go and don't make up on the doorstep; again, he may read this as a reprieve and start all over again. Let him come back the next day, or call you on the phone to make amends.

If a man will not leave your home, after several requests, find an excuse to leave the room or even the house and phone a friend to come to your aid, even the police if you feel adequately threatened. If the phone is in the same room, make an excuse to leave the room and then go to a neighbour and use their phone.

If the situation has become grave, but not violent, and the man is laying a guilt trip on you, perhaps intimating that he may become violent if he does not get his own way, and you are not in a position to use a phone, continue to make it clear that you do not want him to continue and maintain a safe distance between you and him. In some cases it may even be worth developing a few bad habits: picking your nose, talking about your piles or periods, coughing and spitting into a handkerchief. This may well put a lot of men off wanting sex.

If all else fails and the man continues to force himself on you and you are struggling to control the situation, tell him firmly and clearly, 'If you don't stop now, this will be RAPE! STOP! OR THIS WILL BE RAPE!'
Many date rapists claim, post rape, that they didn't think their act was rape, using the old 'No doesn't always mean "no"' excuse. If you tell him that what he is about to do IS going to be rape, he can be in no doubt. The word RAPE will also be very sobering, neutering arousal and possibly stopping a potential rape.

If all else fails, every and any physical response you may have learned will come in to play. All the techniques described so far of deception and cunning should be employed. A man with his genitals exposed is very vulnerable. But it will take courage in bucketfuls to act.

April 1992, Catford, South London.

'A man with previous convictions pushed his way in to a care assistant's home, he took her money and then demanded sex. He tore open her clothes and then sexually assaulted her. When he licked her face she bit his tongue. His screaming alerted the assistant's twenty-eight year old son, who called the police. The attacker was sentenced to nine years. He told police "I chose her because she is a woman. They are soft and can't struggle." In this case he couldn't have been more wrong.'

Unleash the Lioness

Any attempt at rape, whether thwarted or not, should be reported to the police. Many rapists are free and walking the streets today because their victims were either too scared or too embarrassed to report the attack, often even too scared or ashamed to tell their own families of the atrocity. This reticence is understandable, but every time a victim fails to report a rape or attempted rape there is a possibility that somebody else will get attacked or raped as a direct or indirect consequence because the attacker is still at large. If you are the victim of attack, telling some one will also help share the burden and hurry your recovery. A problem shared is a problem halved.

LESSONS LEARNED:

The following expected response graph has been devised from information as taken from my interviews, actual experience and case histories.

Expected Response Graph

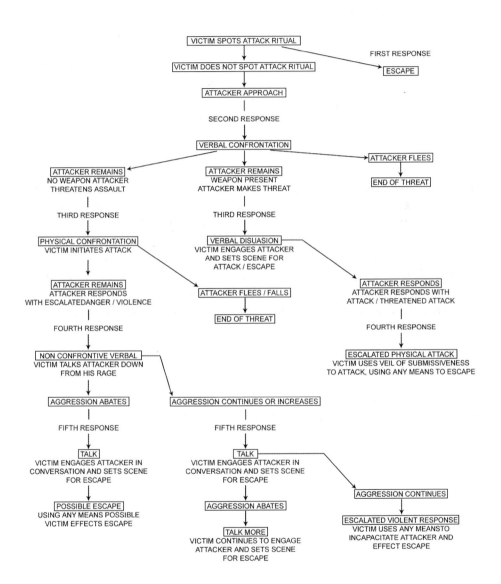

Chapter Three

Fear Control

'When the common soldiers are too strong and their officers too weak, the result is insubordination.'

Sun Tzu

'Courage is grace under pressure.'

Ernest Hemingway

'This is where it's at, this moment before engagement when the adrenalin, the fear, reached its pinnacle and felt like hell, gathering in the cavity of your chest like a burning fire ball of negative emotion that makes you feel like breaking down in a crying quivering heap of jellied shit. It rises from your chest to your nasal passage like toxic gas, gnawing away at you like caustic, tempting you to crack, daring you to fight, questioning your ability to "handle it" telling you to flee, to run, to hide, to GO! GO! GO!'

Watch My Back

This, from my book *Watch My Back*, talks about the fear of a real confrontation and the negative effects of the same. If I, as a veteran of hundreds of fights, struggle with adrenalin, it goes without saying that people with less experience and knowledge of conflict will also struggle. As formerly stated, you cope with fear through the knowledge that it can be a help rather than a hindrance. Mental strength is also a pivotal element of fear control.

Many people practise technique after technique in their bid for physical competence. They become bag punchers and mirror watchers, convinced in their own minds that they can handle themselves. Whilst developing power on the bag and building a sinewy, beach physique in the gym, they ignore the most important factor: the mental physique. This is, of course, not to detract from the physical training formerly mentioned. It is very important, though not nearly as important though as the old grey matter. A strong mind can and will take you, if properly trained, safely through the adrenalin build-up, stress and pain of a physical encounter and the ever-present aftermath that can crush you flatter than a shadow.

Understanding the mechanics of adrenalin greatly lessens its impetus. The shock factor of adrenalin can be scarifying if you do not understand or expect it, rendering many frozen in the face of an ensuing attack.

This unpleasant, strong emotion often causes terror immobilisation, or the freeze syndrome, in the recipient. The key with adrenalin is don't panic. Easy to say, I hear you cry, and you are right; it's not easy, it's very hard. That's why so many people, trained and untrained, baulk at the obstacle of a real fight. The adrenal syndrome needs to be understood and addressed so that it can be harnessed.

Adrenalin is a little like fuel injection in a sports car: action, fight/flight, the metaphoric accelerator.

The car: by engaging the clutch and pressing the accelerator you will utilise the turbo, and the car will move at speed. However, if you sit at the traffic lights pressing your foot on the accelerator without engaging the clutch, there will be no movement and fuel will be wasted.

The human: by engaging action (fight/flight) you will utilise the turbo drive of adrenalin and trigger spontaneous response.

However, if action is not engaged and panic sets in, energy will be utilised negatively.

Body Accelerators

POSITIVE BODY ACCELERATOR

Your positive body accelerator is action. When you act, adrenalin is utilised positively, adding power, speed and anaesthesia to your response.

NEGATIVE BODY ACCELERATOR

Your negative body accelerator is panic, caused when the reasoning process mistakes adrenalin for fear. Adrenalin is utilised negatively, leaving the recipient drained of energy and often frozen in the face of ensuing danger.

If you find yourself in a confrontational situation and do not or cannot act, the adrenalin may be gobbled up by increasing panic, this dissipating your turbo blast needlessly and fruitlessly. Like the car, you will be pressing the accelerator without engaging the clutch. Nothing is gained and all is lost.

In the gap between confrontation and action, adrenalin can be controlled with deep breathing and knowledge, and the look of fear hidden from your assailant with the *duck syndrome* (detailed later).

In primeval days when man (and woman) had to fight to live and eat, the feeling of fear was an everyday occurrence that would have felt as natural and as common as eating or drinking. In today's society, which is very tame by comparison, adrenalin is no longer needed in our everyday lives. In fact some people go through a whole lifetime without ever experiencing it fully. So when a situation arises that causes the adrenalin to flow, we are so unfamiliar with it that we naturally neither welcome, use nor like it. We panic. Psychologists call it the *fight or flight syndrome*. In moments of danger the body injects chemicals (adrenalin being the best known of these) into the blood stream, preparing the body for violent action, making it stronger, faster and sometimes anaesthetised to pain. The more dangerous the situation the bigger the build-up and adrenalin release. The bigger the release the better you perform (run, fight), but by the same count, the bigger the build-up and release, the harder it is to control.

However, fear has many disguises that also need to be understood. I have formulated what I call the *Adrenal Map* to help people better understand the disguises of fear.

It is my belief that we as human beings are far better designed for flight than we are for fight, this is why we feel the innate urge to run away from confrontations rather than meet them. Against many of our early enemies who only attacked prey that moved, the *freeze syndrome* would also have been a good thing. Unfortunately with today's enemy it is not such a good thing because if we do not move we get attacked more readily. The instinct however is still there and has to be overridden if survival is our aim.

In self-defence terms the innate urge to run is a good instinct. I always recommend flight above fight but the grey areas in this syndrome seem to be in abundance and confusion is compounded by a multifaceted society where confrontation, more often than not, demands neither fight nor flight. A run in with the boss, an exam or arguments with the neighbours all bring on the adrenal response but none demand a fight or a flight so, understandably, instinct has become a redundant commodity. We also have a moral dilemma in a paradoxical society where both fight and flight can be simultaneously unacceptable. You fight too often and you are seen by your peers as a thug; you run away from confrontation and you are seen as a coward: a man (or woman) who does not face up to his problems is looked upon as weak. In a way the adrenal syndrome has become antiquated and as a consequence instinct cupboarded; the natural bodily reactions associated with fight or flight, are so misunderstood that they are now seen as signs of cowardice.

The brain, it would seem, cannot distinguish between differing forms of confrontation and so releases adrenalin, carte blanche, for most forms of confrontation, even where life is not threatened. Actors freeze (stage fright) on stage because of adrenalin and over anticipation, kids go blank on exam day because blood is drawn away from non-vital areas of the body (those seen as non vital in fight or flight), one of these being the brain. What we have to do is learn to recognise when instinct is right and when it is wrong. It is right to run away from a violent encounter – that's survival – it might not be right to run away from intangible confrontation because problems have to be met and overcome.

In a long-winded way, what I am trying to say is, don't feel like a coward because your instinct tells you to run away from a violent encounter. That is good instinct, but, if it is impossible to run and you are forced to fight then use the adrenalin to aid you in fight. It takes a strong will to overcome the natural instinct to run away; that can be developed by correct training in self-protection.

If you misread the signs and allow confusion to enter the equation you may well find yourself frozen with fear. Knowledge dispels fear – read on.

Some of the following may seem a little peripheral for self-protection, but there is of course a natural overflow into things in our everyday life so either way the knowledge should help.

The Adrenal Map

FEAR (SLOW RELEASE)

The fear of fear itself

Often you may not know why you feel fear, so you look for the reason or the logic behind your anticipation. Basically if you know why you are scared it can help you to deal with the problem. For instance, if your fear was of consequence (pre-post-fight fear) you could, in theory, look at the worst case scenario of confronting your fear (whatever it might be) and accept that you will handle it. 'If I stand up to the bully and he beats me up, I will handle it.' 'If I fight Joe Bloggs and he brings his three bruiser brothers down to get me, I'll handle it,' etc. If however you cannot pinpoint why you are feeling scared then there probably isn't a reason other than natural anticipation. We all feel it in confrontation, so don't bother trying to look for logic in something where there is no logic, because all it will do is add confusion to discomfort. Confusion causes indecision and indecision in the face of ensuing attack can cause capitulation and/or defeat.

My wife would spend two months building up to a karate grading; she hated them and always experienced think-fight fear that caused her a lot of discomfort. She got so bad that she often felt like giving up karate and never grading again. She'd spend hours trying to analyse why she felt so scared but could never find a reason. The concentration made her very tired and mentally weak because although the brain only weighs 2 % of the bodyweight it can, in times of worry and concentration, use up to 50 % of your oxygen. That's why a champion chess player may lose 7lb in weight over one week of a tournament.

There was no tangible reason for her fear other than natural anticipation, which should be expected in martial arts gradings, so I instructed her to analyse no more and, instead, channel her energies into perfecting her grading technique. This she did and she now holds a fourth dan.

If there is no reason for fear, don't try and look for one, because if you do you'll be wasting valuable energy that could be better employed in fight or flight.

THINK-FIGHT FEAR (SLOW RELEASE)

Anticipation of confrontation

When you anticipate confrontation you may experience slow releases of adrenalin, often even months before a planned confrontation, and often over a long period before. The slow release is not so intense as the fast release but, due to its longevity, it can wear and corrode the recipient. This is not just in combat; things like the anticipation of having to talk in public, an exam, a big sales meeting, a forthcoming karate competition, a planned confrontation with the husband/wife/neighbour/boss etc. will cause slow release.

If my confrontation is not for another week, then although the adrenal release acts as a warning signal that anticipation is imminent, we do not really need that adrenalin until nearer the time. If I am having a fight next Saturday and today is Monday then I do not need fight or flight for another four days. So for four days I am getting adrenalin that I do not want or need. In a week of anticipation that adrenal release is going to take away my appetite, my sleep, in fact, my life is going to go on hold until the confrontation is gone. During that week of anticipation I am going to be like a bear with a sore head and hell to live with, because the adrenalin that has been released but not utilised (don't forget the fight is not until next Saturday) has got to come out somewhere. It will and does find its own way out in the guise of temper tantrums, irrational behaviour, road rage etc. This is why so many doormen and policemen end up in the divorce courts because their spouses just could not live with their irrational behaviour, the mood swings, the impatience.

Adrenalin is a physical syndrome that needs a physical release. If you have a week to confrontation but are getting daily releases of adrenalin, then release the adrenalin on a daily basis. Go through a kind of psychological de-sludge, with a long hard run, hit the bag or swing a golf club. Get it out of your system. Once utilised you will feel the appetite returning and sleep easier. Over a long period anticipatory adrenalin is a metaphoric monkey on your back and monkeys have a habit of getting fatter and heavier by the day. Think-fight fear is responsible for more 'bottle drops' than you would believe. Understand it and deal with it.

PRE-POST-FIGHT FEAR (SLOW RELEASE)

Anticipation of consequence

When you anticipate consequence (aftermath), before a confrontation even begins, there will be fear of that consequence whether it is being killed, raped, beaten up, come-backs, police involvement, etc. and this often forces the recipient to abort. Many women capitulate in rape situations because they are afraid of the consequences of fighting back. 'I was afraid to fight back just in case it angered my attacker more and caused him to really hurt me,' is a common statement from women who have been raped. I once watched the Midlands boxing champion get beaten up outside a nightclub by a criminal who would not have come to scratch with him in the ring. He got a terrible beating off this guy and didn't even try and fight back. Why? Because he was frightened of what might happen after the fight if he fought back and won, as the criminal was renowned for revenge attacks on anyone that angered him.

What the boxing champ failed to understand was, that by not fighting back he got battered anyway, which was all he was worried about if he had beaten the guy, who then decided to come back on him. I was faced with many name fighters in my time and most of them got their reputations by initiating revenge attacks. In the end they rarely had to fight, as people were so scared of the consequences of fighting them that they simply didn't fight, and got battered or intimidated because of it.

The best way to deal with pre-post-fight fear is, and this is what I always did, accept the consequences before you fight. Look at the worst case scenario and say to yourself 'yeah, I can handle that.'

In many cases, the consequences of not entering the arena and bottling out are the same as entering the arena and losing, except when you do enter the arena at least you have a chance of fighting back. If you bottle out you are just a punch-bag, another victim. I'm not trying to tell you what you should do in a self-defence situation, I'm just trying to make it clear that supplication is not a guarantee of a painless encounter – you may and usually will end up getting battered anyway.

PRE-FIGHT FEAR (ADRENAL DUMP)

No anticipation or fast escalation

Psychologists call this 'adrenal dump'. It is what Jim Brown (bodyguard trainer and security consultant) calls 'The WOW factor.' Pre-fight fear generally occurs when anticipation is not present (when the victim is in code white), or a situation escalates unexpectedly fast, or the recipient feels completely out of their depth – this causes adrenal dump. This feeling is often so intense that the recipient freezes in the face of confrontation; the reasoning process mistaking it for sheer terror. Adrenal dump is the most devastating of all adrenal releases.

It often occurs when a confrontation arises that one was not ready or prepared for, usually the same scenarios as those that cause slow release but with no prior notice.

When I interviewed some soldiers for my book on fear, they all said that they had never experienced adrenal dump and this was because they were all constantly in anticipation of confrontation (code yellow). So to avoid this devastating release, that's the place to be.

Because most people in society are switched off to the realities of real attack ('it will never happen to me'), most encounters will be unexpected and therefore cause adrenal dump. Avoidance comes from being constantly aware of both the attack ritual and bodily reaction to confrontation – if you are switched off on either count then adrenal dump is likely to occur.

SECONDARY ADRENALIN (ADRENAL DUMP)

The double tap

Before, during or after a confrontation, unexpected occurrences, things that you hadn't accounted for, can cause a secondary kick of adrenalin as the brain, sensing your unpreparedness, gives you a secondary release of adrenalin that is nearly always mistaken for fear. It tends to happen when you think that a situation is resolved and instead of going from code red back to code yellow, you go into a celebratory state: code white. When the situation that you thought was resolved re-emerges, you get an unexpected kick of adrenalin that forces you to freeze. If you think that a situation is over and you drop your guard you will be left wide open.

My advice is no matter how safe the situation may seem and no matter how sure you are that it is over, go straight back to code yellow and retain your awareness. It is like the story of the guy that got attacked by a mugger and beat the mugger up. He was so pleased with himself that he dropped his awareness; after all, no one gets mugged twice in one night! He did. He was so surprised by the second attack that he completely lost his bottle.

My other friend had a shotgun pulled on him at the door of a nightclub. He fought with the gunman and managed to get it off him and gave the chap a good beating. He was so pleased with himself, everyone agreed that he was a brave SOB and he went into a celebratory state, code white. Later in the night a little 'nobody' started trouble and when my friend tried to stop him the guy offered him a 'square go' (a one on one fight) and my mate dropped his bottle because he mistook adrenal dump for fear. It wasn't because of lack of courage that my friend lost his bottle, it was because of lack of awareness. So, no matter how often it 'kicks off', stay switched on or pay the price.

PERIPHERAL ADRENALIN (ADRENAL DUMP)

When awareness is tunnelled

Often people get tunnelled in their awareness – that is they are so indoctrinated into expecting an attacker or an attack to fit a certain place or type, that they are completely taken by surprise when an attack/confrontation occurs outside of their expectations. Awareness needs to be 360 degrees. What also happens a lot in reality is an attacker works with an accomplice who 'pincers' you whilst your awareness is locked onto him. In simple terms, one person grabs your attention whilst the other attacks from the periphery – simple but effective, especially because once a situation becomes threatening you will be experiencing tunnel vision (a by-product of adrenal release) so are highly unlikely to see an attack that is launched from the periphery.

Tunnel vision is a natural extension of the adrenal release and cannot be controlled so should therefore be managed. The best way to manage it is to keep checking around you when being approached menacingly from the front, just in case. If you are facing multiple assailants, keep moving your eyes from one to the other – it is not always the one in front that initiates the attack, rather it is one of those at the side, so beware.

IN-POST-FIGHT FEAR (SLOW ADRENAL DUMP)

In-fight anticipation of consequence

Unusual this, but, I have seen many fall foul of it, bottling out within a confrontation because they suddenly think about (or if the assailant is a clever one, they are reminded of) the consequences of their actions. This often occurs at a crisis point within the conflict; perhaps you have been pinned in a bad position or taken a heavy blow in-fight. Thinking about the possible consequences of fighting back can cause doubt that triggers adrenalin, and this is mistaken for fear and leads to capitulation.

Many people I spoke to (I also witnessed this syndrome many times myself) said that they had initially tried to fight back against their attackers and were told (by the attacker) that if they persisted in their resistance they would be 'hurt'. This triggered 'in-post-fight fear' and immediate capitulation. A girl that initially fights back against her attacker is punched hard in the face and told 'you try that again and I'll fucking kill you'. This consequence causes adrenal dump and the girl freezes, she becomes so scared and so controlled by her assailant that even when the chance presents itself, she does not try to escape. Victims have been known to have pointed a gun at an attacker and then handed it over to him when told that they will be killed if they do not.

Why is all of this important? Because knowledge is power and if you do not understand your own body and its reactions to conflict you will lose the fight from the inside out. In-fight releases of adrenalin are there to help you, but if you misread the signs they can cause capitulation.

I worked with one chap who used pre-post-fight fear to beat nearly all of his opponents. Before the fight he would tell them that, win or lose, he was going to find out where they lived and come to their house when they were having tea with their mum and bite their nose off. In all the years I knew the guy I never knew him to throw a punch, let alone bite a nose off, but he beat over a hundred opponents by telling them that he would. He threw pre-post-fight fear at his opponents like a heavyweight boxer throws a right cross.

IN-FIGHT FEAR (SLOW ADRENAL DUMP)

In-fight pain or danger

Generally, once you have made the commitment to run or fight the adrenalin is utilised and that horrible caustic feeling disappears. However, quite often during fight you may experience pain, exhaustion or panic if things are not going to plan (or even if they are). The brain, again sensing in-fight danger, offers a second (or third or fourth) kick of adrenalin as a turbo drive or anaesthesia, to help you out. This offering is usually misread for fear, and panic ensues. That's why, so often, people 'bottle out' in-fight, because they do not understand their own bodily reactions to pain and panic and mistake the feeling of adrenal release for terror. An experienced attacker will quickly club down any one who tries to fight back because they know that, more often than not, it will cause intense panic in their victim, which will lead to mass compliance. As I have already said, a victim who struggles with his assailant will get a quick punch in the nose backed by very aggressive dialogue: 'try that again and I'll break your fucking neck for you!'. This is also known to be effective in causing adrenal release followed by capitulation.

Recognise that the adrenal release is there to help and, although unpleasant, it will add vigour to your response.

POST-FIGHT FEAR (SLOW RELEASE)

Aftermath – anticipation of post-fight consequence

After confrontation, whether successful or not, the body often secretes slow releases of adrenalin, this being brought on possibly by the stress of 'scenario overload', when confrontation is so traumatic that it forces the body/mind into overload, leaving the recipient mentally and physically weak, and so vulnerable.

It is also brought on by post-fight anticipation, when the brain senses/dreads another confrontation or a repeat of the earlier confrontation and it again releases adrenalin to prepare the body. Aftermath can cause many sleepless nights. Again this should be dealt with in the same way as pre-post fight. Look at the consequences and accept that you can handle them, and don't forget the long runs and bag work to get rid of the adrenalin that is released. You have to get it out of your system.

ADRENAL COMBO

Pre-, in- and post-fight release

Those working/living in a stress related environment like the Stock Exchange, business or security may experience a combination (combo) of all the releases. Slow release because they constantly anticipate confrontation; adrenal dump when situations unexpectedly occur in their environment; pre-post fight because they constantly have to recognise the threat they face for reasons of personal security; and aftermath, in relation to situations that have already happened.

At once the recipient may experience a concoction of all adrenal releases and, if not checked, this can have a devastating effect on their health and personal life. The most important thing is to recognise what is happening to your body; explain to the people in your life what you are feeling so that they do not think you 'impossible to live with' and make sure you release the stress on a regular basis. If it all gets too much, pull away from the arena and give yourself a good rest, mentally and physically.

Fear Adrenal Map

PRECONFRONTATION

FEAR
The fear of fear itself

THINK-FIGHT FEAR
**Anticipation of confrontation
(slow release)**

PRE-POST-FIGHT FEAR
**Anticipation of aftermath
(slow release)**

PRE-FIGHT FEAR
**No anticipation or fast escalation
(adrenal dump)**

SECONDARY ADRENALIN
**Peripheral interactions
(adrenal dump)**

PERIPHERAL ADRENALIN

CONFRONTATION

IN-FIGHT FEAR
(slow adrenal dump)

IN-POST-FIGHT FEAR

POST-CONFRONTATION (AFTERMATH)

POST-FIGHT FEAR
**Overload/aftermath or anticipation of consequences
(slow adrenal dump)**

DUCK SYNDROME

In confrontational moments, when adrenalin is released, the recipient will experience physical reactions that need to be hidden from the assailant; if not hidden they allow the assailant to see that you are scared and struggling to hide your fear. Hiding the fear is a technique I like to call the duck syndrome.

If you watch a duck it will glide through the water very gracefully with very little outward movement, however under the water, where you can't see, his little webbed feet will be going like the clappers. This is how you should learn to control the adrenalin. On the outside you should show no signs of the way you feel inside; this way the opponent cannot get a measure of your emotional state, even though, on the inside, the adrenalin is going mad. Very often, if the attacker thinks that you feel no fear because you are hiding it with the duck syndrome, he will naturally feel that you are not scared. Quite often this will force him to capitulate. After all, no one wants to fight a fearless opponent. When you understand and can control the adrenal flow it is possible to hide adrenal reaction by appearing unmoved and calm.

ADRENAL REACTION

These are the expected bodily reactions to adrenalin:

Pre-fight shakes

Your legs, and possibly other limbs, may shake uncontrollably. In fight or flight, blood is taken from the non-vital areas of the body and pumped to those that are seen as needy for a physical response (running or fighting). This makes the major limbs, especially the legs, shake. It's a little like a motor car sat at the traffic lights with its engine revving, waiting for green. Your body is revving, waiting for action.

I control leg shaking by tapping the heel of one foot, as though tapping to the beat of a song, as I engage in verbal dissuasion. This conscious leg tapping gives the effect of an unperturbed person who is so in charge he is even tapping his heel like a cool thing.

Dry mouth

Your mouth may become dry and pasty. This is not outwardly noticeable so needs no concealing.

Voice quiver

Your voice may acquire a nervous and audible tremor. This is a bad one. It is hard to sound confident when your vocal chords are doing the bossa nova. A quivery voice says to anyone, in any language, that you are scared; this needs to be controlled or it could be your downfall. Many people actually become monosyllabic; that is they cannot speak coherently or they fall into single syllables or very short sentences.

This is because blood is drawn away from certain areas of the brain, again those that are seen as non-vital in fight or flight, in order to be pumped to the major muscles. In days of old, when fighting the sabre-toothed tiger, the voice was an absolutely non-vital commodity. In effect, and to make a long story short, the voice box cuts off. We have to reverse this syndrome. With today's enemy and in today's confrontational moments the voice is not just a vital commodity, it is also a valid and effective weapon that, with the right choice of words and aggression, can cause an opponent to capitulate.

The best way to learn voice control in confrontational moments is to step into any arena that brings on adrenalin, such as the boxing ring, animal day or public speaking, and practice speaking. Before you enter the boxing ring to spar, talk to your opponent and learn to control the quiver and hide the feeling of fear. It's hard, as when facing adversity instinct wants us to run, it does not want us to have a conversation. It is doubly hard because very few people are able to force themselves into an arena that brings on an adrenal release. It will take courage in bagfuls, but then so does fighting in the REAL arena, so it will be good practice all around.

Tunnel vision

On the positive side, tunnel vision enhances visual concentration. Its negative by-product is the blinkering of peripheral vision, which is not seen as vital in fight or flight. Background and bystanders are lost to cortical perception. The potential attacker appears closer and larger due to the optical illusion caused by the effect of tunnel vision. To widen the peripheral field it is wise to step back a little, but this is not easy because the aggressor automatically makes up any distance you retreat.

If facing more than one opponent, keep glancing from one to the other sporadically. The moment you lose peripheral vision is the moment that you are likely to be hit from the side. Being aware of the fact that you will experience tunnel vision and of its dangers is the important thing.

Sweaty palms

The palms of the hands often sweat profusely. In fact you tend to sweat all over the body, which is why the arms often splay as though you are carrying rolls of carpet under your arms to allow the sweat glands to open and release sweat to cool down the body. Soldiers patrolling in volatile areas like Northern Ireland will often sweat away 7 lb in body weight in 4 or 5 hours of patrolling due to the constant release of anticipatory adrenalin.

Nausea

Adrenalin may cause vomiting or the feeling of vomiting. Undigested food is seen as excess baggage in fight or flight so the body will try to throw it up to make you lighter and more efficient.

Bowel loosening

The recipient may experience loss of bowel or bladder control. Again digested food and drink is also seen as non vital to fight or flight so will be discarded. Working as a doorman in the nightclub, it was not uncommon to see the toilet full of doormen, emptying the bladder when they thought that a fight was going to 'kick off'. In a karate or full contact competition the toilets will also be full of competitors getting rid off 'excess baggage.' It is common and natural. However, it is not socially acceptable in this society to urinate or defecate on the pavement before a confrontation so we have learned to control the instinct. Unfortunately all these natural feelings are now very often seen as signs of cowardice. It's not cowardice, it's natural.

Adrenal deafness (auditory exclusion)

Sometimes the threat becomes so overwhelming that concentration is greatly enhanced, so much so that peripheral noise, even as loud as a scream or gunshot, is completely cut out and not recognised by the recipient.

Fugue state

The adrenal exposure, particularly adrenal dump, can cause the recipient to become anatomic, even robotic in verbal response; sometimes these responses are not remembered after the event. This is partly due also to the memory loss or distortion associated with 'dump'. Sometimes terrifying aspects of a confrontation may be completely blocked out and yet, paradoxically, trivial things loom large in recall, also the sequence of events or words may also be altered in the memory.

The black and whites (amaurosis fugax)

Due to the amount of blood drawn from the brain in fight or flight the recipient often sees whole situations in black and white, and all colour disappears as if you are watching a black-and-white TV.

Total acquiescence

If misunderstood and/or not controlled, the adrenal syndrome, and certainly adrenal dump, can evoke feelings of helplessness and abject terror. Fear of death and/or rape may bring on an extreme feeling of depression and foreboding. Tears and often hysteria may also occur. Many women submit to their attacker because of this overwhelming emotional explosion.

Astral experience (excorporation)

Often the recipient of the adrenal syndrome experiences an out of body experience, a feeling as though they are outside of themselves watching the action like a spectator.

Logorrhoea

It is very common for the recipient to experience, especially after a situation, the compulsion to verbally justify their actions with non-stop and very fast speech.

Denial response

In extreme circumstances the recipient can be temporarily psychologically unable or unwilling to accept responsibility for his actions, for example 'I didn't stab him, he ran onto the knife!' etc.

Time distortion/time loss/memory distortion/memory loss (Tachypsychia)

Many attack victims reported that their assault seemed to last an eternity, when in reality it may have only lasted a few minutes or even seconds. During physical attack time can appear to stand still, one minute often feeling like one hour. Paradoxically, in retrospect, victims of muggings and assaults often say, 'It all happened so fast.'

When interviewing James, the victim of an unsolicited assault, he initially told me that he was attacked without warning. After talking to him at some length it turned out that, in between first seeing his attackers and the attack itself, there was a time lapse of 11 seconds, these being lost to time distortion and memory loss.

After confrontation, memories of the event can become distorted ('my attacker was seven foot tall and 17 stone', whereas in fact he was only five foot eleven and 14 stone) or even lost; this is also partly due to tunnel vision. Sometimes, after a certain period of time has elapsed, the memories might gradually come back though sometimes they never return. So if you find yourself being interviewed by the police, post-fight, don't rush into your statement. If you are not sure don't make a statement at all until you have a professional at your side who can better advise you. You may not remember what happened too well and end up saying things (or having things suggested to you) to fill in the gap. The police do a great job and we all admire their work but they do, from my experience, like to get things tied up as soon after the incident as possible, and may gently push you to complete your statement ASAP. There is another reason for this: if they don't get their statement straight away you might change your mind and decide, for whatever reason, not to make a statement at all. That will leave loose ends and they don't like loose ends. What the police often say is they like to get the statement while the incident is still fresh in your mind; in reality the situation is more likely to be fresher the next day than it is directly after confrontation.

Don't forget you are convicted for what you say and not what you do. You may legitimately defend yourself and then make a statement that absolutely hangs you. I have many friends that have done just that and gone to prison for it, so don't be rushed. Understand what might be happening to you, regarding the latter, post-fight.

All of the aforementioned feelings are usual, accept and recognise them; they are all part and parcel of adrenal reaction and, though unpleasant, quite natural. The feelings do lessen in intensity as you become more exposed to them. If needs be, prepare for them, especially in the aftermath when a police statement might be all that stands between you and a loss of liberty.

The ugly handmaiden of adrenalin is the omniscient Mr Negative; General Sun Tzu called him the inner opponent. That little man who perches on the shoulder of your mind's eye and tells you that you're frightened, scared or that you 'can't handle it' (the situation). The inner opponent is, basically, the voice or instinct that tries to warn you of the dangers that you face and the possible consequences of your actions. In general the inner opponent will advice you to run when danger rears its ugly head.

This is, of course, generally a good thing, and natural instinct should be followed whenever possible. However, in many situations the option of flight does not/ may not present itself or is lost and we are forced to fight. We have no option, and yet the inner opponent still keeps nagging away telling us that there is danger and that we should run and that we cannot handle the situation. In effect he takes over the run of your head, forcing you to bottle out. You lose the fight from the inside out. This is not a good thing.

So whilst we should listen to the voice and allow it to point out our options and the inherent dangers we face, we should not let him take over, which he will if you allow him to. He is, if you like, an advisor to the King and, if we are not vigilant he will take over the kingdom. Listen to his advice once, maybe even twice. After that shut him up or he will talk you into supplication. I want to know the negatives of facing adversity but I don't want it repeated again and again. This may cause the self-doubt that starts the downward spiral to my demise, which in the long turn will lose me the altercation. The inner opponent is an advisor not a conversationalist, so 'kill the conversation'. By controlling the inner opponent – in effect controlling your self – you take charge and the voice becomes an ally as opposed to an enemy.

Training in adverse conditions and learning to confront and conquer your own personal fears is a very good way to draw the inner opponent out in to the open so that he plays his best hands, and you can learn to defeat him. This stallion needs to be broken if you want to be in control of your own destiny. Left to its own devices the mind can be a self-detonating time bomb of negativity that will spiral you down into ever increasing misery. If you allow the inner opponent the run of your head he will often force you into capitulation; you will, as they say, lose the fight in Birmingham. Let me explain.

There was a wonderful old wrestler in the beginning to middle of this century called Bert Asarati. Unfortunately he is dead now, but in his day he was a monster of a wrestler with a fearsome reputation for hurting his opponents, even in a show match. He was seventeen stone at only five foot six. When he sat on a train or a bus he took up two seats; he was a big man whose reputation preceded him.

The story goes that there was another wrestler of repute who was travelling down by train from Glasgow to fight Mr Asarati in London. All the way down on the train journey this Glaswegian kept thinking about the arduous task that lay ahead of him and every time the train stopped at a station his inner opponent would advise him to get off the train and go back to Glasgow. At every station his inner opponent reminded him of the prowess of Mr Asarati, and of how Mr Asarati was going to 'hurt him' when they got in the ring. At every station the inner opponent got louder and stronger; the wrestlers' bottle going more and more until in the end he could take the pressure no longer. At Birmingham station he got off and went back to Glasgow on the next available train. He sent a note to Bert Asarati saying, 'Gone back to Glasgow, you beat me in Birmingham.' His inner opponent had beaten him 100 miles before he even got to the fight venue. This is what often happens to people in street situations. They don't lose to the guy that they're having trouble with, they lose to themselves.

One thing I always like to advise people is don't feel bad if you feel like running away. Our natural instinct is not to stand and fight; rather it is to run. The fight or flight syndrome is geared more to running than it is to fighting. As prehistoric men and women our enemies would have probably been sabre-toothed tigers or grizzly bears, far more fearsome fighters than us, so instinct would indeed have had us running for our lives and only fighting if cornered. Unfortunately, as stated earlier, the adrenal syndrome has not evolved very well and confrontation today is more likely to be a boardroom meeting or an exam – neither demand fight or flight – so instinct (i.e. to run away) cannot be relied upon any more. When you feel like running away from a confrontation don't feel like a coward because that feeling is your heritage and very natural. What we do have to learn though is that, if flight is not an option, we have to override the inner opponent and actuate a physical response, even if it is only to save our skins.

If flight is not an option and fight is on the cards then the voice of reason has to be shut up or, as I said before, he will destroy you and you'll lose the fight in Birmingham. There are three ways of dealing with this tactician of corrosiveness if he gets out of control.

Thought rejection

Reject the negative thoughts by completely ignoring them. Not listening to anything that the inner opponent says, thus leaving him no mental ledge on which to perch.

Thought counter attack

Counter attack every 'negative' thought with a 'positive' thought. This is the method that I practise.

'You're scared.'

'No, I'm not scared.'

'You can't handle this situation.'

'Yes, I can handle this situation. I can handle anything.'

And so on. By doing this you can erase the negative thoughts with the positive.

This is an important factor because each negative thought that penetrates your psyche may, and usually does, erode a small part of your 'will' until eventually it, and you, are defeated. I work on the premise that 'negative begets negative', begets defeat. As a parallel, 'positive begets positive', begets victory.

Your greatest enemy in times of adversity is often your own mind.

Repetitive mantra

Block out the internal conversation with a repetitive mantra. Any will do as long as it is positive and not negative.

'I can handle it. I can handle it. I can handle it. I can handle it. I can handle it. I can handle it.'

or:

'I'm not frightened. I'm not frightened. I'm not frightened. I'm not frightened. I'm not frightened.'

This is a very inspiring extract from James Clavell's best selling book *Shogun* that explains the Samurai way of dealing with inner conflict:

'To think bad thoughts is really the easiest thing in the world. If you leave your mind to itself it will spiral you down into ever increasing unhappiness. To think good thoughts, however, requires effort. This is one of the things that training and discipline are about. So teach your mind to dwell on sweet perfumes, the touch of silk, tender raindrops against the shoji, the

tranquility of dawn, then at length you won't have to make such an effort and you will be of value to yourself.'

By understanding your own body, by understanding the mechanics of adrenalin/ fear you can learn self-control. Panic is often catalysed by ignorance, by not understanding your own body or its workings. Most people in most situations are not defeated by their assailants; they are defeated by their own mind. Whilst adrenalin may be uncomfortable, it is natural and should be accepted without fight. There is no way around these feelings, every one feels them; they are a part and parcel of adversity.

'The feeling of fear [adrenalin] is as natural as the feelings of hunger and thirst or the feeling of wanting to use the toilet. When you feel hungry you don't panic, you eat, when you feel thirst you drink. So it is with fear. Don't panic, act.'

Cus Damatio

Adrenalin exposure

The whole process of adrenal release and internal conversation, elongated here for the sake of description, usually has to be controlled in a matter of milliseconds, so practice is of the essence. It is very difficult to practise something that is not or at least doesn't appear to be present in our everyday lives.

For the practising martial artist this task is not such a difficult one because he/ she can, if he/she wishes, gain adrenalin exposure by facing the top dogs in his, or another, *dojo* (training hall) in sparring or partner work. This alone will spark the infamous adrenal gland, and give exposure to adrenalin.

Only through exposure can you gain desensitisation. As unpleasant as this may seem it's the only way. To learn how to handle the heat you must force yourself to stay in the kitchen. As well as adrenalin exposure, this practice will also help to instil within you that all-important characteristic, self-discipline.

The more that you experience and confront the fear syndrome the more desensitised you will become to it and the easier it will be to control and thus harness. The more that you confront and control, the stronger minded you will become. These exercises will build the mental muscle as a bar-bell and weights will build physical muscle; the same dictum 'no pain, no gain' is also evident.

This gained strength of mind will put your whole life into perspective as all of a sudden those mundane tasks at work or around the home become a simple challenge by comparison. All are relegated to simple exercises in self-discipline, everything that life throws in your way becomes a challenge that you will no longer baulk at, nothing will seem beyond your mental capacity. Also due to the high level of self-esteem that these exercises develop, one is also less likely to be chosen as a victim for attack.

For the non-training person the task of adrenalin exposure, cut out extension and instilling self-discipline is not such an easy or obvious one. Joining a good martial arts club may be a solution. Unfortunately, not everyone has the time or the inclination to do this, so we need to look a little closer to home. Confront things in your everyday life that bring on the feeling of fear, work in a pyramid and build your way up, confronting your smallest fears at the bottom of the pile and working your way up, systematically, until you reach the top. This is slightly out of the context of this book and I would ask you to refer to my books *Fear – the Friend of Exceptional People* and/or *Animal Day – Pressure Testing the Martial Arts*.

'I believe that anyone can conquer fear by doing the things he fears to do, provided he keeps doing them until he gets a record of successful experiences behind him.'

Eleanor Roosevelt

Chapter Four

The Psyche

'A whole army may be robbed of its spirit, a commander-in-chief may be robbed of his presence of mind.'

The Tao of paradox:

'Those who strategise, use the tao of paradox.
Thus, when able, they appear unable.
When employed, they appear useless.
When close, they appear distant.
When distant, they appear close.
They lure through advantages,
And take control through confusion.
When complete, they appear to prepare.
When forceful, they appear evasive.
When angry, they appear to submit.
When proud, they appear to be humble.
When comfortable, they appear to toil.
When attached, they appear separated.
They attack when the opponent is unprepared,
And appear when least expected.
This is the strategist's way of triumph.
It must not be discussed beforehand.'

Sun Tzu

Adrenalin Switches

This chapter deals with the art of fighting on an internal level, the art of intangible fighting if you like. l shall list different ways of operating your opponent's adrenalin, switching it off, begetting overconfidence in the attacker by feigning submissiveness, or switching it on to fool the opponent's reasoning process into believing they are scared (psyched out) by feigning fearlessness, or using physical or psychological stimuli.

For every fight that I have witnessed or have been involved in where a physical response was employed, there have been another three where victory was gained over an adversary with guile as opposed to force, attacking the mind rather than the body. All that is involved is a little acting.

POSITIVE ADRENALIN SWITCH

'When speakers cannot hear each other, act with drums and bells.
When observers cannot see each other, act with banners and flags.
Thus, those that are bold will not advance alone.'

The Chun Cheng

In previous chapters we have already spoken about adrenal dump, how it can affect the human body and how the reasoning process mistakes adrenalin for fear, thus triggering the flight response. By giving an opponent an adrenal release we trigger the natural instinct to either freeze or run, both of which would have been very natural defences against prehistoric beasts that were too fearsome to stand and fight or whose eyesight was poor and would not be able to see a frozen enemy, only attacking when they sensed movement. In this society freezing is not always an option and may only get you battered by an antagonist that will use a frozen adversary as a punch-bag. Neither is society kind to the fellow that runs away from danger. The contemporary enemy and peer pressure force the adrenal syndrome into antiquity.

A person that understands this syndrome can use it to great advantage as an attacking tool, especially against an enemy that understands it not.

While the terminology may appear a little complex, the practice is not.

It is fair to say that it will take great presence of mind to make use of adrenalin switches.

When attempting to switch the opponent's adrenalin on, there are different roles you can adopt: *animal, veteran* or *recognition*.

THE ANIMAL APPROACH

This is the 'mad man/woman' approach, aiming to instil fear into your potential assailant by becoming loud, aggressive and challenging, thus making the attacker feel that he has bitten off more than he can chew. 'When ignorance is mutual, confidence is king.'

MULTIPLE ADRENALIN KICKS

The animal approach may induce adrenal dump in your assailant. If his adrenalin is already in operation it will give it a second or even a third kick. His reasoning process will mistake adrenal dump for fear and possibly force him to abort. As an added bonus your aggression will also draw attention to your dilemma, which can also induce adrenalin, again complicating things for the attacker.

'There were three blokes standing around me, ready to batter me. I was shitting myself, I knew I was gonna take a kicking so I stood in this kind of Kung Fu stance and started screaming

and shouting at them, things like "come on you wankers, I'll fight you all." They all shit themselves, ran off. I couldn't believe it.'

CASE HISTORIES

We are manipulating man's natural instinct to want to run as opposed to fight. By triggering adrenalin in an opponent I am also triggering his flight response. When he feels like running away, because society looks poorly on a runner, it will cause mass self-doubt in the opponent and, hopefully, cause him to capitulate. Everything in life has its opposite and the danger with any positive adrenalin switch is that it can backfire on you. If the recipient overrides the urge to capitulate, the release may make him stronger and faster – a dangerous adversary indeed. I only use a positive adrenalin switch if I see a chink in the opponent's armour. This perception has come from many years of dealing with violence and violent people. If you can't read an opponent then I wouldn't recommend employing this tactic; better to stick with submissiveness and use it as a negative adrenalin switch.

THE VETERAN APPROACH

A guy bumped in to me in the pub, I just turned to say sorry and he said, "Who you fucking pushing?"

'I tried to explain that it was an accident but he wouldn't have it. He said, "Do ya wanna step outside?"

'He obviously meant for a fight. I didn't want to but I thought I'd try and bluff it. I kept really calm, never got angry or nothing and said "Yeah, actually I do." The guy went pale and started to retreat. He ended up buying me a drink.'

CASE HISTORIES

This cool devil-may-care attitude suggests to the antagonist you are, because of your blatant disconcern, unperturbed by his threat or a veteran fighter who has trod this path many times before. This causes opponent adrenal dump, psyching the antagonist out and stopping his intended onslaught. Not many people will enter into a confrontation if they think there is a chance of them getting hurt. The story below about Master Abbe is a classic example:

Master Abbe, a world-renowned martial arts teacher, was walking down a quiet suburban street on his way home after his usual nightly teaching session. He noticed three hoodlums hovering, several yards away on the opposite side of the street. When they approached him he was ready. 'Give us your money or you'll get hurt,' said the leader of the three. Master Abbe looked at each one in turn, then casually took his wallet out of his jacket pocket, throwing it on the floor between him and his antagonists. He pointed to the wallet and said, 'I'm prepared to die for that wallet. What about you?' The three would-be attackers looked at the wallet on the floor, then at Abbe, then at each other. Without further ado they all ran away, obviously not prepared to die for the wallet. Master Abbe picked up his wallet and calmly walked home.

I have known this approach work hundreds of times, I have used it dozens of times myself. There is a danger however. If you throw a challenge it may be met and accepted; if it is you had better be able to back it up or be able to back-pedal in a hurry. I never throw a challenge unless I am totally committed to following that challenge through, should it be accepted. I train to take that challenge so if it is accepted I will know what to do. Many people do not and are completely flummoxed when their antagonist says 'yeah, I'll have some of that!' What this does is cause an adrenal rush in you and the whole process is reversed. So if this approach is employed be committed to follow it through – just in case.

A friend of mine, he shall remain nameless, tried the veteran approach; he told his antagonist in a very calm manner that if he wasn't happy that they would have to 'sort it out on the common' not really expecting him to meet the challenge. 'All right,' came the reply, 'let's do it now!'

My mate dropped his bottle quicker than a greasy-palmed milkman. The bottom line was that my mate had no idea of how to do a square go (a match fight).

THE RECOGNITION PLOY

I often teach people, as a pre-cursory action trigger to pre-emption, to ask their assailants a question to engage their brain. The question can be relative to what is happening or abstract: 'Is your mum's name Elsie?' or 'How's your mother/family/ brother these days?' Many of my students have found this effective. An excellent by-product of this is that the potential attacker doesn't realise that it is an engaging ploy and often thinks his chosen victim has recognised him, and really does know his mother/brother/sister, etc. Again, they often beat a hasty retreat before attack.

Warning: This kind of ploy is only useful in the very early stages of the attacker's ritual and only if the locale is right. If you have been abducted or are completely detached from the herd it could be dangerous. Many attackers kill their victims if they think that they have been recognised.

One young lady I teach told me the story of how the ploy saved her and her friends from what could have been a nasty attack/rape:

We, myself and two girlfriends, had come out of the nightclub at about 2.15 a.m. and couldn't get a taxi. We don't live that far from the town so we decided to walk. A few minutes out of town we noticed a group of lads, about six in all, following us. We all felt very scared. As they got closer they started shouting and jeering, they were really crude. We all felt as though we were going to be attacked or something. As they were almost up on us I turned round and smiled at the one nearest to us, 'How's your mum these days?' I asked him. Well, he nearly fell over. He obviously thought I really did know his mum. They couldn't get away from us quick enough after that.'

CASE HISTORIES

In all these cases your intention is to frighten the adversary, via your portrayal, into aborting his attack attempt. The common street term for this process is *psyching out*.

Whether you opt for the animal, veteran or recognition approach it is always wise to prepare for its failure by 'lining-up' the antagonist, in preparation for pre-emption, just in case.

The *Kiaa* spirit shout, (a loud shout employed by Karate practitioners to reinforce technique and spirit), is also very effective for psyching out a would-be attacker. The American Red Indians used a similar principle of war cries and war paint to instil fear into their enemies before battle, with great effect. Also eye contact, a sharp poke into the opponent's chest, a firm push, even a slap across the face can cause adrenal dump in an opponent that often leads to capitulation.

THE NEGATIVE ADRENALIN SWITCH

'Hence, those skilled in the use of strategy evade when the spirit is sharp,
And confront when the spirit is idle or withdrawn.
When able, appear unable. When prepared appear unprepared.'

Sun Tzu

As a parallel to the psyche out you can attempt to disarm your opponent by switching his adrenalin off. This ploy is used when you feel that a physical confrontation is definitely on the cards or you can't read whether the opponent might fall for the psyche out. By being submissive and switching the attacker's adrenalin off with non-confrontational verbal, an attacker can be talked down from his rage, or primed for your pre-emptive attack.

So, if you can't get to grips with the psyche out, for whatever reason, you may wish to adopt this approach and play the situation down by feigning capitulation. This is often ideal when all other options are exhausted. Again acting is employed. This time, you are trying to relax and mentally disarm the attacker. You do this by pretending that you are more scared than you really are, even to the extent that you tell the attacker you are scared and don't want any trouble: 'Please don't hurt me'. This will fool the attacker's reasoning process into believing that you are already beaten, thus switching off his adrenalin, causing overconfidence and probably even effecting premature endorphine release (the body releases a natural morphine into the body after adversity). This will drop his defences long enough for you to make a pre-emptive escape or attack and escape.

This ploy can be devastatingly effective because the antagonist will be so mentally disarmed that your unexpected escape/strike will have maximum effect. Because the attacker's body has prematurely dropped its defences (thinking that the danger has gone), your pre-emptive strike will be undetected and unopposed. If you can convince the antagonist that you are going to capitulate and are therefore not a danger to him he will, consciously or subconsciously, drop his mental guard. If you attack at this moment of disarmament your success rate increases immeasurably. Again we are presuming knowledge here. Dropping your opponent's defence and creating a window of attack is of little use if you are not skilled in attack. The following story is a lengthy yet perfect example of a negative adrenalin switch. It is taken from my autobiographical book *Watch My Back*.

'Kev, the best right-hand puncher on God's earth, was a master of 'talking distance'. He's only about five foot six tall, with an ever so receding hair line, but with bulldog-like shoulders. His face was gruff but handsome, with a very soft voice and respectful manner. He was very similar to myself in that he didn't seem the doorman type. He was a gentleman of the door, but my goodness, could he have a fight. A classic example of talking distance, or switching 'adrenalin off' was when Kev was working the door at the infamous Reflections, where five dead was just a stag night.

'Two name fighters, who were also brothers, had started fighting with a couple of other lads on the dance floor of the nightclub. When Kev arrived on the scene the brothers were just finishing off their victims. The brothers were bullies. Kev and the other doormen ejected the battered and bruised men from the club, then told the brothers they also had to leave. They refused, point blank. Knowing their 'rep' for violence, Kev went into his time served and hard practised routine, "Come on lads, don't be like that. I'm only doing my job. Look, I'm supposed to be head doorman here. If the manager thinks that I'm backing down to you I'm going to look a right idiot. Just come up to the bar and we'll talk about it. You don't have to leave, it's just to look good in front of the manager." They bought it, hook, line and sinker, probably thinking what a "softy" Kev was and revelling in their embryonic victory. They were both well and truly disarmed.

'At the bar Kev made his play, "lining them both up" with a right, "Look lads, we've thrown the other two out, now you've got to go as well," he said sternly.
'Anger hit their faces. The first brother launched himself into an attack at Kev, but Kev was already primed and cocked.

'"BANG!" They were both in sleepsville.'

Climbing inside the opponent and switching on/off his fight or flight response to beat him with guile as opposed to force is advanced play and needs great understanding to employ with conviction. Practice is of the essence if you want it to work and not backfire on you.

Chapter Five

Line-ups: The Fence

Priming – putting a fence around your factory

'Attack is the secret of defence: defence is the planning of an attack.'

Sun Tzu

In this chapter we are working on the premise that you have already exhausted all other options, i.e. avoidance, escape and verbal dissuasion. Most self-defence situations and attack scenarios, as mentioned in the previous chapters, issue rays of prior warning if you are perceptive enough to spot the attacker's ritual. If you are foolhardy enough to heighten your vulnerability by placing yourself in a dangerous situation (like walking down a dark alley at night) you cannot expect any prior warning and will have to make the best of a bad situation. You then fall into the ambush attack. Most people in society are so switched off, both mentally and environmentally, that many attack scenarios fall into the ambush variety. If this is so, and it so often is, you will be fighting tooth and nail for your very existence. The majority do not survive the ambush attack.

Previously I talked about the verbal communication (four 'D's) that nearly always precedes an attack upon the person and the victim who is quite often disarmed or shocked rigid by it. The time lapse between the disarming or scarifying verbal (which can be very short) and the attack itself is your time. During these seconds the victim may seize the moment, as it were, and be pre-emptive, effecting attack/ escape, or elongate the verbal by replying to the aforementioned dialogue with aggressive counter-verbal, unbalancing the attacker's psyche.

These seconds before battle are absolutely pivotal and must be managed quickly and without demur; remember, hesitancy begets defeat. This arena is that of the three second fighter.

When the police talk about self-protection the key is target hardening – we mentioned this earlier in the book – that is, making yourself a hard target by means of placement and awareness of environment and the enemy. When I talk about the physical aspect of self-protection I am always working on the premise that, for whatever reason, a situation has gone beyond this and reached dire straits and the possibility of escape is no longer an option or that option has been lost.

As I have just said, pre-fight management is vital if you want to survive intact. Who wins and who loses in most situations is usually determined by what happens pre-fight as opposed to in-fight. Most situations start at conversation range, this being talking or handshake distance. If this is mismanaged it degenerates rather quickly to vertical grappling range and then ground fighting – not a good place to be if you don't know the arena. While conversation distance is not the chosen range of the majority – most people feel safer at about four or five feet – it can be maintained so that it does not degenerate further into grappling range by 'putting a fence around your factory'.

If you had a factory that you wanted to protect from robbers the most sensible thing to do would be to place a fence around it to make it a hard target so that a potential robber has got to get past that fence before he can even think about attacking the factory. While the fence might not keep him out indefinitely it will make his job decidedly harder. Rather like a boxer who constantly flicks a jab into his opponent's face, even if that jab does not hurt his opponent it still keeps him at bay, and if his opponent wants to employ his knock out blow he first has to find a way past his opponent's jab. To the boxer the jab is the fence around his factory.

In self-protection the fence around your factory is your lead hand, placed in that all-important space between you and your antagonist to maintain a safe gap.

Like the factory fence the lead hand will not keep an aggressor at bay forever – just long enough for you to initiate an escape or a pre-emptive attack – but it will place you in charge, even though your aggressor may not know it. Placed correctly the lead hand will not only maintain a safe gap but it will also disable the attacker's armoury of right- and left-hand techniques/ head-butts etc. Though he may not know it on a conscious level he will instinctively realise that, until that fence has been removed or by-passed, his techniques have no clear way through.

SENSORY TENTACLE

The lead hand should be held in a non-aggressive way (see illustrations) and should not touch the aggressor unless he makes a forward movement and tries to bridge the gap between you and him. It acts as a sensory guide to your aggressor's intentions; if he moves forward he will touch the fence and set your alarm bells ringing – this forward movement should be checked so as to maintain the safe range by using the palm of the lead hand on the aggressor's chest. Don't hold the touch as this may be seen by your assailant, on a conscious level, as a controlling movement (while of course it is a controlling action, it's better at this stage that the aggressor does not feel that you are in control). This will force him to knock your hand away or grab your wrist and possibly cause him to attack you prematurely, so as soon as you have checked him return the lead hand to its stand-by position.

One of the final subliminal precursors to an aggressor's attack is distance close down. If he tries to bridge the gap that you are maintaining it is usually because he is making his final preparations for assault, so if he does move forward and touch the fence you should, as well as checking range, be getting ready to make a pre-emptive attack or suffer the consequences should he break down the fence. In my opinion the maximum amount of times that a potential attacker should be allowed to touch the fence is twice – after that you've got big problems and will probably end up in a match fight situation or on the floor with a crowd around you, depending upon the calibre of fighter you are facing. Every time the attacker touches the fence the danger doubles.

The fence should look and feel natural; this will come with practice. If it doesn't and the attacker notices it on a conscious level he will try to knock it away and bridge the gap. Ideally the fence should be fluid, always moving, like you are using your hands to talk.

A professional may notice the fence no matter how well you disguise it and try using deceptive dialogue or body language to bring the fence down. Once down he will act. This often entails telling you that he does not want trouble, or that he just wants to talk; he may ask directions, the time, your name, anything to disarm you enough to lower the fence. An experienced fighter will offer to shake hands to get rid of the fence or try to close the gap by putting his arm around your shoulder in a pally kind of way. Don't have any of it – if there is the slightest chance of threat then don't let anyone touch you; a good fighter will only need one shot once the fence is down, so keep it up. If he still persists in coming forward and you don't feel ready to strike, or indeed are not even sure that a strike is called for, don't hesitate to back-up the check with a firm verbal fence: 'Just stay where you are'.

With the modern enemy the rule of thumb is 'if his lips are moving he's lying' so don't believe a word that he says. If he still persists in coming forward then he has given you the 'go'. Having said all that, if the potential attacker has already made his intentions obvious by demanding your wallet or threatening you then there is nothing to contemplate: you should go the first time he touches the fence.

RANGE FINDER

The fence also acts as a range finder. Many trained fighters misjudge the distance of their attacks in a real situation because the range is foreign to them. By touching the opponent with the lead hand before initiating your attack you can judge the exact distance, giving you a more accurate and solid shot.

ACTION TRIGGER

If and when you have decided to initiate an attack the lead hand also acts as a physical action trigger. You touch the opponent with the lead hand, finding the range, and bounce off the touch using it to trigger your attack. This should be coupled with the verbal brain engaging action trigger detailed earlier.

MULTIPLE ATTACKERS

The fence can also be used to maintain the range and even position of multiple attackers, but this is tantamount to fighting on more than one front. It is very difficult to maintain the range of more than one attacker and a speedy decision to attack or escape should always be sought.

The fence can be constructed in any way you choose as long as it blocks the gap and looks inoffensive. You can use a stop fence by placing the palm of the lead hand in front of the opponent, but this will bring the control to a conscious level and may catalyse alarm in the opponent. Where possible it is best to control him without him knowing it.

HERE ARE A COUPLE OF SUGGESTED FENCES:

The pleading fence (PF)

This is a nice fence because it is submissive and inoffensive but it blocks range beautifully. It also leaves the fingers ideally placed for an eye attack should it be needed. It is often best to underline the fence with firm dissuasive dialogue: 'look, just keep away from me, I don't want trouble' or a more assertive 'stay where you are – don't come any closer.'

Being submissive is ideal if you have decided that you are going to employ a pre-emptive attack or you are using the deception to escape. It will mentally disarm your opponent, making him an easy target. It has a bad point, however. Many attackers will see submissiveness as a meal ticket to an easy victim and spur on their assault, which is OK if you are setting the trap but not so good if you are not expecting it. Personally I use the submissive approach quite a lot because it really does disarm the opponent and give you a clear line for the sniper attack option, whereas other times I will use an assertive, even aggressive fence, to psyche out the opponent.

Assertiveness can be a good thing and a bad thing. If the attacker thinks that you are confident it may cause him to abort his intended attack, but if he is committed to attacking you no matter what, your assertiveness may trigger his aggression and you may lose the element of surprise and give him added adrenal turbo.

Having spent a lot of time working with and controlling violent people, I have learned to judge the right time for assertiveness and the right time for submissiveness. Not every one will be able to do this, so if you have to choose and there is no other way, use submissiveness to disarm and then attack and run, or use firm (but not aggressive) or submissive verbal dissuasion.

Both hands are placed in front of you, palms facing the attacker and several inches away from him but not touching.

The staggered fence (SF)

Similar to the PF with palms facing forward but with the hands staggered by about one foot, the hand at the back would be the ideal one used to attack though with practice the lead hand would be ideally placed for a finger strike to the eyes.

The exclamation fence (EF)

The hands, palms upward, are held as though in exclamation, the lead left hand pushed forward as fence and the right hand, cocked to strike, to your own right hand side (left if reversed).

The verbal fence

The verbal fence is an excellent tool if you can see menace on its way in and works well pre-fight, in-fight and post-fight. I have used it successfully many times. An extract from my book *Watch My Back* exemplifies a post-fight fence rather well:

'The fight with "The Karate Kid" had been on the cards for several months, I'd tried to avoid it but was unable. I pick up the situation as it reached its conclusion – the post-fight fence comes in at the end of the fight when one of his friends becomes involved [this was a match fight by the way].

'I'd spent two months trying to avoid this situation and was fed up with trying, I had no more chances left in my "chance bag".

'As The Karate Kid got closer his face began to grimace and I sensed he was going to strike at any moment.

'"BANG!"

Almost in slow motion, I hooked my right fist onto his advancing jaw, pushing it backwards, shaking his grey matter into the realms of unconsciousness. As he fell I volleyed his face and he spiralled, like movie strobe. I kicked him so hard that it hurt my foot. I felt hate leaving my body; he landed face down and forlorn on the cruel, black tarmac of defeat. Many people were watching, so I thought I'd give them a display, not for exhibitionism, nor fun, nor ego, I just wanted to take out a little insurance. Making the onlookers [mostly his mates] think that I was an animal would, in the future, insure that they did not tangle with me. It's what the Chinese call "killing a chicken to train a monkey".

'"Kiaaa!" I screamed as I brought an axe kick onto the body of my sleeping quarry. To the onlooker, it probably looked barbaric [which is how I wanted it to look], but in reality the kick was empty, I pulled it on impact, just as I had a thousand times in training.

'The man with the weasel face [The Karate Kid's mate] ran at me, from the crowd of onlookers, with ill intent and I stopped him in his tracks with a lash of my tongue [the verbal fence].

'"GER OUT 'F MY FUCKING FACE BEFORE I DESTROY YA!"

'I pointed at him to underline my resolve. He stopped like an insect on fly paper.'

Unlike the varying genres of physical fence the verbal fence is best aggressive – the more so the better – it has to pierce the opponent's subconscious and register danger with the brain, causing an adrenal reaction in him that, hopefully, he will mistake for fear.

In America they have a saying in the prisons: 'give me five feet'. This means 'keep at least five feet away from me', five feet being the distance they feel they are relatively safe at. This only works if you're aware enough to spot menace at a very early stage. More often than not a fight will come through an argument or some kind of aggressive verbal so the five feet rule is already lost and the physical fence comes into play.

If you are using the verbal fence you must, as I have said, be very firm, even aggressive.

'Stay where you are, don't come any closer, stay!'

This would be underlined by placing your lead hand in front of you in a stop sign.

This can even work in-fight if someone tries to attack you whilst you are fighting or defending yourself. I have been grappling on the floor with one opponent when his mate has tried to join in against me. Noticing this I used an in-fight fence by telling the guy that if he joined in I was going to batter him afterwards. He quickly changed his mind.

Pre-fight verbal fence

I'm trying to find a way to write this now so that it does not sound over-complicated. Here goes. If you use the verbal fence pre-fight it is important to create a gap – about five feet would be good – between you and him with a sharp shove, using the lead hand fence. It's very hard to control an opponent with a verbal fence when they are already in your face. So if the situation has reached an impasse and you think it is going to become physical, but you do not want to make a pre-emptive attack for whatever reason, then shove him hard on the chest so that it knocks him backwards and out of immediate attacking range (this may take some practice in the gym with training partners). This minimal physical contact will also cause an adrenal release in the opponent. Then back the shove up with a very aggressive verbal fence, even using expletives to add aggression. The reason for the gap is many fold but not least that it takes the opponent out of his striking range. What it also does is take the opponent from a state of reaction to a state of response. Let me explain. If you shove the opponent but not out of range he may automatically react to the shove with an attack of his own. He'll do this without even thinking; it will be very easy for him because it'll be an automatic response. In effect, by staying within strike range you are forcing the opponent into a fight response. His instincts will inform him that he is cornered and that he should fight his way out. That is not a good thing for obvious reasons. If however you shove him out of attack range you will trigger his flight response and give him the instinct to run or freeze. Even if he does not run away, the fact that he feels like running away will cause confusion, which triggers more adrenalin, and then you have the downward spiral to capitulation.

Once you have created the gap and the confusion, the opponent is forced out of a reactional mode and into a response mode, which means that now, if he wants to attack, he has to be able to consciously override all natural instincts and move forward. This very often leads to the sticky feet syndrome. He may really want to move forward but his feet appear stuck to the floor, his body lurches forward as though trying to move but his feet stay stuck firmly to the ground. To add to this effect and to make yourself a hard target you can add ballooning or stalking. This is done by pacing left to right without taking your eyes off the opponent, at the same time shouting out verbal commands, 'stay there, don't move!' and pointing to the opponent, this acting as a back-up fence to the verbal.

Interestingly, the ballooning triggers innate fears within the opponent that go right back to the dawn of man when we were not at the top of the food chain and were the prey of bigger animals. This will only add to the opponent's woe if he thinks that he is being stalked like a wild beast. If you watch the cheetah when he hunts the antelope he balloons or stalks before he attacks; in fact most animals do it, we are no exception. It can be used by us as an attacking tool to trick the opponent into a flight response, or against us – often inadvertently – to effect the same freeze tendencies.

The psychological fence
The psychological fence is a fighter's reputation or confident/aggressive gait – this places an invisible fence around you that only the very brave will try to pass.

The negative psychological fence
Deliberately dropping the physical or psychological fence by pretending to be scared or unthreatening can draw the opponent forward onto your intended attack. He walks into a trap.

The invisible fence
An experienced player will use what I call the invisible fence. That is, he will have the confidence and experience to face an opponent or opponents without employing a physical fence. He knows his range and his enemy so well that he can sense when there will be movement and he can feel bad intent. If his opponent moves forward he will move back or use a stop hit attack instinctively.

On the one hand the physical fence will control range and prime your attack. On the other hand, if you are not sure whether to strike or not, the fence allows you time to maintain a relatively safe range whilst you plan a course of action – bearing in mind that decision-making this late in the game is not a good thing, though sometimes it is unavoidable.

Sir Winston Churchill once said that occasionally people stumble upon the truth – and then get back up and wander off as though nothing happened. The truth is that in the three second fight, the fence is one of the best, if not the best, little techniques available for controlling the early stages of an altercation, but it is so simple that many people often fail to see its importance. It is too easy and they are looking for something more advanced or fantastic. To be honest the advanced stuff, the fantastic stuff, only works in the James Bond films. The fence should therefore become the bedrock of all your physical self-protection work. Ignore it at your own peril.

ATTACKING OFF THE FENCE

As formerly mentioned, if you find it necessary to initiate a pre-emptive strike, then attack off the fence. What you use as an attacking tool is your personal choice; out of necessity it is best to employ your strongest, most comfortable attack. There is nothing to gain and everything to lose if you throw anything less.

The attack is your chosen main artillery technique and whilst many techniques should be practised and perfected, one or two, the ones that work best for you, should be taken to one side and isolated. These will be the techniques used in your sniper option.

There is no sense in beating about the bush and saying that main artillery can be taken from any range because they can't. If punching range is the one most often given in a real situation then that is where the main artillery should be drawn from. Having said that I always think it is wise to have one or two very strong techniques at every range; after all a chain is only as strong as its weakest link.

So hand techniques are the order of the day, and there is little point in manufacturing another range when the one you are in is the most clinical anyway. Kicking and grappling range are far from clinical: they are, at best, elongated ranges where it usually takes several blows or seconds to finish an adversary as opposed to the split second it can take to finish a fight with a good hand technique. Punching range is also a very mobile range and a good puncher can move through several opponents in as many seconds. If you beg to differ then I respect your opinion but please don't try and convince me, have an animal day (a training session where the participants fight all out with very few rules and any range is allowed) at your own club and see for yourself. When you watch someone like the brilliant Rick Young teach trapping it makes you realise what a valid part of your armoury it can be, but even Rick will probably tell you that it is an incidental range used to back up main artillery technique. Basic trapping therefore is a valid (though very small) part of the support system. A fight goes from talking distance to in-your-face in the blink of an eye.

People often ask me what is the best means of physical defence and I always reply 'learn to hit fucking hard', and that's the bottom line. Learn how to hit very very hard and you'll come out of most situations on top, but please learn to do it from the right range. It's one thing being able to hit hard from a comfortable range and from a guard position or perhaps even using combination to build momentum and power, but how well will you fare when the distance you are used to is halved and you have to punch from a no-guard position? It's a completely different ball game so it is important to train your techniques as close to reality as possible. Then the step from dojo to street is not such a big one. If you are used to compliance in training you've got a very big shock coming to you when the shit hits the fan.

In the vast majority of situations I have been involved in I have used a left lead fence to set up a right-handed punch – sometimes a cross, sometimes a hook. My base was, and is, almost always a very small left lead forty-five degree stance and I always ask a question before I strike to trigger my action and to engage the opponent's brain. Other people I have worked with preferred a left-lead stance and a right-hand fence, punching with a left hook off the lead leg; others still favoured a left-lead fence from a left-lead stance and attacked with a pummelling head-butt. The lead hand or reverse hand finger strike is also a good stopping technique.

It's worth remembering that your opponent will be experiencing tunnel vision as a by-product of adrenal reaction. In real terms this means that by placing your attacking hand, left or right, slightly outside of his tunnel vision you can strike him without him seeing the blow.

The following illustrations are some of the favoured off-fence attacks.

Here are a few of the more common 'line-up' techniques taken from a fence:

RIGHT CROSS/HOOK

Thrown from the rear of a left-leading stance: can be tremendously powerful and effective. Its only real infirmity is that, because it is thrown from the rear leg, it can be slightly telegraphed.

From a right-lead stance this technique may be executed using the left-hand.

LEFT HOOK

Thrown from the front leg of a left-lead stance. If employed by a 'practised' pugilist, this punch can be very destructive. Because it is thrown from the front leg it is less telegraphed than other techniques and it has less distance to travel to the target. Because of the high skill factor involved it is not a recommended punch for the novice.

HEAD-BUTT

An attack method that inflicts a huge amount of pain, usually directed at the opponent's nose. If executed correctly utilising the body weight it can cause enormous damage to an adversary, though it is not known as a knockout technique.

As a final point on attack, don't ever pull your technique. If a situation has got so bad that you are forced to hit someone to protect yourself then they deserve everything they get. Pulling your technique is the quickest way to the graveyard, so either attack all out or do not attack at all. The only exception to this rule is if you are very experienced and feel you can judge the potency of your attacker. I was often faced with people that were not enough of a threat to demand a good hiding so I would use an adrenalin switch to psyche them out and thus beat them without coming to arms. This takes a lot of experience and unless you are very experienced, don't take the chance.

It is also my recommendation that, once you have hit your opponent, you make good your escape. The only time you need to finish off an opponent is when he is still a threat; if he is not then there is no need. I know this contradicts some of the things I have said in

Watch My Back but that (bouncing) is a different arena where many rules have to be broken to keep the peace long term. I have seen many people go for a finish when a finish was not necessary, and lose as a consequence. Use the distraction of your attack to make good an escape. That's my advice if the situation is a self-defence one; if it is a fight situation you may need to stay and finish off.

ACTION TRIGGER

This is a word or sentence that you can use to trigger action. When facing potential menace it is very often difficult to initiate a physical response, never quite knowing the right time to attack. A key word or sentence will take away decision making. Your chosen word/sentence will automatically initiate your attack. The trigger word/sentence can be any of your choosing. Preferably it should be a submissive question as opposed to a flat statement, as this will serve the triple purpose of switching off the opponent's adrenalin, brain engagement and action trigger. The submissive question is also a subliminal intimation that you wish to prolong the conversation, whereas shorter sentences, certainly single syllables, send the message that conversation is coming to an end.

While the flat statement, 'I don't want trouble', is submissive and can act as an action trigger, it does not adequately engage the brain because it does not demand an answer. Neither does it suggest that you wish to prolong the conversation. Even an abstract question has that triple purpose because of the confusion factor, for example 'how did the City get on today?' What has the City result got to do with the situation in hand?

Of course this all works nicely in the context of the four 'D's, your multi-faceted question being deception and distraction before a decision to fight (destruction) or flight. If the antagonist proffers a question, you may wish your pre-emptive blurb to be in the guise of an answer to it, or you may wish to feign deafness by saying, 'Sorry mate, I didn't hear you. What did you say?'

SUMMARY

Once you have put up the fence and lined up the antagonist with your chosen technique (this should be done within the first seconds of any confrontation) and you are sure that an attack upon your person is imminent, utilise the response sequence previously detailed. If you have to attack, distract and engage your opponent's brain with your chosen trigger then, if no other option is open to you, make a pre-emptive strike from your pre-cocked 'line-up' position. Your engaging verbal should veil your attack.

I also try not to ask a question that can be answered 'yes' or 'no', e.g. 'can we talk about this?' It does not engage the brain as well as a question that demands a longer answer, such as, 'what are you trying to say?'

One thing is certain: the longer you take to act, the graver the situation becomes, especially when faced with more than one antagonist. Time is of the essence, so don't waste even a second.

Chapter Six

Attacking Tools

'Security against defeat implies defensive tactics: ability to defeat the enemy means taking the offensive.'
Sun Tzu

Having got this far in to the book you should already be well aware of the fact that if a conflict reaches a physical response only the strong will survive. Even the highly trained and experienced martial arts practitioner struggles with a physical response. It is my hope that the techniques herein will help to lighten the load somewhat. Realistically, unless you make them a part of your everyday life, they will not. It is my advice to the reader that he/she makes a conscious effort to practise and perfect attacking techniques so that they become instinctive.

Attacking tools: there are many, and different schools of thought adhere to and promote different tools. Some talk of the indomitable boxer, with fast, punishing hands, others about the cripple-shooting kicker or mauling grappler. In fairness every discipline has its strengths and its weaknesses, its good exponents and its poor ones. To be a good all-rounder you need a compilation of all the disciplines. You need to be able to wrestle, box and kick. For 'blood and snot' self-protection, economy of movement is the name of the game. Why risk a high kick, when a poke in the eye would suffice? I have been there and tried it all, and what I am left with is a small nucleus of techniques that have and will work in a live situation. This text will show you what I deem to be the most effective, along with those techniques that are less frequently used, though are still effective for the odd occasion.

In this chapter I have listed various attacking tools without too much attention to detail; that will be left to the specialist chapters where each individual tool will be isolated and dissected. In this chapter I want to try and smash the myths regarding what is and is not effective, so I shall be very honest in my evaluation of all the forthcoming movements. For instance, it is a popular myth that, once learned, certain attacking techniques are guaranteed to work and will stop any attacker dead in his tracks. Frankly this is folly. To make a technique work against a determined attacker you will need many hours of practice – even then there are no guarantees. I have no bias to any one art so my evaluations will be unbiased and apolitical.

Pressure testing. No adversary is ever going to just let you apply a movement/technique. To be effective your moves must be both cunning and ferocious. Anything less will fail. For this reason it is important that your techniques be practised under pressure. A compliant training partner is fine when first learning the mechanics of a given move; after that, compliance will only serve to instil a false sense of reality and security.

So, gradually increase partner resistance, building up your confidence with each technique. Eventually practise against full partner resistance. While it is not reasonable to expect a training partner to take full contact blows during every practice session, you may use training aids, focus pads, punch-bag, etc. to develop impact.

Pressure testing is also excellent for gaining exposure to adrenalin, developing self-esteem and a strong will.

For greater detail of pressure testing please refer to my book *Animal Day: Pressure Testing the Martial Arts*, which specialises in this very subject.

THE BODY

HEAD
Best when used inside punching and wrestling distance. May be used to butt from the right, the left, the front or to the rear, using the corner, front or rear of the head to attack. Also effective if executed in an upward manner using the crown of the head to attack. While grappling the cranium, hair may be rubbed into the opponent's eyes. The head is an under-used attacking tool, which is surprising because it is one of the most effective and, especially when used by a woman, often totally unexpected. The danger with using the head to attack is that if you hit an opponent above the eye line, or anywhere on the skull, you are likely to hurt yourself just as much as your opponent – even knock yourself out. So always keep your attacks below the opponent's eye line.

TEETH
Only effective within wrestling distance. Bite anything, especially protruding items of the anatomy: e.g. nose, ears, etc. (false teeth may be thrown at an assailant).

MOUTH
Spitting into an opponent's face or eyes can be a great distracting factor that may lead you onto a better grip, attack etc. Shouting is also a good tool; use to attract attention or psyche out the assailant.

SHOULDER
Effective for close-in fighting if thrust into the opponent's windpipe or face.

ELBOWS
Effectively used from any angle whilst in close range.

HANDS

May be used to punch in any direction with power. To pull and twist whilst in grappling distance, to palm, heel or, with the fingers extended, to gouge.

HIPS

Pivotal when executing throwing techniques. If thrust into the opponent's mid-section ensures depth and unbalances the opponent before the throw.

KNEES

May be used to thrust inward, upward and around to the body or the head or by dropping knee-first onto the 'felled' opponent as a finishing technique.

SHINS

May be used to attack any part of the opponent's anatomy, especially the knees and thighs.

FEET

May be used to attack front, side, back or round to any part of the opponent's anatomy. Particularly effective while attacking the opponent's lower regions: lower abdominal, pubic bone, groin, knees and shins.

INCIDENTAL WEAPONS

'He who only sees the obvious wins his battles with difficulty, he who looks below the surface of things wins with ease.'

Sun Tzu

This list is by no means comprehensive. Anything, be it a handbag or a forlorn piece of brick on the floor, may be employed as an incidental weapon. Some will fall within the realms of the law, others outside it. All are uniform in one way: they are extensions of you. It is impossible to include every conceivable weapon within this text, because almost everything may be used as a weapon. I will try to cover the main weapons that you may carry on your person.

The greatest drawback of most incidental weapons is availability. Most are concealed in pockets or bags, so are not readily available, at least not quickly enough. You can look pretty conspicuous walking down the street wielding a stick or bat.

Rape alarm

Anything that makes noise and attracts attention is excellent, though useless if stuck in the bottom of your handbag or if you have heightened your vulnerability by placing yourself in a remote area with no chance of attracting attention. When choosing a rape alarm try to get one that does not sound like a house or car alarm. People are so used to hearing these that they will hardly bat an eyelid.

Hair spray/deodorant

They say that this is great as a hit and run implement. One spray in the eyes of an assailant would prove very painful, distracting him long enough for you to run. They must, for obvious reasons, be aerosols.

A sturdy aerosol canister would also act as an effective bludgeoning tool, if in close to your assailant. I have to say here that, although in theory this would be effective, I have never known anyone use it so I cannot be emphatic. I would also say that, unless the can is a heavy one and you can hit very hard, it is not that likely to stop a determined attacker.

Umbrella

A sturdily built brolly (they are few and far between, let me tell you) with a point could prove a very effective attacking tool for gouging into the eyes, throat or by swinging, baseball bat style, at the assailant's face. Lacks the solidity of a bat or stick and in my opinion is unlikely to do the job.

Handbag

The classic joke weapon, so often portrayed in comedy sketches. In reality the bag, if sturdily made with metal rims etc., might be effective as an attacking tool. Its greatest weakness lies in the fact that it must be swung to attack, deeming it telegraphed, and most bags are not sturdy enough to even begin to hurt someone who is determined.

Pepper

If you are ever attacked whilst having your dinner (a friend of mine was, he never really got mad until the guy stood on his steak) then a small pot of pepper with an easily detachable lid might come in handy. When thrown into an attacker's eyes it becomes a fine hit-and-run implement. If it doesn't blind him it might have him sneezing to death.

Newspaper

Famed by the great eye-spy writers as a lethal weapon. Due to its celluloid fame, it is often looked upon as unrealistic, and I would say that that just about describes it for me. I'm not saying that it is impossible – just unlikely.

Pen/pencil

Inconspicuous, accessible and potentially deadly, if aimed at the softer, more vulnerable areas of the assailant's anatomy, i.e. eyes, cheeks, throat, etc.

Credit card

The fine razor edge of a credit card makes it a potential killer if purposely or inadvertently aimed at the jugular or other main arteries or veins. Very accessible, extremely legal. However, it would take a lot of practice to become proficient with this weapon.

Chapter Seven

Areas of Attack

'Emerge from the void, strike vulnerable points, shun places that are defended, attack in unexpected quarters.'

Sun Tzu

Due to the anaesthetic qualities of adrenalin and the assailant possibly being under the influence of drink or drugs, pain per se is not usually enough to stop an attack. Most of the time they won't feel pain. For this reason attacks should, in the case of body shots, be penetrable, striking the nervous system, or in the case of head/eye shots, accurate (jaw, eyeball). Then they will cause deep-seated pain, disorientation or unconsciousness.

IN THEORY

In medical terms, a severe attack on any one part of the anatomy could potentially prove fatal. Even if such a blow was not a death-dealing one, the accidental consequences of it may result in death. For instance, a blow to the nose may render an opponent unconscious. If in falling the relaxed head strikes the pavement or another hard surface, which from my experience it very often does, a serious concussion or skull fracture may occur. This could result in a possible brain clot or haemorrhage, ending in death. Death may also result, in this instance, from the huge amount of blood from the nose clogging the throat during unconsciousness, which in turn stops the flow of oxygen to the brain, causing death. Even a kick to an opponent's shin could, in an extreme case, result in death, either from shock or due to an 'arterial embolism'. In the latter, small particles of the decimated bone splinter into the torn blood vessels and become lodged in a vessel too small to permit their passage. This forms a blood clot that could mean circulatory failure of a section of the body, causing gangrene and/or ultimately death.

IN REALITY

In real terms, broken bones, unconsciousness and death are not so common, or likely. The human body can be very durable and is not an easy vehicle to stop once it is charged with the pain-reducing influence of adrenalin.

As the potential victim in a self-defence scenario, one should never worry about the medical implications of a counter-pre-emptive attack on an antagonist; to do so would cause indecision on your part, indecision begetting defeat. Even one second of indecision can mean the difference between life and death, survival and destruction.

The bottom line here is that he is trying, for no reason, to hurt, rob, rape or kill you. To pay him any consideration would be foolhardy and dangerous.

Undoubtedly, the three most vulnerable areas of attack are the eyes, throat and jaw, though not necessarily in that order. Vulnerability depends largely on how they lie in relation to your attacking tools at the time of a particular altercation. You would, for instance, have little chance of attacking any of the three if you were grabbed from behind. For this reason, it is wise to learn other vulnerable areas so as to cover all situations. So, again let's get rid of some of the myths because I am sick of people saying stupid things like 'just kick him between the legs and he'll drop like a sack of shit!' Oh, if only things were that simple.

HEAD

Anywhere above the opponent's eye-line is a no-go area (unless you are using a weapon). To strike the skull with your fists or head is usually futile. The cranium, being of thick and strong construction to protect the master muscle, the brain, does just that, though it is vulnerable to kicking techniques if your assailant is horizontal. The temple is, of course, very vulnerable, but strikes to the temple take pinpoint accuracy to be effective. The head is also vulnerable if you grab it and smash it against a wall or a curb (or anything harder than the skull itself).

EARS

Attacks to the ears, especially when both ears are attacked together, can be potentially fatal if unconsciousness and concussion occurs. If both are attacked simultaneously with cupped hands, rupture of the ear drum would theoretically ensue because of large amounts of air being forced into the internal canal of the ear. In reality, this is unlikely to happen, though the pain inflicted by such an attack would likely be enough to stop your assailant long enough for you to make your getaway. The ears can also be ripped by gripping and pulling, though this can be difficult if the ear is sweaty/bloody. The most effective attack against the ear is the bite. This causes panic and extreme pain, stopping even the most ardent attacker. Also, a one-eared assailant would also be very easy for the police to trace, though I doubt they'd thank you for that.

EYES

The most vulnerable, accessible and sensitive part of the human anatomy. You may either scrape, poke or gouge them using the end/s of the finger/s, depending upon how you are situated in relation to the eyes. Any connection between finger and eye will cause extreme pain and more often than not stop your assailant. Strikes to the eyes could result in a collapsed eyeball, lacerated eyelid or even the eyeball being pushed completely out of its socket. Accuracy is the predominant factor when attacking the eyes, and needs much practice to obtain. Most attacks to the eyes are thwarted because humans have an instinctively fast reaction where the eyes are concerned. Your attacks are more likely to work if you attack up the face and into the eyes as opposed to a full frontal attack that will almost always be seen.

NOSE

Because the nose protrudes from the face it becomes an obvious target, though not a favourite of mine. A strong aggressor would shake off such an attack and carry on. Because of its protrusion it is a very good target for biting. From a rear bearhug the nose is a very vulnerable area for the rear head-butt. As was formerly mentioned, a severe attack to the nose could prove fatal; however, pain and watery eyes are far more usual.

THE JAW

Most people who have experienced and participated in real fighting with any degree of success will tell you that the jaw is the ultimate target for the ultimate fighter. Not because it causes pain or fractures, but because, if struck correctly, it causes unconsciousness. This, in a defence situation, is the ultimate goal, especially if you are facing more than one aggressor.

An accurate punch to the jawbone will shake the brain, causing unconsciousness. Accuracy is of the essence if this is to occur. A severe knockout that sees the opponent unconscious before he falls can easily result in a fatality if the head strikes anything harder than itself, e.g. the pavement.

More on in Chapter 18 – 'The Knockout'.

THROAT

Vulnerable is not a descriptive enough word to depict this accessible, susceptible area. Although only partially protected by the jaw and neck muscles, it still takes accuracy to strike a telling blow. Chopping and straight finger strikes are most effective when attacking the throat. A strong, accurate attack may cause any one of a myriad of contusions, from contusion of the internal jugular through to contusion of the larynginal nerve, a fracture of the spinouse to a possible injury to the branchial plexus, which would cause partial or complete paralysis of the arm. All of these could be fatal.

For close-in fighting, grabbing the windpipe around the Adam's apple sector and squeezing the larynx tightly may cause choking, extreme pain and unconsciousness. Be warned: many fatalities occur as a direct consequence of attacking this vulnerable area.

SOLAR PLEXUS

Medically speaking, a severe blow to the solar plexus can cause anything from a deep fissure in the liver to a torn gall bladder or even a complete rupture of the stomach, which may culminate in massive internal bleeding. Due to severe shock or blood loss this can end in death. More realistically, you can expect to knock the wind out of your opponent, at the most, which would give you enough time to run. From my own experience in these matters, body shots (unless employed as a finishing technique to a felled opponent) are not usually stopping techniques and should only be employed when there is no other option or target open to you. Adrenalin, with its pain-reducing qualities, builds a brick wall around the body, often making it impervious to punches and kicks. You may break ribs or cause internal damage to your foe and still not deter him at the time of his attack. As a paradox, an attack to the face/jaw will at the very least cause disorientation in your assailant, because of the simple fact that it 'shakes' the brain.

JOINTS

I've lost count of the amount of times I have heard people saying 'take the knee out, take the elbow out, etc. etc. etc. As though it were as easy as picking apples off a tree. Let me be very honest here and blunt – it's a lot of horseshit. Breaking limbs with attacking movement is very hard and very unlikely. The time they are vulnerable of course is in *newaza* (ground fighting) where arm and leg bars do, have and will break bits off an opponent so easily that it often happens by accident in the dojo (training room).

All joints – finger, elbow, knee, etc. – are in theory vulnerable to attack, but, and this is a big but, they are very well protected by surrounding muscle and tissue. Knees can be attacked with kicking techniques, but you'd have to be a very proficient exponent to find the accuracy that is necessary to do so. Paradoxically, it takes no skill at all to break fingers, only the opportunity to bend them back.

GROIN

Anywhere around the lower abdomen and pubic bone area is very vulnerable to knee, foot or fist attacks. A severe attack to these regions may rupture the bladder causing shock, internal bleeding or thrombosis or even a clot in the femorial vein, which could ultimately lodge in the lungs, causing death.

Again, though possible, these are unlikely in reality. If no other target is available to you though, this is a good option.

TESTICLES

In my time I have kicked, punched and grabbed this supposed vulnerable area in a bid to stop an attacker, usually to no avail. My lack of success has been largely due to the testes being so well protected. Attempted infiltrations with foot and fist have been lost to either the large front leg muscles that sentry the testicles or the assailant's instinctive thrust-back action. In the case of the 'grab and squeeze', the assailant's underpants and trousers demand an iron grip to get even a whimper. Paradoxically, if you are fortunate enough to score a direct hit, that is an entirely different matter.

These, to my mind, are the major attack areas of the human anatomy. As you can see I am not a great believer in body shots for the aforementioned reasons. When you have a choice, always attack the jaw, eyes or throat. If these areas are not available for attack, aim for the most vulnerable area that is. Never expend energy on non-vulnerable areas like the skull, back, chest and shoulders. Whilst some of these areas do conceal major organs that may be susceptible to attack, they are too well protected by major muscle groups/bone to penetrate.

You may only have one shot so don't waste it.

Chapter Eight

Hands and Elbows

In my opinion there are no better instruments to employ as attacking tools than the hands, whether punching, poking or grabbing. The hands are to physical self-protection what Nureyev is to ballet.

Elbows are also a valuable asset, though more of a rainy day technique than the irreplaceable hands, which are the most natural and accessible tools for defence on the human anatomy.

The knuckles are, when the fist is clenched, an extremely solid and durable element. When abetted by transferred body weight they become very destructive as an attacking tool. The fact that our hands are endowed with the sense of touch also aids the accuracy of an employed technique.

There are many ways in which one may practise and polish hand techniques, some of which I will explore in this chapter. Some of the techniques and methods of practice may seem a little basic for the advanced or practising martial artist who, unrealistically, sees complex as synonymous with effective. In real terms, complex is synonymous only with unpractical. To be effective the chosen self-defence technique must be economical – and what is economical if it is not basic? The beginner will find no problem in practising the prescribed techniques because of their fundamental qualities.

THE MAIN ARTILLERY

'The Fox and the Cat were standing on a hill, talking about how many ways they know of escaping from a pack of dogs. The Cat, feeling rather inadequate, said, "I only know one way. I run up the nearest tree." The Fox gave the Cat a sardonic smile and said, "Well, actually, I know fifty different ways of escaping a pack of dogs." Just then a pack of dogs appeared on the horizon and ran in the direction of the Fox and the Cat. The Cat, utilising his only escape technique, found sanctuary up a nearby tree. Whilst the Fox was busy deciding which of the fifty escape techniques he should employ, he got ate by the pack of dogs.'

Game plans

THE TRAINED FIGHTER

We have a paradox here. In the main, the trained fighter has a huge support system and yet no main artillery and no game plan. He has too many techniques to chose from. When a situation becomes live, like the Fox he is often defeated whilst he is in the process of choosing the right technique /game plan to employ.

On the other hand, the novice has no artillery, no game plan and absolutely no idea. When a situation becomes live for him he has nothing to chose from and very often comes out of the altercation badly.

Form a game plan. How will you react and what techniques will you employ when confronted by an attacker? Decide, and then mentally rehearse your game plan, over and again. This process is enlarged upon in the chapter on visualisation.

SPONTANEOUS RESPONSE

I am often told, by the uninitiated, that in an attack scenario the victim should be spontaneous, their response varying according to the attack. This would mean having to wait until the assailant actually attacks, spontaneously reacting thereafter. Too late. I have to say that no one with any real experience has ever said this to me.

Action is faster than reaction. If you allow the assailant to attack first, your chances of defence are minimal.

If you are blind-sided and the first you know of a situation is the attack itself, then yes, you will spontaneously respond. Unless you are highly trained and pressure tested that response will often be capitulation or collapse. If you wait to be attacked you have left it far too late.

If, however, you are coded up it will be pretty difficult for an assailant to utilise a blind-side attack. His attack is therefore likely to come from the front, and usually through deceptive dialogue. This allows you to take the initiative and determine the state of play.

My advice to the novice who has no formal fighting background is to choose his strongest side (right hand if you are right-handed, left if you are left-handed) and perfect one or two techniques. Make them, via conscientious practice, your own.

Practise until you develop power and accuracy, then, especially if you employ the technique as a pre-emptive attack, you will have a good chance of defending yourself successfully.

My advice to the advanced or practising martial artist is exactly the same: choose your strongest technique and make it stronger, work it until it is absolutely natural and comfortable. This will be your main artillery. Of course, you should still practice all your other techniques and perhaps add to your main artillery as they improve. These will be you support system.

Your game plan should be the aforementioned sequence of positive responses, from avoidance right through to physical confrontation, and, if and when necessary, responses five and six, as detailed in the chapter on attackers and attack rituals.

In your bid to attain good hands you will be looking to develop accuracy, speed and power; accuracy rising slightly above the other two necessaries, because an accurate attack can be effective with minimal power and speed. Later in the chapter I will go into depth about the development of the three foregoing elements. Firstly, I would like to look at the different attacks available via the hands.

Left jab/finger strike/claw

As a punch the jab is generally used as an opener, a lead punch that lacks real power. Very good for causing irritation in an opponent through the stinging pain inflicted. Presence of the former and latter also help to make openings for the bigger punches that you might wish to follow with.

The same attack used with open hand transforms a weakening technique into a stopping technique. This may be attained by either clawing the hand or by coupling/spearing the fingers together to form a point then directed at the eyes. One of the most basic, effective and accessible techniques on the curriculum.

Left hook/palm heel

Thrown (as a right-handed person) off the leading left leg and aimed, ultimately, at the opponent's jaw. Very powerful if abetted by the transferred body weight. All hooking punches are thrown in the same style as a slap attacking with knuckles as opposed to the flat of the hand.

For maximum power push your right hip forward and slightly to the left before the strike. As you throw the left fist toward the target, pull the hip back to its original position and push your left hip sharply across and to the right, following the path of your punch. This hip movement will ensure maximum weight transference into the punch.

With the palm heel the foregoing criteria is the same using the heel of the hand to attack as opposed to the fist.

Left uppercut/palm heel

Thrown from the leading left leg and aimed, ultimately, at the jaw. Very powerful if correctly employed. For maximum power, push your right hip forward and to the left before you strike, slightly bending at the knees so that you are just below the target (jaw). Throw your left fist upward, twisting the fist on impact with the jaw, so that the palm is facing inward (to your own body). Simultaneously retract the right hip sharply to its original position and push upward from your crouched position, thrusting the left hip forward and upward, following the path of the punch. On connection with the jaw, follow through with the punch and hip for maximum effect.

Right cross/finger strike/claw/palm heel

A most powerful technique utilising (if correctly executed) nearly all of the body weight. Thrown from the back, right leg whilst in a left-leading stance. Throw the right fist toward the target (jaw), simultaneously thrusting your right hip forward and in the same direction as the punch. Your hip should fully thrust in conjunction with the punch's connection with the jaw.

Use the finger strike, claw and palm heel to attack as opposed to the fist. With the finger strike and claw the target area would be the eyes as opposed to the jaw.

Right hook/palm heel

A powerful, accessible and natural punch. Applied with the facsimile of a 'slap' using the knuckles as opposed to the flat of the hand to attack.

Thrown from the back, right leg whilst in a left leading stance.

Throw from the outside-in, in a semi-circular motion toward the target (jaw). Throw the fist toward the target, simultaneously thrusting the right hip sharply forward, following the route of the punch. As it connects with the jaw follow through with the punch and the hip for maximum power. With the palm heel the foregoing criteria is the same using the heel of the hand to attack as opposed to the fist.

Right uppercut/palm heel

Thrown from the right leg whilst in a left-leading stance. Bend slightly at the knees so that you are just below the target (jaw). Throw your right fist upward, twisting the fist on impact with the jaw, so that the palm is facing inward (toward your own body). Simultaneously push upward from your crouched position and sharply thrust your right hip forward and upward following the path of the punch. On connection with the jaw follow through with the punch and hip for maximum effect. With the palm heel the aforementioned criteria is the same using the heel of the hand to attack as opposed to the fist.

Elbows

The elbows are almost as versatile as the hands, though usually employed from a shorter range. Because of their close proximity to the body they are, potentially, more powerful than the hands. However, they lack the 'feel', accuracy and cunning of the hands. They may be used off the front leg or rear to uppercut, thrust (sideways) reverse strikes or (whilst in grappling range) as a downward strike.

For hooking and uppercutting with the elbow, from front or rear, the foregoing criteria in the section on hook and uppercut punches is the same, using the point of the elbow as opposed to the fist to attack.

Downward strike (against a waist or leg grab)

Lift your right (or left) arm up high with the palm of your hand facing away from you. Pull it down in a rapid descent aiming the point of the elbow at and into the target (spine, neck, ribcage).

Side thrust (against an assailant attacking from the side)

Bring your right (or left) arm across the front of your chest, palm inwards, as far as it will go, then thrust back along the same route, aiming the point of the elbow into the oncoming or stationary attacker. Target the solar plexus, throat or face.

Reverse elbow strike (against an opponent at your rear)

Downward elbow

Stretch your right arm out in front of you. Turn your head and look at the target behind. Sharply retract your arm back from its outstretched position until behind you, aiming the point of your elbow at and into the assailant. Simultaneously step back with your right leg to add weight to the attack. Target the solar plexus, throat or face.

Technically speaking, the elbows are just a shortened version of the 'hands', effecting tremendous power if sponsored by body weight transference.

Equipment

Focus pads (hooks and jab pads)

Potentate amongst training aids is the focus pad. Excellent for the development of accuracy, power, distancing and multi-angled punches.

Each pad is centred by a one and a half inch (in diameter) spot that acts as the target area. Anything but a direct hit on the spot looks, feels and sounds wrong. An accurate shot will feel solid and emit a definite thwack, letting you know that you are on target. They are excellent for anyone wishing to develop a knockout punch.

It is necessary to have a partner when practising the pads. He should fit one pad to each hand and then angle them to meet the demand of your desired punch. Spot facing inward for hook punches, downward for uppercuts and forward for straight punches. The person punching the pads should lead with his left leg (right if right-handed) and punch the pads with his left hand to his partner's left side, and his right hand to his partner's right side. The 'puncher' should employ a guard in normal practice and no guard in 'line-up' practice. The holder should vary the height and distance of the pads (from the puncher). As the puncher hits the pads he should exhale through his mouth or nose, this will regulate the breathing, feed the working muscles with oxygen and aid *Kime* (body focus), forcing ones muscles to tense on impact of the punch or strike.

Once the puncher becomes familiar with hitting the pads and the holder with holding them correctly, the holder may dictate and control the play by shouting out strikes for the puncher to execute, such as jab, cross, right hook, left hook, then change the angle of the pads to receive the designated strikes. The experienced puncher may attempt more advanced combinations: left jab, right uppercut, left hook. Again the holder moves the pads in time with the strikes. The holder should not stay in the same position all the time, but should move, forcing the puncher to employ footwork. Each time the puncher finishes his punch or combination the holder should move to a different position.

When practising the line-up, pre-emptive strike, it is important to precede each strike with a disarming or engaging statement (as covered in the fence). You must line-up, disarm/engage and then strike as though it were the real thing.

Some people may feel a little foolish talking to an inanimate object (the pads), but realism is of the essence in practice, so I feel it is important to get as close to reality as is humanly possible.

Top and bottom ball

Suspended in mid-air via a length of elastic from floor to ceiling, the top and bottom ball emerges as a wonderful piece of equipment that is excellent for the development of timing and distancing. Some argue that it is the closest one can get to a live opponent; I am not inclined to disagree. It is also a hugely enjoyable method of practice. May be used to practise jabs, crosses, hooks and, for the advanced player, uppercuts.

Line-ups may also be worked on this versatile training aid. The height (and thus the speed) of the ball can easily be altered by tightening the straps above and below the ball. In practice, if you stand close to the ball it will, if you are not vigilant, hit you on its return or bounce back, adding to the realism of the practice immeasurably.

The punch-bag

Probably the oldest method of practice known to the fighting man. Despite its ancient heritage, it is still the very best power-developing implement on the market. Also known to be excellent for developing good technique, stamina and combination punching. Also good for practising line-ups. Because of the punch-bag's mass, accuracy development is not aided here, though everything else is.

If you dress the bag in a sack or even drape some old clothes around it, it becomes a fine implement for practising grabs and combinations of grabbing and striking.

The greatest form of practice, without a doubt, is to be had with a live opponent/ partner with whom you can communicate, learn and progress. Tell each other when a technique feels right, wrong, realistic, unrealistic, powerful or weak. If you do not or cannot train with a partner, make your bag or pad work as realistic as possible using visualisation (see Chapter 20). Imagine the bag, ball or pads are real antagonists and that you are in a real situation. Try to charge every blow with aggression, imagining that your life depends on the success of the said strike.

This method of practice not only adds realism to the training session, it also makes the session therapeutic.

Chapter Nine

Legs

As attacking tools the feet are both powerful and accessible, though less immediate than the hands, and harder to master. Basic, low kicks are favourable if you choose to employ the legs as attacking tools.

Kicking techniques can be invaluably destructive – in theory. In reality, live situations lack the space and distancing to employ the kick to its full potential, and just the fact that you are using your legs as attacking tools renders you less mobile.

Great kickers (they are few) will doubtless disagree with me, and work effectively every kicking technique and theory that I would deem as ineffective. But they are an exception to the rule. The techniques that I promote and practise are aimed at the greater majority who would or could never, even given the right distance, employ a successful kicking technique, and not at the minority who probably could. To the minority I apologise profusely before I start, because I am sure you will not like what I have to say. Even the minority would, I'm sure, agree that when aiming at the masses one is obliged to promote techniques that will not take a lifetime to learn. I can get a complete novice punching hard and accurately on the focus pads in one session, preparing them, in a small way, directly for the street. To do that with a kicking technique is a near impossibility.

Personally, I use kicks to bridge the gap (when the gap between you and your opponent is too great to employ punching techniques), or as a finishing tool (to finish off a felled opponent). In these scenarios feet are unrivalled, especially in the latter. As independent attacks, in most circumstances, I do not endorse them. I only kick if there is no other option open to me, though I always, without exception, finish off with feet.

Front kick

Very basic and effective, especially when directed at the lower regions such as groin, knees and shins. Balance is not impaired (if kept low) and little skill is needed in execution.

May be used as a thrusting kick attacking with the heel by pulling the rest of the foot back; as a snap kick attacking with the ball of the foot by pushing the ankle forward and pulling back the toes; or by attacking with the in-step by pushing the toes forward.

Any area below the waist is a safe and legitimate target; more specifically the groin, pubic bone, testicles, kneecaps and shins.

The most important aspect of the front kick is the utilisation of the hips. Forward hip thrust is pivotal if any power is to be generated. A fast recovery of the spent kick is also imperative (this applies with all kicks), as a lazy kick will be grabbed by an adversary.

Side kick

Very powerful and accessible, though restricted by its high skill factor. May be executed to the front or the side attacking with the heel or the side edge of the foot by turning the attacking foot inward and pulling the toes back tightly so that the side of the foot is taut and prominent. If attacking to the side: lift the knee of the attacking leg upward and thrust the foot sideways at the target whilst simultaneously pivoting on the supporting leg so that the foot of the supporting leg is pointing in the opposite direction to the target. This will ensure full hip commitment. After connection with the target, recover the attacking leg quickly along the same route as it was aimed.

Roundhouse kick

Very powerful and accessible, with a much higher skill factor than the front kick. Any target below the chest is a safe and legitimate one, more specifically the ribs, kidneys, lower abdomen, groin, pubic bone, testicles, thighs, knees and shins. The higher the target area aimed for with this kick, the more danger there is of impaired balance and a slow recovery, unless you are highly skilled.

The attacking part of the foot can be the in-step or the ball of the foot. If employing the ball of the foot, pull back the toes and foot so that on impact with the target the heel is higher than the toes. If employing the in-step push the toes and ankle forward and strike with the bone at the front of the foot. It is important to lift the knee of the attacking leg high and to the side, throwing the designated leg around and into the target by pivoting on the supporting leg and thrusting the hips behind the technique on impact with the target. After contact with the target, quickly retract the leg by pivoting back on the supporting leg and pulling the hips back to their original position.

Back kick

Potentially a very powerful kick. Accessible whilst attacking to the rear, a high skill factor if aimed at a forward-facing opponent. The latter is therefore not recommended for the novice.

When using the heel of the foot to attack any of the lower anatomical regions, more specifically the solar plexus, ribs, groin, pubic bone, testicles, thighs and knees, hours of practice is needed if accuracy is to be gained.

Attacking to the front: a potentially hazardous kick because it is necessary to turn your back, for a split second, on the opponent when twisting around. Due to this 'twisting' action disorientation often occurs.

If using the right leg to attack, lead with the left leg. From this small compact stance lift your right leg up and toward your left leg, wrapping the in-step of the right foot tightly around the back of the left calf muscle. Pivot around on the left supporting leg so that your back is directly facing your opponent, simultaneously turning your head so that you do not lose sight of him. Thrust the heel of the right foot, propelled by the forward thrust of both hips, into the target. After connection with the target, twist your body around and place the attacking (right) foot on the floor so that you are now facing the opponent.

Attacking to the rear: turn your head around so that you can see the target/opponent. Lift your right knee up to waist height and directly in front of you. Thrust the attacking heel directly behind you and into the target/opponent, propelled by the forward thrust of both hips following the route of the kick. After connection with the target, retract the kick sharply back to the 'knee lift' position in front of you. Replace the foot on the floor. Alternatively, after connection with the target, twist and place the attacking foot on the floor so that you are now facing the opponent.

Stamping kick

Simple, accessible and very destructive. Used mostly as a finishing technique, but may also be used in vertical grappling as an ankle or foot stamp. Effective on any part of the horizontal human anatomy, more specifically the head, neck, ribs and legs.

Lift the knee of the attacking leg high and directly in front of you. Stamp the heel of the attacking foot into the target.

Sweeping kick

Used to sweep an opponent's legs from under him. Devastating if followed up with a stamping kick. May be used to attack and sweep the opponent's front leg, or both legs by attacking the opponent's rear leg.

Front leg sweep

Used to attack an opponent who has one leg leading (right or left). Attack the shin of the opponent's lead leg with the in-step of your right foot (left if attacking his left leg) sweeping his leg across the front of his own body, spiralling him to the ground. Especially effective if the opponent is transferring weight onto the leg as you attack it, or if he already has weight on the leg.

Back leg sweep

This attack relies heavily upon the opponent who is standing with his legs/feet close together. Attack with your strongest side, again using the in-step of the foot. Attack the back of the opponent's knees, lifting him completely off the ground, toppling him to the floor.

Equipment

All kicking techniques, for realism, are best practised on or with a 'live' partner. However, other implements may be used for the development of power, distancing and accuracy.

Punch-bags

Ideal for practising front kicks, roundhouse kicks, side kicks and back kicks. If you lie the bag flat on the floor it is also good for practising stamping kicks.

When executing front kicks, side kicks and back kicks on the punch-bag you may swing it, kicking it with the designated kick as it comes back toward you. This is excellent for practising distancing on a moving target.

For low kicks and sweeps, a long 6ft bag that hovers just above the ground is recommended.

Focus pads

Specifically good for practising front snap kicks (using the in-step rather than the ball of the foot) and roundhouse kicks, will help to develop power, distancing and more importantly accuracy.

By holding one pad to the thigh, target area pointing outward, it may be used to practise low roundhouse kicks. If tucked under the opposite armpit, target area pointing outward, it is ideal for mid-section roundhouse kicks. If held at groin level, with the target area pointing to the floor, it may be used to practise low front snap kicks, using the in-step of the foot to attack. If held across and slightly in front of the body, target area pointing outward and at face height, it may be used for face height roundhouse kicks.

Strike shield

Excellent for developing power in all the kicks because the shield is held along the contours of the holder's body, the practice has the added bonus of realism. If the holder tucks the shield tightly to the backs of the legs and bottom, the attacker may practice realistic low roundhouse kicks and sweeps.

Chapter Ten

Knees

Made famous by the ferocious Thai boxers who use the knees as naturally and as effectively as the western boxer uses the hands. Their use is relegated to close-in fighting or grappling, though they are unsurpassable when appropriate. They may be used to attack upward, forward, around or, to a felled opponent, as a finishing technique downward. They can be used to attack as low as the opponent's knee or high as his head. Very basic and very accessible with, in some cases, a low skill factor. As stated, the problem with kneeing techniques is that you generally have to be close to an opponent – close enough, in fact, for him to grab you and drag you to the floor – not the best place to be in a violent encounter, especially when facing multiple opponents or indeed one determined opponent that wants you on the floor in the first place. I get sick of seeing kneeing techniques as the flagship of so many hypothetical self-defence productions that intimate that this technique will guarantee to finish an encounter should it be employed. Not so. No technique holds such a guarantee and to think they do is to ill prepare yourself for an arena that is ferocious and ugly.

My first couple of attempts at kneeing techniques in real encounters failed abysmally because my attacks were clumsy and pushy. This was not helped by the fact that I was wearing trousers that stuck to my thighs as I tried to lift my knee. In theory and in perfect conditions it should be easy to generate power with the knee. In reality, with adrenal shake in the legs and constrictive clothing, it is far from easy. For a knee attack to work it needs to be sharp and forceful; this means much practice.

Upward knee

A slow technique not only lacks power but is also easy for an aggressor to catch. If he grabs your leg you are as good as on the ground, and if that is where he wanted you in the first place then you are in a world of trouble, as they say.

I'll talk through the different attacks you can employ with the knee.

Upward knee

To the groin or testicles this is a simple but effective technique. Lift the knee upward as sharply as possible. A slow pushy movement is likely to be ineffective: the quicker the ascent, the greater the impact. If applying the same technique to the opponent's face or head, first grab his head by the hair or ears or by coupling the fingers of both hands at the back of his skull, and pull his head down rapidly toward your knee. Simultaneously, bring the attacking knee upward to meet the descending head. As they meet, smash the head through the knee.

Forward knee

Much the same technique as the thrusting front kick, using the knee as the attacking tool as opposed to the foot. Relies heavily on the grip you have on the opponent. Grab the opponent's clothes tightly at about shoulder level and vigorously pull, the opponent's body quickly toward your knee, via the said garment.

Simultaneously, thrust the attacking knee upward and forward to meet the opponent's body on its descent. At the moment of impact, thrust both hips forward and into the opponent's body while still pulling downward with the grip.

Forward knee

Roundhouse knee

Much the same as the roundhouse kick, using the knee as the attacking tool as opposed to the foot. Also relegated to grappling distance and relying much on the pulling/grabbing support of your hands. May be used very effectively to attack the opponent's knee, thigh or body. The advanced exponent may even attack to the head.

To the knee, thigh or body, lift the attacking knee up and slightly away from your body then thrust it downward toward the target and at the same time pulling the opponent via his attire toward the attacking knee. On impact, thrust your hips forward and slightly drop your body weight into the technique.

Knee drop

A very damaging technique to finish off an opponent who is already lying of the floor. Logically, the heavier you are the more effective this technique will be, although it doesn't rely entirely on body weight for its effectiveness. It can be dangerous for the person attempting the knee drop because of the danger of being pulled into grappling range by the person on the floor.

You literally drop all of your weight forward and down onto the opponent, landing on the target area (ribs, head, etc.) with the point of your attacking knee (left or right). The quicker the descent, the more effective the technique. For added effect you may jump up so that you land on the opponent from a greater height.

The danger here is obvious. If the opponent is not finished by your attack he will probably grab you as you drop and you could easily fall into ground fighting and be beaten by a stronger, more experienced person. As a point of fact I do not recommend the use of finishing techniques in self-defence, unless the assailant is still a danger to you. Always try to hit and run. It's popular, again, for self-defence teachers to recommend a second and third strike to an opponent who is already stunned. Forget it. Don't even think about it. Anyone that has actually been involved in a real situation would not, or certainly should not, recommend this. If one attack stuns an assailant then use those two or three seconds to make good your escape. Unless you are highly skilled, a stunned or semi-conscious assailant may instinctively grab you when you move in for the kill. Then you have got problems.

Equipment

Punch-bag

The best way to practise knee attacks on the punch-bag is to clothe it, either by tying a loose sack around it or dressing it in old clothes, so that you can grip it like you would a real opponent. Then grab and knee as you would a real person. As with kicking the bag, you may, if you wish, swing the bag and knee it as it swings toward you. If you lie the bag down on the floor you can practise the knee drop on it. A six foot bag is great for practising lower region strikes.

Focus pads

Not as effective as the bag, but still quite good. The holder holds one pad tightly against his thigh with the target area pointing outward whilst at the same time the attacker thrusts his knee, (roundhouse), into the pad. To practise the upward knee, the holder should put both hands (padded) in front of himself at about groin height, right hand overlapping left with both palms facing toward the floor. The attacker may take hold of the holder's hands and pull them downward into the uprising knee, or alternatively grab the holder's clothes at shoulder level and pull on them as he executes the knee attack on the pads.

Chapter Eleven

The Head

'I didn't do anything at first, except try to get up. As I did our heads clashed. The back of mine with the front of his. I felt the weight lift as he rolled over and groaned. I don't think I've ever moved so fast in all my life. I was up and away down the towpath like a shot.'

Unleash the Lioness

The head can be one of the most effective weapons available if used correctly. If used incorrectly it can be as dangerous to the bestower as to the recipient. The key factor in the success of the head-butt is to keep the attack below the opponent's eye-line. Anywhere above the eye-line is no-go and potentially dangerous for the butter. Paradoxically, the person employing the butt must use only that above the eye-line to attack with, or again they get more damage than their opponent.

You may attack with the head in five ways:

1) From right to left using the left corner of your forehead to attack.

2) From left to right using the right corner of your forehead to attack.

3) A forward thrusting butt using either the left, centre or right of your forehead to attack.

4) You may attack upward with the crown of your head, or-

5) Backward with the back of your head.

They are all close range attacks that can be employed with or without the support of your hands to pull. Power in the butt relies on the combination of two things: the whiplash effect, whereby you lurch the body forward slightly before the head, thus forcing the head to follow, creating a whiplash effect, and the propelling body weight which should still be travelling in the same direction as the head as it strikes its target. This momentum will add great weight to the attack.

A good head-butter, and I have worked with a few, will often go through hundreds of fights with nothing more than the head and destroy opponents large and small with the one simple technique. Employed correctly, it can have a devastating, face-demolishing effect on would-be antagonists. Again, as with everything really, it takes much practice to perfect. Let's have a look at the different methods of butting.

Left to right

Lurch your body forward followed by the head. The right corner of your forehead whiplashes into the right side or front of the recipient's nose, face or jaw. If you are actually gripping the opponent's attire at the time of your attack, pull them rapidly toward the head-butt.

Right to left

The same applies, though here the left corner of your forehead whiplashes into the left side or front of the recipient's nose, face or jaw. Again, if you have a grip on your opponent's clothes, pull rapidly toward the head-butt.

Forward-thrusting head-butt

Lurch your body directly forward followed by the front of your head, whiplashing it into the opponent's nose, eyes or jaw. Care should be taken when attacking directly from the front not to hit the opponent's teeth. Although it is very painful for the recipient, it is also potentially dangerous to the attacker. Use a grip on your opponent's clothes to pull them rapidly toward the attack.

Upward head-butt

Generally employed from within grappling range when your forehead is in the region of your opponent's chest. From this position thrust rapidly upward, attacking your opponent's chin with the front crown of your head.

Reverse head-butt

To be executed when an opponent is standing directly behind you or is holding you in a rear bearhug. In the case of the former, lurch your body rapidly backward followed by your head, whiplashing the back of your skull into the opponent's face. In the case of the latter where the body weight is locked in the bearhug and therefore redundant, bring your head slightly forward, then throw it backward as quickly as you can, hitting the opponent's face with the back of your skull.

Equipment

Basically, to practise the various head-butts with any realism you need a partner. If this is impossible (not everyone wants to be used for head-butting practice!), then a punch-bag will suffice. Treat the bag practice exactly the same as you would a person, standing yourself in the correct position in relation to the bag according to which butt you want to practise. Beware, though, of prolonged practice and over-zealous butting. It can cause extreme headaches.

Some people, certainly many women, might feel the head to be an unlikely weapon, or the type of attack they would not employ. In a life or death situation a good butt can and may mean the difference between winning and being battered, robbed or raped. Please don't discard it just because of its unsophisticated demeanour.

Especially ladies. Firstly, a good head-butt is a stopping technique (the pain can stop an attacker in his tracks) and secondly, no attacker will ever expect a lady to use a head-butt, it's unheard of. That's why you must be prepared to use it – it could save your life.

140

Chapter Twelve

Chokes and Strangles

Ah, the stories I could tell about what the Japanese Judoka call *shime* (shime-waza – strangling technique). In-close the strangles and choke are the most devastating, underestimated and misunderstood of all the finishing techniques.

As a nightclub doorman, my associates and I employed these techniques successfully on literally thousands of occasions. It is a brilliant and hugely effective technique. Its major drawback is that chokes and strangles can only be employed at very close range, and that is exactly where you do not want to be in a real situation. You need to work from and off a fence and never get closer than punching range. However, we all make mistakes – even monkeys fall out of trees – and when we do they have to be addressed. So the shime is an excellent part of the support system.

A good headlock or choke, if employed correctly, is a definite stopping technique, usually rendering your opponent unconscious. Very accessible and not over-complicated with a low skill factor. Some are employed from the back and side while others are used direct from the front. Some of the strangles use the opponent's jacket or shirt as an aid and for leverage, whilst others (naked strangles/chokes) work independently without the use of the opponent's clothing. Many may be executed while in the vertical position or in the horizontal, ground work position.

When familiarity with chokes and strangles is gained it is probable that one may flow into another giving you a bastardised choke or strangle of your own invention or design. This matters not as long as it stops your opponent.

Due to the potency of shime-waza, the techniques should be treated at all times with the utmost respect, and I do not recommend its practice to minors. Fatality is the possible consequence of misuse or misunderstanding. A good choke/strangle can take a man to unconsciousness in under three seconds; if held on after unconsciousness it can start brain death in around fifteen seconds. In a real situation, with time distortion brought on as a part of the adrenal syndrome, fifteen seconds may go by in the blink of an eye and before you know it you have killed the opponent and you could be facing a murder or manslaughter charge. Understanding this at the offset is imperative so that practice and actual use can be tempered with control so that unfortunate accidents can be avoided.

In the controlled arena we use the tap system to avoid unconsciousness, the recipient tapping himself, his opponent, the floor, etc. with his hand or his foot to signify submission, at which point the move should always be released. Outside of course there is no such practice and the opponent's response to a choke or strangle will be unconsciousness. After this, remember, every second could prove fatal.

I remember one situation when I worked as a doorman in the Diplomat pub in Coventry, a great little place right in the heart of Coventry city centre. I was actually with Sharon, my wife, on this particular night. We were talking away when I noticed a couple of men arguing. Trying to be pro-active and stop the situation before it started I moved across and politely asked them to discontinue the argument otherwise I would have to ask them to leave. Now I don't quite know whether they just didn't hear me because they were so deeply engrossed in the argument (adrenal deafness is not an uncommon side effect of the fight or flight syndrome) or whether they didn't take my warning seriously, but either way they totally ignored me. Just as I was about to ask them again they kicked off and started fighting with each other. They moved about five feet in the blink of an eye, locked in a ferocious vertical grappling embrace, and ended up on the main dance floor just by where Sharon and her friend were standing.

I tore after them like a very fast thing, grabbed one of the men in a rear choke and pulled him from the other. By this time my partner Kenny the body builder had come to my assistance and grabbed the other guy. The one that I held in the reverse choke was going crazy trying to get me off. I turned him from a rear choke to a side choke/headlock and increased the pressure to control his thrashing. I whispered into his ear that if he didn't calm down I was going to have to knock him out. The hold was now secure so I was in the right position to do so if need be. Again he refused to listen and went crazy trying to throw me off; he was a strong guy. I tightened the lock once more and his struggling ceased. When I gently released the grip to see if he had gone he fell to the floor in an unconscious heap. He didn't come around for a couple of minutes and when he did I helped him up and showed him to the door, he asked me who had sparked him (knocked him out). I told him that I had. He said 'Oh!' and left without further ado.

I personally have had very many KO's in the street with these techniques and I am in no doubt of their potency. It's a good feeling when you have secured the hold (whichever one you are employing) and you know that the fight is over because once secured the chance of escape is almost non-existent.

In my early days I knocked several people out with chokes and strangles by mistake because I did not appreciate their potency. By holding opponents with what I considered restraining force I knocked them out because the force was too much. Through experience I learned to use enough control to restrain an opponent when ejecting him from the club without knocking him out, though I was always then in a position to take the hold to unconsciousness if the need arose.

They say that a little knowledge can be dangerous. This is true: many people have been killed in street encounters through the misuse, most often an inadvertent misuse, of the choke and strangle. The hold has been secured and then not released after unconsciousness. Not always gratuitous, it is usually a misuse through fear and inexperience, fear that if the opponent gets out of the hold he may batter you senseless so you hold on for dear life. It's what I call the panic grip. The way someone grips you in the dojo or gym will be very different from the way that they grab you in a real encounter. Even breaking the opponent's gripping limb may not release the panic grip and often nothing less than unconsciousness will do it. It is an incredible thing to witness, and I have been witness to it many times.

When one of my friends got stabbed outside a city nightclub he grabbed and gripped his attacker so tightly that when he fell to the floor, as a result of the knife wound, he pulled his attacker down with him. Even though four of the attacker's friends laid into him on the floor, it was not until my friend lost consciousness that the grip was released.

Sadly, my friend died in this unprovoked attack.

What I'd like to do in this chapter, indeed in this book, is offer enough knowledge to enable you to use these techniques, only in times of self-defence, with the control that they demand.

Often in practice, as you will see if you do any degree of live ground fighting, your arms or even legs can get tied into a position that disables you or your opponent from being able to tap out. It is for this reason that I recommend training under supervision – this is very important. A third party will be able to observe and stop the practice should one of the fighters get into trouble and be unable to signal.

Basically speaking, the difference between a choke and a strangle is that the choke cuts off the airways in the windpipe at the front of the neck and the strangle cuts off the flow of blood to the brain in the carotid arteries at either side of the neck. Both the choke and the strangle stop the flow of oxygen or oxygenated blood to the brain and thus cause unconsciousness. Depending upon how long and how tight the technique is held this can vary from very mild unconsciousness to deep unconsciousness or death. The most efficient strangle depresses the superior carotid artery, preventing oxygenated blood reaching the cerebral cortex. The compression usually has to be very strong because the carotid artery is protected by the muscular band of the thick sternocleidomastoid muscle, on the sides of the neck.

Often when you employ the choke/strangle it may be neither one nor the other. Rather you have gripped the opponent partly across the throat and partly across the neck, part choke and part strangle, slightly cutting off the blood and partly cutting off the air – it doesn't really matter too much, as long as it still does the job, which it will.

Personally, I have found the choke to be far more dangerous and prone to accidents than the strangle. With a strong naked choke using the bar of the wrist as the depressing implement it is very easy, even by accident, to collapse the opponent's wind pipe and/or severely damage the larynx or the trachea. Again, care should be taken at all times in the controlled arena and the knowledge should be taken to use as a tempering yardstick into the pavement arena.

People often ask me, 'how do you know when to let go of the opponent in a real fight so that you don't kill him?'

In theory, if you have taken the choke/strangle from a vertical position the opponent will let you know that the move is on by falling over (unconscious); in practice this is not always the case. In my early days on the door when I didn't really understand the mechanics of the techniques I knocked many people out without intending to and then, afterwards, wondered what I had done. On many occasions I held a thrashing, violent attacker so tightly that I never felt the drop of body weight when he went unconscious because, in an over-zealous bid to control him, I actually held the KO'd opponent off the floor. When I slightly released the hold to see if he had gone (as I always do), he plunged to the floor in an unconscious heap.

When you are on the ground it's even worse because when the opponent does finally go there will be no plummet of body weight. Later I learned to look for the signs of imminent unconsciousness so that I could take a person, if I wanted to, very close to unconsciousness without actually completely knocking him out or, if I felt it needed it, into a mild unconscious state. If I thought it was called for (sometimes it really was), I'd take them right out of the game.

Most untrained people go through the same ritual when you apply the choke, though the more sensible people just capitulate, innately knowing that they have no chance of escape. Firstly they go crazy and buck like an unbroken stallion and try to rip your arms from around their throat. For these few seconds the enemy will be very strong as his in-fight adrenalin goes to work (more about that in my Fear book). When their energy dissipates and they realise that they cannot escape, they go through a kind of pleading ritual (they can't usually speak because you are crushing their throat) where they almost pat your arms in an instinctive version of the tap system, their breathing at this point a sickly gurgling sound. These are the precursors to unconsciousness. A couple of seconds after this and they will not move at all. If they are standing you will feel a drop in the opponent's body weight as his legs abandon him. When he stops trying to escape and his hands are no longer touching your choking arm, he is out of there and this would be a good time to release the hold. If you're unsure maybe hold it for a couple of seconds longer but no more than that or death will be knocking at the door. In your adrenal haze it is very easy to miss all of these signs, even though they will be staring you in the face, but the more you learn to temper and fine-tune the hold in the controlled arena and spot the same signs in your training partners just before they tap out, the better you will be able to judge the right time to release in the real situation.

I have also found the choke/strangle ideal for controlling someone that perhaps did not need knocking out or beating up, but did need calming down. Once I had them firmly in the hold, sometimes standing, other times on the floor, I would talk to them and calm them down. It always worked because, to the people that have never experienced it, choking is a very frightening feeling. Panic usually brought on capitulation without actually hurting the opponent, and if the little chat did not work then I was in a very good position to put their lights out. If I was dealing with a very nasty person I would even whisper in his ear, just before I knocked him out, 'good night'! Psychologically this frightens the pants off the opponent because it intimates to him that you are in complete control (which you are) and that not only are you capable of knocking him out but you can actually tell him when you are going to do it. When he comes around, and probably for the rest of his life, he will remember you and that particular incident.

So to reiterate, give the chokes and strangles the utmost respect in practice and in reality, learn to know them well so that abuse does not become a by-product of ignorance.

Many of the positions that you find yourself in on the floor may leave you in a good position to get back to your feet while your opponent is still in the horizontal position. If this is an option I feel that, as a rule of thumb, it should almost always be taken. In a self-defence situation it should be your prerogative.

If the situation is a match fight then there may be contributing factors that need to be brought into the computation, just because you're vertical and the opponent is horizontal does not guarantee that the victory is automatically yours. If he is a strong fighter, someone prepared to take a few kicks to get back to his feet, he may do just that: get back up and kick your arse.

You may have spent five minutes trying to get the opponent to the floor because he is out-punching or kicking you, he may be far superior to you in vertical fighting – if that's the case then the last place you want to be is back on your feet. Often brilliant vertical fighters, boxers and kickers especially, are like upturned turtles on the floor. If that's the case then keep them there until you have finished the fight. If you are fighting numbers then the floor is absolutely the worst place on earth to be – get back up as soon as possible. If you can't get back up, and he's not just going to let you, then you have to make the best of a bad job no matter how unfavourable the odds may be.

Reversed naked choke

Standing, kneeling or lying at the rear of your opponent, place your right arm around and across his throat, clasp your right hand with your left and apply pressure to the throat by pulling backward with the combined force of both hands. It is important for maximum effect to make sure that the bony part of the right wrist is against the throat as opposed to the softer forearm. It is also beneficial if you can pull the opponent backward and off his feet, as this lessens his 'fight back' chances.

Sliding reverse collar lock

Standing, kneeling or lying at the rear of your opponent, place your right arm around and across the opponent's throat and grip hold of his jacket or shirt. Place your left arm under your opponent's left armpit and seize his right lapel (or jumper/shirt). Apply pressure by choking in a wringing action.

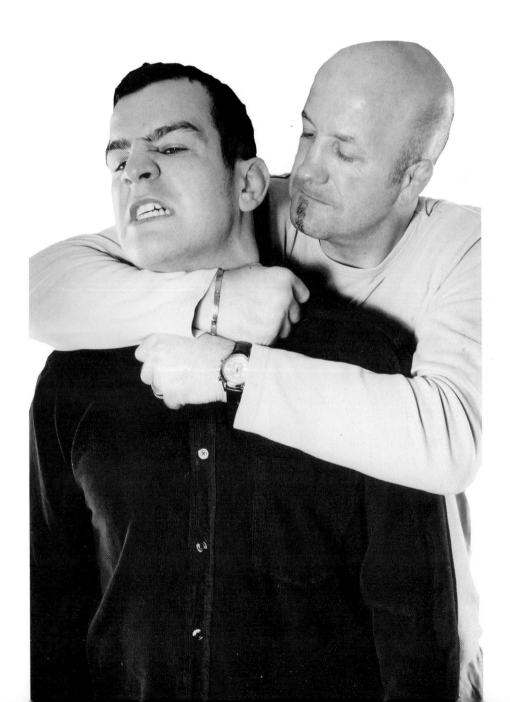

Side headlock/strangle

Place your right arm around your opponent's neck and hug his head tightly into the side of your own body. The palm of your right hand should also by facing inward so that the bony part of your right wrist is into the opponent's neck. Place your left palm heel underneath your right fist and apply pressure on the neck (jugular) by pushing up with the left hand and squeezing in with the right hand.

Upper throat lift

Place your opponent's head under your right armpit and slide your right arm under and across his throat. The palm of your right fist should be facing into your own body to ensure that the bony part of your wrist is along his throat. Place your left palm heel under the right fist. Apply pressure on the throat by pushing the right arm up and into the throat with the left hand whilst at the same time pulling the right arm into the throat.

Upper throat lift

Claw squeeze around the larynx

Simple and highly effective, especially if the opponent and yourself are grappling on the floor. Grip the larynx, which is situated at the top of the windpipe just below the chin, and squeeze tightly.

Scissor choke

While sitting on top of and astride your opponent, cross your hands with palms down and grab the opponent's lapels as deeply to the back of the neck as possible. Apply pressure to his neck by pushing both elbows simultaneously downward, forcing both wrists into either side of the opponent's neck.

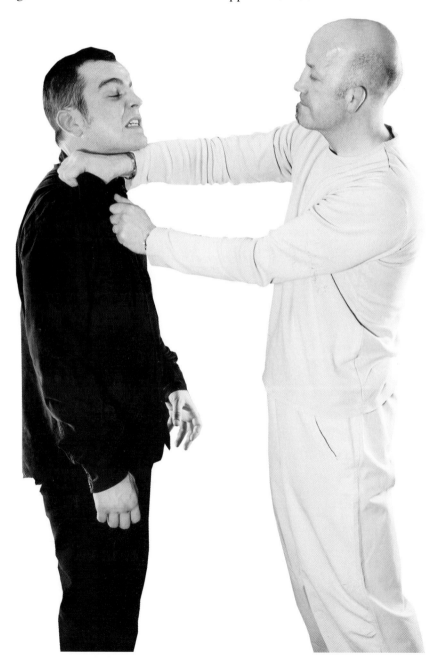

Equipment

The only equipment available for the practice of chokes is the live partner. Extreme care should be observed in all practice of chokes. The tap system should be employed at all times and a choke should always be released immediately if the opponent taps. There is no real set situation where you may use a choke or lock: it is just a case, when grappling, of remembering them and looking for appropriate openings.

The tap system in practice

When a choke, lock or hold is on, the opponent taps the floor, himself, his partner or anything close enough to tap, to signal submission.

Chapter Thirteen

Throws

A good throw can be spectacular and effective (although it is only the latter that we are concerned with), and for the advanced Judoka or wrestler, very accessible. In reality their accessibility is dulled by the very high skill factor that is demanded in pursuit of competence. They are far more effective in my opinion if preceded by a strike (head-butt, bite, etc.) as a weakener. As a singular attack, the throw can often quite easily be neutralised, even by a strong novice. If, however, you bite the opponent or butt him before you throw, the success rate of the throw elevates markedly.

It is also usual in a live situation for the assailant, if thrown, to also drag the thrower to the floor. Clean throws are not always possible unless the thrower is expert. Having said all of that, I do know judoka and wrestlers that can and have thrown many opponents in street confrontations without any problem, and finished the guy with the throw alone.

As with all applied techniques, use cunning and ferocity for the best effect.

Naturally, a throw can only be employed realistically whilst in grappling range and it is fair to say that if you are in grappling range it is because of an error on your part. Grappling, especially to the non-grappler, is unique. It is the non-grappler's quicksand because, unlike kicking and punching range where you may move in and out at will, once you're in grappling range you will very rarely get out of it before the culmination of the fight. So it is best avoided. Being human, of course, we do make mistakes, and to not prepare for such circumstances would be a major shortfall.

There are a myriad of different throws to be explored. Some may suit, others may not. The more complicated movements would not be applicable (for the beginner) in the street. The more basic the movement, the easier it is to apply. As with punching and kicking combinations, a bastardisation of the throwing techniques may be, accidentally or on purpose, sought and executed. As long as it is effective, use it.

It goes with out saying that to really get these throws 'off' you will need proper tuition.

Major outer reap

From the grappling range this throw is both simple and highly effective, though it relies, as do all throws, on a fast explosive attack.

Break the opponent's balance backward to the right corner as you simultaneously advance your left foot forward. Continue to draw the opponent's balance outward as you reap your right leg to the back of the opponent's right leg, throwing him backward. Always try to precede with a butt, bite or stamp to distract the opponent from the throw. To attack to the left side, reverse these instructions.

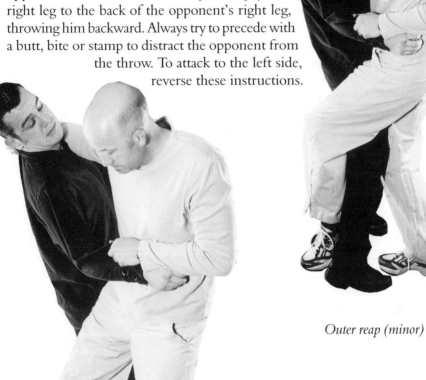

Outer reap (minor)

Outer reap (major)

Hip throw

Break the opponent's balance forward to the right front corner, as you simultaneously advance your right foot toward the opponent's right foot. Make a body turning in entry and place your right arm around the opponent's waist (or neck). Make sure that both of your feet are inside his, your bottom is tightly into his groin and your knees are bent. Throw your opponent forward fast and explosively over your hip. This throw can be reversed.

Major inner reap

Break your opponent's balance backward as you simultaneously reap your left leg inside and around the back of his right leg, lifting his leg off the ground. Push the opponent (or butt him) violently backward.

May be reversed.

Inner reap

Shoulder throw

May be used on an opponent who grabs from the back as well as the front.

Break the opponent's balance forward as you simultaneously advance your right foot toward his right foot. Make a body turning in movement as you simultaneously pass your right arm under his right arm, gripping hold of his clothes. Try to keep both your feet inside his and bend at the knees, then throw the opponent over your right shoulder fast and explosively.

May be reversed.

Minor outer reaping ankle throw

Break your opponent's balance to his right back corner, as you simultaneously advance your left foot forward and bring up your right foot. Reap the back of the opponent's right heel with your left foot. May be reversed.

Sweeping ankle throw

Advance your right foot forward forcing your opponent backward on his left foot. Take a wide left step as you advance your right foot inward to support your body weight. Break the opponent's balance to the right side and simultaneously sweep his feet together as you lift him upward. Throw him with speed and force. May be reversed.

Body drop

Break the opponent's balance to his right front corner. Advance your right foot toward his right foot. Position your body so that your right foot blocks the opponent's right ankle and your left leg is bent. Throw the opponent directly forward and over the back of your right ankle quickly and forcefully. May be reversed.

Inner thigh throw

Break the opponent's balance forward to his right front corner. Advance your right foot toward his right foot. Make a body turn in movement so that the left foot is positioned in the centre of gravity. Sweep your right thigh upward on the inside of the opponent's right thigh, continue sweeping your right thigh up and back, throw the opponent directly forward and over your right thigh with force and speed. May be reversed.

All the throws may be executed from your right or left side depending upon which you favour and your position in relation to the opponent at the time of the throw. Of course in theory, if at all possible, you ideally want to throw the opponent clean and clear of yourself. But more often than not, when you throw an opponent in the street situation, he maintains his grip upon you, even though he's been thrown, and pulls you down with him. The only solace one can extract from this fact is that you, the thrower, will usually end up on top: an enviable position.

Don't expect an opponent to just let you throw him, it can be a battle. For best results always try to distract the opponent with the aforementioned blow (butt, bite) before attempting the throw. If he does maintain his grip after the throw and pulls you down with him, try to land upon him with the point of your knee or elbow, and break free at the first available moment.

A word of caution: never deliberately seek grappling distance in order to execute a throw. Only attempt to throw if you find yourself trapped with no other options open to you. The element of surprise is pivotal in the execution of a throw: it must be fast and explosive. Neither speed nor force will come without a lot of practice.

Chapter Fourteen

Ground Work

Ground work is split into two categories: grappling on the floor and fighting from the floor. The former is when you and your opponent both fall to the ground; the latter is when you fall, or are knocked, to the floor and your opponent is still in the vertical position.

Both are very dangerous fighting areas to find yourself in, especially the latter. Some schools of thought advocate the latter as a first line of defence, advising their practitioners to throw themselves to the floor before an attacker and fight from there. This is about as sensible as telling someone to throw themselves into a fire to get warm. Don't do it. If I could find one word to describe this kind of advice it would have to be BOLLOCKS! Throwing yourself to the floor in front of an attacker is tantamount to throwing yourself at his mercy: after all, isn't the ground where he wants you to be in the first place?

Basically, if we are fighting from the floor it is because we are in the shit and trying desperately to fight our way out of it. I've been there, and it's not pleasant – so avoid at all costs.

It would be easy, again, to theorise and show illustrations and demonstrations of how a felled person may attack and break an advancing assailant's shin or knee-cap with a low-line thrust kick, or sweep him to the ground with a scissor throw. In reality, if you are on the ground and your attacker is standing, your chances of getting back up, especially as a novice, are minimal. Even an experienced fighter is facing defeat if he is on the ground. If both of you fall to the ground you have at least a 50 % chance of winning. If only you are on the floor, your attacker will almost definitely go in for the kill, so it is imperative that you quickly find a good defensive position. This may be lying on your side, left or right, where both arms and legs are used to provide support, enabling quick movement and position change.

The right knee and right elbow are easily available to provide cover for the body, groin and head. From this defensive position kick out rapidly at the attacker's groin or knees every time he approaches to attack. As soon as is possible, get up. The longer you stay down the less chance you have of getting back up again. If you find it impossible to get back up, try to catch hold of the attacker's legs or arms and pull him down to the floor with you, where you have a more even chance.

If you both fall to the floor it is important that you fight back hard and fiercely by striking the attacker in his vital areas: eyes, throat and groin. Try to make the attacks calculated and accurate; don't waste time and energy on attacking the more muscular areas of the body. Bite, pinch, gouge, butt, knee – do anything and everything.

Remember, the attacker needs a quick result. He cannot afford to be rolling around the floor with you, scrapping it out. As soon as he realises that he's got a fight on his hands, the sooner he's going to want to get away. If you are severely pinned down and cannot move, feign supplication, pretend you've had enough and that you will let the attacker have whatever he wants. As soon as he releases his grip on you, strike him hard in the eyes or throat with your fingers or fist, then run.

Chokes and headlocks come into their own in ground work. All of the chokes and headlocks illustrated in Chapter 12 are hugely effective in ground work, as are the eye gouges, head-butts, bites, etc.

These are a few illustrations of ground work techniques that I have successfully employed over the years.

The best way to practise these techniques is with a friend or your husband/wife or partner, using the tap system as a safety measure.

Infliction of pain upon your foe will give you valuable extra seconds to flee.

Protect groin/head

Block kick

Kick on knee

Biting

I personally only bite as a last resort, when all else has failed or is not available. Other fighters I know work the bite as a first resort attack when inside grappling range, even seeking grappling range to employ the bite. The former is my personal recommendation, but the choice is yours.

What I will say is that today's enemy is a biter and if you do not know or are not accustomed to defending against bites in your training then the chances are you will fall victim to the bite in a real encounter. My reason for insisting on biting in training is twofold. One, it teaches you to use the bite to effect, very handy if the bite is all that you have open to you and the attacker is going to rape your wife or daughter after he has bashed you. And two, it teaches you to defend against people that bite. Omit it from your curriculum at your own peril.

Note: In training, biting should be used with control. It is enough to bite and release so that major injuries are avoided. There should only be a minimal use of force, not enough to cause a bruise, just enough to let the opponent know that he has been caught.

With the inherent danger of AIDS and blood-related diseases, one must be aware of the possible consequences of biting an adversary. However it is not always necessary to draw blood to stop an assailant when you bite, just bite deep enough to secure your release and escape.

Chapter Fifteen

Defence Against a Weapon

'As she put the key in to the ignition, her driver's door was wrenched open and she found herself looking at a man who was a total stranger. He produced what she believed to be a hand gun with a barrel about six inches long. Bending his head into the car and thrusting the gun against her side, he said, "If you do what I say you won't get hurt." He pushed her as if he wanted her to move into the front passenger seat while continuing to push the gun at her.
'With great presence of mind, Julia Holdman swung her legs around and kicked out at him, at the same time pushing him off balance with her hands. She also shouted at him and let out a loud scream. As the man straightened up, she slammed the car door shut, started the car and rapidly drove out of the car park.'

Ladykiller

'A knife-wielding man forced his way in to a mother's flat, held a knife to her throat and ordered her to take her clothes off. For 15 minutes whilst still clutching her six month old son she refused. The man departed leaving the victim uninjured. The detective constable in charge of the investigation praised the victim saying that "Her brave defiance had stopped an even more serious assault from taking place."'

Unleash the Lioness

The use of weapons is getting more and more common place these days and attacks of this kind are always potentially fatal, especially with edged weapons such as knives. The first line of defence here is, always, avoidance. In a real encounter there is no similarity to the movies where the attacker makes a deliberate strike with his weapon and you skillfully defend with a textbook block and counter attack. Attacks with a weapon are nearly always frenzied and multiple. To pick out one of such a myriad to grab or block is nearly always impossible, and therefore impractical.

From my experience with knife-wielding assailants, 'a stabber rarely shows and a shower rarely stabs.'

Those that show the weapon do so to frighten the victim into capitulation, those that do not usually intend to stab.

Knife defence is a highly-skilled art; in all honesty it cannot be learned through the pages of a book. I also have to be honest and say that knife defence is not my speciality. I have faced attackers with knifes and been glassed several times, and while that certainly qualifies me to talk about the reality of knife defence, I'm not sure that it qualifies me to talk about how best to defend against it other than to avoid or escape an armed attacker. What I have done is enlist the help of someone who is expert in the field, Peter Robins of S.T.A.B. (Strategy and Tactics Against Blades). This is what Peter had to say:

S.T.A.B. Strategy & Tactics Against Blades

Thoughts on Attacks from Edged Weapons

by Peter Robins

The mention of a knife in an everyday conversation would pass off without a second thought, but the mere mention of a knife in any connection whatsoever to a criminal or combat situation makes alarm bells start ringing! In the latter example, with criminal or combat connections, it is understandable that one starts to feel alarm. What is it that triggers a basic instinct in us all to fear the very thought of a knife (or any edged weapon) being used against us? That fear even extends to the thought of a knife being used anywhere near us.

A knife (and for the sake of brevity I will refer to any edged weapon as a knife from here) is an implement that we all use, usually every day, without giving it any consideration. These can be extremely sharp pieces of cutlery and even quite fearsome if we cared to look at them in that way, yet we feel no danger.

One of my former instructors made a very good point in a class one day when he made us think about a knife in a different way to the setting in which it was presented. This was during a martial arts class and so the mention and sight of a knife put us into the 'alarm bell' mode. Yet there was no threat or danger involved. The basic instinct rising again. We were asked what we thought of the knife and how we would describe it. Most answered that they considered it to be a weapon. Yet that same knife could have been produced in another place and or time and it would have been considered to be just an everyday implement. We were asked to think this, that the knife was an implement or tool. Nothing more or less than that. How was this done? By placing the knife on the floor in front of the whole class and then suggesting that if it remained there for a thousand years, save someone falling on it, it would do no harm to anyone. What turned it into a weapon was the person using it. Of course what really turns it into a weapon has much to do with the intention of the person wielding it. That simple lesson has stayed with me. Why? Because it stops me from becoming paranoiac. I say this in view of the recent knife amnesty brought on by the tragic and cowardly killing of a headmaster in North London. It is right to want to do something positive in the light of what happened but just how much of an effect an amnesty is going to have in stopping this kind of thing I am not wholly convinced.

Let me explain: to ensure that no one is ever stabbed or slashed on our streets again it would take a national amnesty that would mean every single one of us taking every knife we possess to the bins provided. After that we would need to take every edged implement that we have in or around our homes and places of work. It cannot be done, can it? Even if it were possible would it solve the problem? What we have to do is take away the intention of a person to use a knife against someone else. It is as simple – or as difficult – as that.

This brings me to the point behind this chapter. To make us all think about what an attack from an edged weapon consists of I have brought back the term edged weapon into the text. This is deliberate as it applies to many everyday objects, just like the ones that are actually used against the victim. Of all the weapons used, fewer fall into the combat-cum-fighting knife group than people imagine. Many people have been attacked and injured, even killed, with our everyday kitchen knives; screwdrivers; chisels, nail files, steel combs, craft and Stanley knives, bottles and glasses, and the list goes on. We must focus on the intention and view it from our own individual perspective as it applies from a self-defence standpoint.

I have also to make a point about that particular terminology – self-defence as it usually implies does not really exist.

If nothing else after many years looking at this frightening problem I have learnt this simple truth – that there is a vast chasm between two small but very important words – defence and offence. Defence can have a suffix 'less' added to it which sadly can often sum up the mental and physical state that it is all too easy to slip into (defenceless). Offence can never be anything less than trying your best to take the fight back to your attacker. There is no such word as offenceless! If this sounds extreme, I apologise, but ask the reader to think about it. Nothing was ever won by remaining on the defensive, you have to counter attack at some time. In the case of an attack from an edged weapon offensive action, sooner rather than later, will go some way to win the day. I must qualify that statement by saying that in the case of a knife being produced in any kind of altercation, dispute or potential attack, the age old advice RUN LIKE HELL is the first that comes to mind. Do not let anyone try to convince you that there is an easy solution. Beware the instructor that tells you he does not fear the knife!

We must be clear in such a discussion as this that there is a vast difference in a mugging situation and an actual attack with a knife. If the knife is present and used as a threat to induce you to hand over money, do so and get away as fast as you can; if a knife is going to be used to attack, your first option always is escape! If unable to escape you have to counter attack, but wisely. Fools rush in and all that!

What I also must make clear is that my comments are based on what has been a long road of research and some practical discovery along the way of looking at the vast subject of edged weapon use. I do not claim to be speaking from any base of authority. I view myself as a life long spectator and player. Very much the amateur! On this subject, we all are...

Now we have been truthful and admitted that there is a problem with potential knife attacks, not just because of their frequency, real or imagined, but because of the great physical and mental stress placed on us; let us examine it as far as we can.

It is a strange quirk of fate that in spite of the recent media focus on the subject of people carrying knives, buying knives and even collecting them, that for all the perceived danger as of now there is very little documented evidence on the subject. The Home Office Statistical Department only has documentary evidence for the number of times that edged weapons/sharp instruments have been involved in homicides, although they have the figures for crimes of violence recorded by the police in 1992, which are as follows:

Out of 284,000 crimes of violence, minor wounding totalled 184,000 and serious wounding (including homicide) totalled 18,000. They can not break the figures down into how many times an edged weapon was used nor which particular types.

The one thing we can look at is that in the 1994 homicide figures the stark fact emerges that of the 677 cases recorded, some 236 (35%) involved an edged weapon of one type or another. Up to 1994, the previous ten years have shown that the fluctuation in this percentage varies between 32% and 37%. Unless 1995 shows a dramatic upsurge in these figures we are left wondering has the problem actually exploded or is it the media focus that would have us believe that? This is said neither to trivialise these figures nor should we exaggerate them. What we must look at is this, that edged weapons are used in many fatal attacks, so it is very likely that they might be used in those attacks that end up as minor or serious woundings.

One thing we must bear in mind as martial artists, practitioners or aficionados, call us what you will, is that just one stabbing is too many and one stabbing that can in any way be attributed to us is way too many! I say this because it is seemingly becoming very fashionable and almost popular in training circles that the emphasis has swung from talk of knife defence to 'knife fighting'. This last term is a bit of a misnomer because what people are actually referring to is one of two things – knife attack or knife duelling. Let us deal with these two options.

Knife attacks are in the realms of what we are discussing very important, it should be thoroughly understood but not taught in isolation. The attack is one that we should be concentrating on from a defensive viewpoint. Why? Because it makes a lot sense when the old saying is quoted in this regard – you cannot destroy that which you cannot create. Taken simply you will not have the faintest chance if you have no idea what a knife attack may consist of. You would not teach only blocking to a student in the impact arts, would you? Imagine only teaching trainees blocks. If they were attacked how long could they purely block for? Try it. A very honourable thought, but completely unworkable. Well it would be for us mere mortals. To look at the subject in isolation and working only on the attack lays us open to much misunderstanding from those outside the martial arts.

The second presumes some kind of duel or fair fight where two men would face off and draw their knives and go to it. Not very likely and not very welcome in our society. And rightly so.

So what can and should be taught? First of all we should try to make our students aware of the potential problem. Make them aware what is possible and what is not, and what is clearly nonsense except if they are someone very, very good or very, very lucky. Only lottery winners are a certainty in the latter category.

The subject of knife defence is vast, complex and most certainly controversial. I do not wish to get into a debate about which system is the best, which is the fastest, which is the most powerful, the oldest and so on. They are just matters of opinion and as I was always told you can argue on opinion but not on facts. So are there any facts regarding knife defence? I think there are. I think there has to be.

So what are the facts about knife defence? From my viewpoint I would perceive them as not just facts regarding particular moves or techniques, but how to discern the problem in the first place. What first interested me in the first instance, with reference to the knife in martial arts training, was its very absence. It just did not exist. It was all punches, kicks and blocks. Perhaps we all lived in a safer environment, but I think not. It was much to do with the general perception at the time. (In a similar way paralleled today by the media milking a problem for all it is worth) I do not deny that there is a potential problem in knives being carried but it would seem that it is a phenomenon that feeds upon itself. The chances of getting attacked with a knife about 30 years ago seemingly was not a great threat. If it were, then few martial arts schools taught moves with this in mind.

Knowing that people did carry weapons and were prepared to use them and have done since time immemorial, made me want to work on some kind of defence against them. I looked around and saw very little out there. Yes there were a few systems that had knife defence moves in their syllabus and yes it did look nice to watch it being practised. But nice is not always effective and practical. Things have not changed all that much. Consider this, in any of the systems that you have seen or practised yourself, is the knife 'attack':

1. Arranged so that one of your set moves will work against it (and also look good against it)?

2. Done as a single arm move (in isolation)?Or

3. Does the attacker 'freeze' once he has carried out this single move?

4. Does the attack start off from a good distance (a non-realistic distance)?

If the answer to one or all of these is 'yes', I would advise you to seriously re-examine what you are being taught. Why? Because no real attack includes any of the above-mentioned factors. Let us examine these factors in detail.

1. As with unarmed moves it is an easy trap to fall into where all defence are executed against the type of attack as done within your own system. What are the chances of that happening out in the real world?

2. Many attacks with the knife are made only with that arm – not so in the real world. The other arm will most certainly be involved in the action, as a feint, strike, push or pull.

3. The 'pillar of salt' syndrome (as Bob Kasper in the U.S. terms it) is again very common in many defence system's syllabus. Why? Because it looks neater and enables the usually complicated follow up arm/wrist lock/throw to be executed. In an all out knife attack the wielder will not stay still, on the contrary he will move like the devil.

Many moves are practised against an attacker at a comfortable distance thereby giving the defender time to prepare his move. This does not happen very often out on the street. Many attacks will be from close quarters and with no notice given and no time to get into a good start position.

I realise in saying this that I risk being classed as a know-all. I sincerely trust not, but you have to see the potential pitfalls of what has been and what is still being taught today. There is no simple answer to the problem. If there were, someone would have made a fortune by now by producing books, making videos and conducting seminars. That has not happened nor is it likely to.

If your instructor tells you that a knife attack is a situation to be avoided and even feared then listen to him. If he tells you that is quite easy after you have learned some of his moves then start to wonder! He is one of three things – very good, very stupid or very insulated from the outside world. One might say in the latter two instances he is to be avoided and in the first instance only to be listened to if he can make you as good as he is. He won't be there if you ever get attacked, I can tell you that. More than likely you will be completely on your own. In most instances that could well be an advantage – there will be no one else to see how fast you run away, or, if you decide to stay whether your feet were in the correct position, your hands at the right angle and so on.

If you have not seen for yourself first hand, then believe me and anyone who tells you on this subject that a knife attack is usually very, very fast. Not quite like the controlled speed of many a demonstration in the dojo. If you have not been at the business end of a knife then believe me that it is quite unlike a dojo setting, no matter how warmed-up you are. Time slows down and you are working in a vacuum. A quiet unreal setting. The one thing you will hear is your heart pounding fit to burst and your laboured breathing, no matter how fit you are.

So what have I learned from this study of knife defence? To examine very carefully what you are told, what you see and what you are shown. Question it all, not necessarily out loud, but certainly in your own mind and in your own time.

The most frightening factor about a knife attack is that there is no requisite on the behalf of an assailant in a skill level. He will need no training to pick up a knife and use it on you. A knife is just as dangerous if he stabs/cuts you or if you run on to the knife and stab/cut yourself. Bear that in mind when considering a counter attack! You must choose the moment and carefully. That moment only comes when you are unable to run!

In the 1990's we have several martial arts that concentrate a good deal on knife work in their syllabus. Escrima (Kali) and Pentjak Silat spring to mind, I apologise if I have missed any other schools out. The former certainly is one of the very few who start off teaching the knife and then go on to empty hand techniques. Most arts go in the reverse order if they include knife work in their teaching. I underline this, for as I mentioned before, it is not taught in all systems. One could say that the ideal would be that in what you were taught your method of halting or redirecting a strike coming in would be the same if the hand was empty or contained a weapon. This does not seem to be the case in many instances.

The reader may like to be drawn to this fact before reading on. I shall be quoting or mentioning many people in the coming paragraphs regarding knife work and I do it not for the sake of name dropping, although I must admit that it is pleasing to do so as many are old training partners and friends from along the 'way', but because they talk sense and reality on the subject. Keep those factors in mind and you will be doing your best to keep an open eye and an open mind.

With a background of early experiences and also experiments within a training environment I began to carry out research into this very extensive and emotive subject. What I found was quite educative. It was this; most of the practical knowledge and development of knife defence had come not only from the martial arts schools in the orient but from the police forces from all around the world, not just in the East. From these sources it had evolved into a wartime science for military purposes. It is just the same today. Find that hard to believe? Think about this. Save that of wartime what organisation or body has ongoing and extensive hands on experience in the face of danger and personal violence? Yes, mainly the police.

The development of Close Quarter Battle (CQB) in the last war was directly attributable to the work done and practical experience gained in the face of extreme violence by a police force stationed half away across the world in China. Where and how you may well ask. The answer is to be found in the International Settlement of old Shanghai. This most unique metropolis gained a reputation as being the world's most dangerous city. Their police force, the Shanghai Municipal Police (SMP) comprised of Chinese, Japanese, Russian and 'Foreign' officers (mainly British). In the 1920s and 30s it became one of the best trained forces of all time. This was almost entirely due to the work of one remarkable man – W. E. Fairbairn, who had joined the force in 1907 and served until he retired in 1940. During these years he trained the force in all their self-defence, both unarmed and armed. He devised, trained and led the famed Riot Squad, which has rightly been dubbed the very first SWAT unit. He also made a special effort in researching the offensive and defensive aspects of the knife. Why study both sides of the coin? Because he also believed in the old saying – you cannot destroy what you cannot create.

That is a good base to work from. To understand how you might be able to defend you must understand how it might be that someone would attack you. Again we go back to the dojo and your set piece defence. Will it really happen like this you must ask yourself. If your answer is no then you should perhaps practice that which is set and also that which is not!

Today, especially in the United States and Canada, much research is going on in regard to police defensive training and a great deal of importance has been attached to the subject of a knife wielding assailant. This should be of important note to us in the UK, as US police forces are routinely armed. If they find the threat of deadly force with a knife to be very real when in theory their officers have the ultimate deterrent (!), what chance have we got?

One should ask why the American police have doubts about the effectiveness of a gun against a knife. It was assumed for many years that there was no contest until a series of experiments were carried out in regard to a knife attack and a gun defence. In this experiment I can assure you that the attacker was really moving in and not stopping to thrust from a static position. The findings were that a gap of 21 feet was required between the two, as a starting position, before the police officer could draw and fire at the assailant before the gap was closed and the knife was in close enough to slash or stab the officer. This was a minimum distance! Dwell upon that.

In Great Britain the subject of knife defence for the police has seemingly taken a back seat until recently. Thankfully the situation is now being addressed. As has been said before there is no easy solution, but the problem must be looked at. It will not go away simply because it is ignored.

What influence does this have on the ordinary citizen? Simply this, if the carrying of guns and batons is no proof against a knife attack for police officers then what chance do we stand, unarmed as we are. Not much I must admit. But we do have some chance and in the event of an attack it might be the only recourse.

One of the greatest of all the modern studies into knife attacks and possible means of defence has been done by an American pioneer in police defensive tactics (PDT) training, Bruce Siddle of PPCT Management Systems Inc. of Illinois. Mr. Siddle has been researching and experimenting in PDT since the 1970s. His great work resulted in what today is called Pressure Point Control Tactics. The principles of which date back to the first recorded traces of martial arts evolution. Right back to Dharma in the Shaolin Temple period. Regardless of the actual historical facts the principle stays true and it was due to Bruce Siddle that this ancient research has a modern forbear. His intuitive research was carried out long before the fairly recent interest in vital point striking as shown by such luminaries as George Dillman. Of course we in the martial arts know that this esoteric art was always there but not until Siddle researched and documented it for modern police use has it become a tangible asset again.

In 1988 he put together a training package, helped by his senior instructors and Dan Inosanto, that focused on utilising these nerve points in regard to his knife defence programme. It was titled 'Spontaneous Knife Defence'. It was based around the principles of Filipino attack and defence lines and since its inception has undergone four revisions. I have been taught one of the earlier versions and attest that it is everything it sets out to be – simple, direct and retainable under stress! It is the last factor that perhaps is the most important in the equation. What Bruce Siddle did was to prove again, that under stress the body loses a great deal of its dexterity and movement. What are termed fine motor skills are lost. That is why many of the defences that are commonly shown just would not work in the stress of combat. Why do I stress again? Because as he will agree, he was not the first to notice (and comprehend) this phenomenon but he was the first to research it and explain it scientifically. The early pioneer in this century was the aforementioned W. E. Fairbairn out in Shanghai. He did not go into the scientific explanations for it, for many reasons, but he built his method of self-protection around it. It was called Defendu and it was this art that was taught to the SMP, but I digress.

Mr. Siddle makes a valid point in his teaching that his method is to be regarded as a last ditch attempt at defence and only to be followed if previous measures were not effective. By that he means if all else fails then you have to resort to empty hand tactics to take the opponent out of the frame. No reliance on the wrist or arm lock on its own to end the encounter. Of course we know that there are wrist locks and arm locks that could be put on by certain masters that would end the encounter, but we are not talking about the gifted few. We are talking about the majority of us. There are very few masters!

Another important aspect underlined by Siddle and others who look at self-protection from a realistic point of view is that which Peter Consterdine and Geoff Thompson call the mental log-jam. This is important in any encounter and even more so in connection with a knife attack. What is this log-jam? Simply put, it means that your subconscious has been overloaded with information and choice of techniques. For defensive purposes it is best to rely on a few practical methods that can be used at any time and under the maximum of stress rather than a multitude of attractive moves that can only be carried out in optimum conditions. The above mentioned and those that follow have proved without doubt that under pressure the skill level of an individual quickly drops away when the pressure is on. Siddle has proved that the optimum heart rate is around 145 beats per minute. Above that and the fine motor skills rapidly diminish. You can rest assured that your heartbeat will easily exceed that figure if someone attacks you with a knife.

It seems to me that a sound basis for effective defence is that your range of techniques or options should have some common ground. To underline this I fell into a trap some years back of thinking that to know 10 defences against a punch, 10 against a kick, 15 against a front strangle and so on made one a more effective player. It does not, it makes you a more knowledgeable one but that it is not the same as being effective. To underline this an experiment was carried out in the States with a group of trainees, they were shown one defence against an attack and timed doing it. They were then shown several more possible defence against the same attack. When the group were attacked in the same manner there was marked drop-off in their reaction time. Proof of the log-jam effect. It makes one think.

Reaction time is a very important ingredient in the formula. If you think you are fast in your response then you may be interested in an experiment carried out by my pal in the States, Bob Kasper. He took a group of his students and timed their movements in an exercise that had them drawing from a concealed position either a fixed blade knife (Kasper Kombat) or a folder (Benchmade AFCK). The students had to draw and slash through a special target. The times for their moves were between .75 to .83 seconds for the former and between .95 to 1.05 seconds for the latter! The latter times are a trifle slower because the trainees had to open the folder whilst drawing it. When I look at those times and contemplate some of the so very complicated moves I have seen demonstrated and taught over the years, it makes me shudder! Why? Because I know that the quickest reaction time is around .5 of a second and can stretch to over a second. Not much of a differential is there? How much movement (body shifting) could you attempt? What chance to reposition yourself with the much vaunted side-step or jump away? Although these moves might be possible, if that is your first line of defence (or should I say your last?) or your only one, shouldn't you be looking at something a little simpler and direct? Something on the lines of the worst case scenario. What would that be – if your defence is to side-step or jump away – it is that you cannot do it, either because of the time factor or a physical barrier to prevent you from doing so? Never assume that because you have practised that way that you will always be able to move away from an attack. Your base line should be some kind of protective measure that can be done from you being rooted to the spot. Now that is a real possibility.

All the research I have done on this subject brings me back to one simple truth – and that is you have to counter attack. To rely upon a 'defensive' move only will not give you enough of a chance to get away. By this I mean that there has to be a definite attack on the knife man. His mindset has to be changed and quickly. It is not enough to divert his attacking limb, not enough to unbalance him, not enough to rely upon a joint lock to deter him. He has to be hit. That is the simplest and most direct way to alter his thought process. His mind must be taken off his first avowed intent – to do you harm. He must be bought to the point where defence of his own person is required. This does not mean just hurting an arm or a leg, you must take him over physically and mentally in as short a time span as possible. He must get a sensory overload that will take his mind completely away from his knife. It calls for multiple hits delivered as fast and hard as is possible. These must target the correct areas on his body.

It may be of interest to the reader to know that I have come to the conclusion that in these circumstances the conventional punch may not be the best strike to use. Why? Because most of us have trained in punching techniques that tend to make us pull away to gain the optimum distance for maximum power. In a knife encounter once you have started to close an opponent down to move away to deliver a strong punch is not always the best avenue. Although we are only talking about a relatively short distance it is very crucial in this regard. Another point with punching is that most of us wish to be square on to our target to deliver a punch. Of course most of these factors occur subconsciously, but nevertheless it will happen.

I know that many readers will strongly dispute my comments, but please carry out this experiment. You can do it on a bag. Stand square on and strike it. Move yourself slightly to the left of the bag and punch again. Move more to the left so that the bag is gradually being moved to your right flank and then gradually to your right rear. You will see that the power of the straight punch rapidly diminishes and you will start to alter from a straight punch to something resembling a hammer fist or a back fist strike. No big deal you will say, but have you not proved that a punch is limited to its angle of application?

I emphasise that many of the conclusions I have come to are not entirely my own but those that are have been echoed by many better informed people than I. Bob Kasper, the Director of the GHCA, an organisation dedicated to keeping the teachings of the wartime USMC alive agrees with many of the points I make. Why is that important in this context? Because he is highly regarded in the States with his work on the knife; he has been trained extensively by their Patriarch, Charles Nelson of New York City, who also holds strong views on much of what is taught today. Recently Bob has been in touch with Col. Rex Applegate of wartime OSS/CIC fame who gain agrees with what the GHCA preach. The Colonel was taught by Fairbairn in Canada and the US and his partner Major E. A. Sykes over here in the UK during 1942/3 before he went on to do his own teaching.

Fairbairn and Sykes held similar views on the subject of a knife attack. Their first line of advice on the matter was if you got the chance – RUN. Sage advice. Here is what Major Sykes said on the subject '... you would do better to have no shame about it but run like hell, hoping that the other man won't catch up with you until you have secured some sort of weapon with which to deal with him'.

Bob Kasper – 'I've found through extensive research, and trial and error, in which I have not changed my view for many, many years, is that the best way to defend against a multiple slash attack is to cover, trap and immediately follow with a brutal offensive attack to vital areas.' He also added that if one is fortunate enough to have halted a stabbing attack – 'Then counter-attack with everything you've got. Don't even attempt a lock or release [from his grab] until the assailant is, or almost is, unconscious.'

LEARNING CURVE:
Friends and enemies from the 'outside world' Jim Shortt (IBA) and Brian McCarthy (BBD)

Various instructors / friends in the Bujinkan

Bob Campbell and indirectly Jim Maloney from Uechi-ryu Jay Dobrin and assistant instructors (Escrima)

Ken Pence / Mel Brown of Nashville S.W.A.T. unit

Levi Montgomery of Priority One John Urwin and instructors of Pro-teet

Bob Kasper and fellow instructors of the GHCA – Charles Nelson NT, a good friend in Canada

SMP veterans

Instructors and veterans of WWII Special Forces Influence of Col. Rex Applegate; Col. Biddle; John Styers The inspiration and spirit of W. E. Fairbairn and E. A. Sykes

Last but not least to two good friends, Steve Carter and Paul Child and all those who train with us I thank you all for opening my eyes and keeping them that way!

You will have gathered that I have not endeavoured to pass on specific techniques through the pages of this chapter. For one, it could not be done in a single chapter, it would have taken over Geoff's book completely! Hopefully what I have been able to do is to clear away some of the mist surrounding the subject and given a clearer view of it. For those who already have a good grounding in an art that focuses on the knife then most of what I have said may be common knowledge or it may clash with your own teachings and belief If so, then please disregard this and carry on. If this is not the case, then I have achieved what I set out to do. None of us can shortcut experience, but you can certainly learn from others. So, stay alert and stay safe.

Since the first draft of this book Peter Robins has tragically died. My love and best wishes go out to all his family and friends.

Chapter Sixteen

Defence Against Multiple Attackers

'When facing multiple opponents you must attack first and keep attacking until the danger subdues.'

Miyomoto Musashi

'February 1993, Salisbury, Wiltshire.

'After leaving a nightclub at 1.15 a.m., a twenty-two year-old married woman passed two men in the shadows on her way home.

'Following a brief exchange of words she continued walking, but the two men quickly caught up with her again.

'While one man stayed behind the women, the other stepped in front of her. He then grabbed her, ripped her clothes off and raped her.'

Unleash the Lioness

We've all seen the films and TV programmes that show the good guy dispatching a crowd of baddies one at a time, systematically and with textbook technique. Looks good doesn't it? In reality – forget it. Forget it in a big hurry because it's comic book stuff. I have faced multiples on more occasions than I care to remember and it frightened the shit out of me every single time. Your only chance of survival in these scenarios is either to break the minute mile and run away, or attack first and hit everything that moves.

If you are fighting one person and you make a mistake you can always fall into the support system and use the back up of the techniques therein. If you muck up when facing numbers you'd better get a liking for camping because you may be looking at living in an oxygen tent. I have seen many men kicked to pieces, and know many of them died as a consequence of beatings involving more than one opponent.

Before detailing my theories on dealing with multiple attackers, I feel I must be brutally honest and inform the reader of the high skill factor and sheer bravado needed when attempting such a feat. The only truly safe cure is prevention. It's OK me talking about the fact that you should be pre-emptive and attack first, but that is not much use if your attacking tools are not up to scratch. If you are going to be first your attacking movement needs to be ferocious, not just enough to stun the guy that you hit but also to frighten the shit out of his partners in crime. If you do not sufficiently put the fear of God into them then the chances are you are still in the mire.

An effective physical response is not always about being fast, strong, accurate, trained or even brave, though they are all, of course, important factors. First and foremost it's about being cunning, ferocious and, above all else, 'first'. This is especially so when dealing with two, three or more attackers. If you're not first, you will most likely be last. As we all know, 'last is lost' in the pavement arena. I have been involved in over a hundred fights where the numbers were against me; I won because I was first to initiate the physical attack.

As detailed in earlier chapters, most assaults are preceded by verbal entrapments. These may be short to blunt or long to prolonged. Former or latter, it is present and you must – if all other options have been exhausted – act by attacking as soon as you are sure an attack upon your person is imminent.

With the lone assailant you may prolong the verbal and control range using a simple fence whilst concentrating upon him and your attack/escape. With multiple attackers this is not so easy. While it is possible to control the range of one assailant it can be very difficult to control the range of several at once, so time is of the essence. The longer you take to analyse the situation and prepare, the less chance you will have of effecting a pre-emptive attack because the attackers will gradually be surrounding you and getting closer in order to make their assault a little easier. When they do attack, it will not be one at a time like in the films, but all at once and with brutal ferocity, leaving you very little chance of fighting back.

The concept of blocking an attack rarely works, especially with multiple attackers.

THE RED LETTER SYNDROME

Beware! For every 2-3 seconds (variable) that you delay your first pre-emptive strike you will be fighting one more opponent. With every passing second they will get closer. If you manage the pivotal seconds effectively, your first attack will be to the opponent in front, then to the next closest/most dangerous opponent. If you mismanage your allotted seconds your strategy must change. I call it the Red Letter syndrome. If you have three Red Letters (bills), which do you pay first? You don't pay the one that fell through the letterbox this morning, you pay the one you've had the longest, the red one, the one that is threatening to cut you off. So, if you mismanage your allotted time, your fighting strategy must change accordingly.

If the opponent on your right or left moves to your blind-side, he becomes the most dangerous opponent. Due to the tunnel vision that accompanies adrenalin, the victim often does not see the offside opponent. Ironically, he is the one most likely to initiate the attack.

As detailed in previous chapters, part of the attack ritual is the pincer movement. One attacker, usually the one facing and threatening you, will deploy your attention whilst the other/s attack you from your blind-side.

I have never found a cure for tunnel vision; it will, it seems, always be a part of conflict, so it is most important to be aware of this ploy. If you are faced by numbers, deploy your vision so that you do not lose sight of the other antagonists. If they try to move to your off side, change your position slightly so that you can still see them and use your outstretched hands to control the range between you and them. If you feel an attack on you is imminent pre-empt it by attacking them first.

This is the absolute pivotal factor in such a scenario: attack first. Attack is your best means of defence. After your pre-emptive strike, it is best to make your escape, if possible. If not, hit everything that moves and scream using 'Kiaa' to underline your resolve, to psyche out your antagonists and to attract attention to your dilemma. What weapon you use to attack is your own choice; whatever it is it should, as always, be your best shot aimed preferably at the vulnerables: eyes, throat, jaw, etc.

As with every scenario that begins with dialogue, use the four 'D's; only make a pre-emptive attack if no other option is open to you.

If the attackers have not heeded your warnings to back off and are still forward moving, then use your lead hand fence to keep a safe distance. Be submissive, engage the opponent's brain using your action trigger, and attack.

Personally, my own pre-emptive strike would be a right cross/hook to the jaw, preceded by some kind of mentally disarming verbal. Hopefully, having neutralised the first person, I would then attack the remaining antagonists with head, punch or kick, depending upon my distance from them.

There seems to be a big ego problem with confrontation, especially with men and especially when they are with their women. They feel that to avoid is to bottle out. Not so. Even Sun Tzu, a great warrior general some twenty-five centuries ago, advised flight when the numbers were stacked against you. Ego does not or should not come into it: you are not defending your ego, you are defending your life. So if you can run then run for your life. There will be another day, another arena where the odds will not be so great. Remember the sequence: avoidance, escape, dissuasion, attack.

Chapter Seventeen

The Knockout

'So in war, the way is to avoid what is strong and to strike at what is weak.'

Sun Tzu

There are many contributing factors that combine to form a knockout on an adversary. Rising above all as the most important is not, as you would imagine, a powerful strike, but an accurate one. A powerful attack that is not accurate is very unlikely to knock an adversary out. Neither is it a matter of being big or heavy: size is irrelevant. An eight stone woman who punches her weight will have no trouble knocking a much larger adversary unconscious, if she is accurate.

The next important factor to accuracy is surprise. The adversary who does not expect the punch cannot prepare for the punch; therefore the impact of the punch is maximised. To attain a KO you rely heavily on the looseness of the adversary's neck and jaw muscles. If they are not braced when you strike the jaw, a huge shaking of the adversary's brain will occur. It is this shaking of the brain that will cause unconsciousness. If, however, the adversary sees the strike coming, he will brace himself (consciously or subconsciously), the shaking is minimised and unconsciousness does not occur so readily. This is where we tie in with the chapter on fence work. Verbal disarmament and brain engagement are pivotal in the execution of an effective KO The fence allows you to utilise your entire body weight from a stable, balanced posture; the verbal mental disarmament engages the adversary's brain for the split second. This is your window of entry to launch the pre-emptive attack. While the brain is engaged, even for a second, the adversary will not see the attack coming. Because he doesn't see it coming, he does not brace himself for the strike – the jaw and neck muscles are relaxed, maximum shaking of the brain occurs followed closely by unconsciousness. Also, brain engagement will cancel out any spontaneous response that your antagonist may have in-built. He will not react during brain engagement.

As mentioned in the chapter on fence work, attacks that are launched outside of tunnel vision also have a great effect for the same reason, the attacker does not see, so cannot prepare for them.

For best effect you should strike anywhere along the line of the jawbone, from the ear to the chin. This, if struck correctly, will cause the brain shaking that brings on unconsciousness. If you strike by the ear this will cause minimal shaking of the brain and a short spell of unconsciousness. The further down the jaw you strike the bigger the brain shake and the larger the probability of unconsciousness; if unconsciousness does occur, the longer the spell of unconsciousness. By the same count, the further down the jaw you strike the smaller the target area becomes.

A punch on the point of the jaw will have maximum effect but holds the smallest target.

The jawbone, when struck along the jaw line, causes a shaking of the brain. However, when it is struck on the point of the chin the knockout occurs in two phases. First the clivius and the anterior edge of the occipital bone are pushed against the lower portions of the pons and the anterior surface of the medulla oblongata. Next, by virtue of the 're-bounding effect', the medulla oblongata bounces back against the internal surface of the occipital bone and the posterior edge of the foramen magnum. In essence, the double impact causes the medulla oblongata, the most sensitive part of the brain, to concuss, thus causing temporary cancellation of the functions of the central nervous system.

THE APPLE TREE HYPOTHESIS

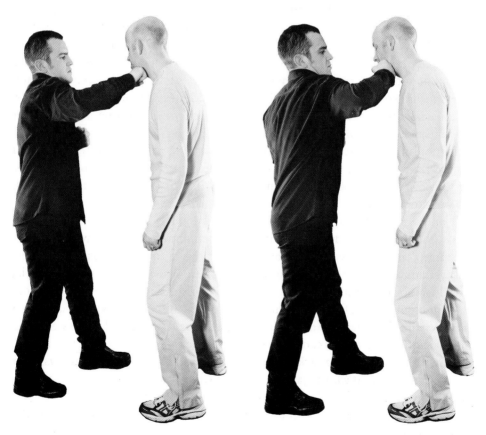

Right cross   *Right hook*

The chances of such a strike are lessened by the fact that the target is only around one inch in diameter. I call it the apple tree hypothesis. If you shake an apple tree at the base of its trunk, heavy shaking of the upper branches will occur, and lots of apples will fall. If, however, you shake the tree high up the trunk, minimal shaking of the upper branches will occur, and very few apples will fall. It is recommended, therefore, that you aim your blow at the middle of the jaw line (on the curve), where the target area is larger and the effect of an accurate blow will cause unconsciousness of a reasonable duration, certainly long enough to effect escape.

The first thing to do, before you strike, is look at the target area on the jaw; if you do not, you are not likely to hit it. When you strike, do so with your best technique, preferably off the back leg to ensure maximum body weight utilisation (an experienced fighter may throw the technique off his front leg). Don't stop the punch and merely strike the target, punch through it with your blow and your body weight.

There is a school of thought that says punching off the back leg is telegraphed and slower than punching off the front. Let me tell you that the time difference between punching off the back and the front leg would not register on a normal clock – we are talking about a difference of split seconds. So attacking off the front leg may be quicker but not enough to be caught by the naked eye. Speed of punch is not the major factor anyway. I know slow punchers that get KOs in every encounter because they are so good at engaging the brain before attack. While the brain is engaged time stops for the opponent, probably for a split second: this is the window of entry for your attack. If time stands still for a second your attack need only be as quick as that and you are in.

A direct hit will cause unconsciousness in an adversary immediately; his fall will then add to his defeat, because the unconscious head will usually meet the floor very heavily. If you are on target, but not right on the button, your adversary will, likely as not, fall to the floor in a semi-conscious stupor from which he usually recovers quite quickly, so get away as soon as possible. Even a blow that is off target should at least stun the adversary, giving you enough time to run. Always, as a matter of course, try to verbally and mentally disarm and engage the adversary before you strike, as this will greatly enhance the chances of a KO I would always, when possible, advise you to use a punching technique as opposed to anything else, because the hands are economical, fast and usually closer to the target than most other attacking tools. When using the fist to strike, for best effect, strike the line of the jaw with the two major knuckles. If you cannot or do not use the fist then make sure you use the hardest part of whatever attacking tool you do use. Bone to bone is always most effective. You may attack the jaw underneath (uppercut), around (hook), straight (cross), or overhand (hook), depending upon your preferences and strengths, all will have the desired effect if accurate (though hooking punches seem to be the most effective).

Summary

1. Line-up the adversary using your 'fence' to control range and trigger attack

2. Mentally disarm him and engage the brain, using your verbal action trigger

3. Look at the jaw

4. Strike

5. Escape

Chapter Eighteen

Hurdles and Pitfalls

'On the long journey from A to Z you learn an awful lot about B to Y, because there is often a lot more merit in what you learn on the journey than what you find at the journey's end.'

'The end matters most in the journey,
But it's the journey that matters most in the end.'

Old proverbs

This chapter is aimed, in the main, at those training (in whatever sphere) for the physical response, though the values and theories herein cover a far wider spectrum. No matter what it is you are trying to achieve in life, whether it is competence to excellence in the martial arts, faster track times in the world of athletics, building up a successful business, selling, even maintaining a healthy relationship with your spouse, you are always going to meet hurdles and pitfalls.

The inner opponent, in your own mind, can and will hinder your chances of success in any field, if not taken to task and controlled. The mind can be like an overbearing parent, frightened to give his child too much control.

As soon as you are starting to gain a little competence and get a little way up the mountain of self-realisation, your mind throws something tangible or intangible in your way to slow you down or stop you completely.

The further you get up that mountain, the more hurdles you climb over and pitfalls you cross, the stronger you become and thus the more control you gain over your own mind.

At the top of the mountain is the ultimate goal of complete self-control.

On the journey you will have developed, because of your overthrow of the hurdles and pitfalls, an iron will and an indomitable spirit. You will also gain enlightenment, because in order to get over some of the more difficult hurdles and pitfalls it is necessary to mentally dissect yourself, admitting and recognising your weaknesses in order to be able to confront and overcome them, and thus get past whatever stumbling block it is that's holding you back. This mental dissection is what develops enlightenment. This is why hurdles and pitfalls are, in essence, a godsend: without their challenge you wouldn't find enlightenment, you wouldn't develop the iron will that is necessary to confront them, nor the indomitable spirit that is developed by never giving in to them when the going gets tough.

The 'journey' is, metaphorically speaking, like a bowl of water, and you are like an inflated bicycle inner tube. You immerse the inner tube (yourself) into the water (the journey) to find out, via the bubbles, where there are any leaks (your own weaknesses).

Once you have found the leaks you can patch them up. Ultimately, you will have no leaks.

Hurdles and pitfalls can be many-splendoured things. They may be tangible or intangible. Sometimes, when there are no hurdles imminent, the mind, wishing to abort the journey, will invent silly ones. Basically speaking, hurdles and pitfalls come in three categories, but are uniform in one element, they are all reasons to give in, and are nearly always thrown in when the recipient is just starting to gain some kind of realisation and competence. Recognising them as hurdles and pitfalls and realising that the real benefits to be had from training are gained only by overcoming them will help immeasurably in your bid to do so.

The three categories of reasons not to continue the metaphoric journey are tangible, intangible and silly reasons.

TANGIBLE REASONS

These are incidental hurdles and pitfalls that are responsible for more 'lay offs' from training than any other reason. Broken bones, torn ligaments, twisted ankles, illnesses (one of my students once missed two months training because, and I quote, 'Me mum's got to 'ave an 'isterectomy') – the list goes on. With a serious injury it is foolish to keep training as the injury may become aggravated as a result. However, minor injuries should not deter you from conscientious practice.

You can quite easily train around such injuries. If your left hand is injured, train your right. I was in and out of hospital, and plaster, for two years, and had two operations in that time for a broken right wrist. I never missed training once and used the time to perfect my left-hand techniques. I have also had broken bones all over my body, but still managed to train around my injuries. Training under such adverse conditions requires and develops real will-power and is a great character builder.

With the more serious injury/illness that does lay you off, the danger lies in whether or not you get back to training after your convalescence. From my experience, most people do not. While you are recovering, try to visit your training establishment to maintain your ties and enthusiasm, as this will greatly help in your re-start program when the obstacle of bad health is removed.

A lot of people use their injuries to opt out because they found the going getting tough anyway, but remember this: if it was easy, everybody and his dog would be walking around with a black belt tied to his waist. If there is no adversity there is no advance.

INTANGIBLE REASONS

These can be as destructive in your advancement as the tangible, and in a psychological sense far more painful. Also, because they are mental as opposed to physical, they can quite often be very difficult to admit or detect. The greatest intangible is 'physical contact' – sparring or getting hit. A great percentage of people leave training because they are frightened of sparring. Even at the boxing club I coached at, it was common knowledge that you lost 85 per cent of your new starters after you put them in the ring for the first time.

The only way to overcome this fear is to confront it again and again until you become desensitised to it, and take heart, it does get better. The more you spar and put yourself in the firing line the better and more confident you will feel. In the world of real fighting, pain is unfortunately the ugly handmaiden, so it is imperative that you develop at least some tolerance for it if you want any chance of surviving a real situation.

BOREDOM

'It's getting boring.' If I had a penny for every time I've heard this excuse! Boredom is another major pitfall that loses many people from the martial arts arena and, in my opinion, it is a lazy excuse. Developing a technique into an instinctive reflex, developing power, speed, endurance, footwork or anything else worth having for that matter, requires repetition, and what is repetition if it isn't boring. From revising for a doctorate to perfecting a bayonet attack, both require repetition. Swimmers will practise hours and hours a day perfecting a stroke and jugglers will juggle until their hands bleed, all in pursuit of excellence. As martial artists, we are no different. For one technique to be effective in a 'live' situation we must do a thousand in the gym.

Boredom is the lazy man's excuse not to train. You must treat boredom as another challenge, hurdle or pitfall that must be bettered if advancement is to be attained. When boredom sets in you must use concentration to push it back out again. Sheer concentration on the technique you are practising will erode boredom. You must practice a technique until you are sick to death of it, then you will get good at it.

LACK OF ENJOYMENT

Lack of enjoyment in training is brothers with boredom. Another feeble excuse. Enjoyment in training comes and goes; nobody enjoys it all of the time. The real enjoyment comes from the fruits of training rather than the actual training itself. After all, to become proficient we must push ourselves through the pain of a gruelling training session. Who in their right mind enjoys pain? (My profuse apologies to all you masochists out there!)

If you are going through a bad patch of not enjoying your training, stick with it and try to treat the training as a mundane task that has to be done, the enjoyment will return. It's unrealistic to expect enjoyment all the time out of something so physically and mentally demanding. When the enjoyment is there, make the best of it, when it isn't, cope. It's all part of the character building process.

LACK OF IMPROVEMENT OR SUCCESS

Another favourite excuse for throwing in the towel is, 'I don't seem to be getting any better.' This is one of the mind's best finishing techniques: it kills off the enthusiasm of many students with the suddenness of cyanide tea. After all, what is the point of continuing in training if you're not getting any better? If I may use a metaphor, it's a bit like a propelling spiral that picks up momentum very quickly then, just as it seems to be reaching its pinnacle of speed, it seems to start going backwards.

So it is with training in the martial arts. In the beginning you are learning something new every session and improvement can be as fast as this metaphoric spiral. All of a sudden your advancement seems to be slowing down and in some cases you seem (like the spiral) to be going backward instead of forward, but it is only an illusion. After such a quick advance, even a slight decrease in speed may seem like a backward spiral. Usually it is only the person himself who sees or thinks he sees this supposed decline, and everyone else around him will be seeing his improvement – everyone but him. From my experience and as irony would have it, it is usually the better student who thinks he isn't improving. Every day and every session that you train will bring you some advancement, visible or invisible, large or small. The child that you see everyday will show no visible change or growth, but to the person who only sees the same child every few months the change is so obvious that they sometimes can't believe it's the same child.

And so it is with improvement in training. Sometimes it is so gradual that on a day to day basis it is almost not noticed, but it will be there.

SILLY REASONS

These are the most infuriating and are always employed by people to cover a deeper, underlying reason or problem, probably one of those in the last category. These are the worst (and sometimes the funniest) reasons for missing single sessions or even packing it in all together, because it means that the person employing the 'silly excuse' cannot come to terms with the real reason.

To my mind this puts him right at the bottom of the proverbial mountain with a long way to go. He'll probably never make it.

Here are my favourite 'silly' reasons, all of which have been used to me, by my own Karate students, over the years:

I can't train because:

1. My cat died.
(A great excuse because it can be used nine times)

2. My mother is having a hysterectomy.
(I think he was getting sympathy pains)

3. My Karate suit is in the wash.
(As coincidence would have it, the Cup Final coincided with my training time. This was just one of the many excuses used that night)

4. I haven't got any money.
(Saw him in the pub drunk later that night)

5. My granddad died.
(Third time this year)

6. I had to go to a funeral.
(Hope it's not his granddad again)

7. My wife's ill.
(My club is on Wednesdays and Sundays. Coincidentally these are the only days that she gets ill)

8. It was raining.
(He must be made of sugar)

9. My mum's varicose veins are playing her up.
(What?)

10. I can't take my grading because my flat's flooded and my daughter fell off her bike.
(The grading wasn't for another 6 weeks)

Every reason not to train, with a few exceptions, can be turned into a reason to train. The real strength to be attained is hidden within the hurdles and pitfalls, if you want that strength then you have to overcome and defeat them.

Chapter Nineteen

Visualisation

'Seeing is achieving! Whatever the mind of man can conceive he can achieve.'
Samuel Johnson

'It's been said that imagination is stronger than will-power and by not trying, by just visualising the goal accomplished it can be easier to achieve in real life.'
Takayuki Kubota

Top golfers are unanimous in their praise for it, champion body builders put it on a par with diet, and it is used with great success universally by doctors and psychologists, yet it still lies largely in the shadow of disbelief and ignorance. Some sceptics may laugh at the very thought of programming your mind, via visualisation, but who can argue with documented fact (or Tak Kubota for that matter). I think that visualisation is best summed up by Samuels & Samuels:

'What people visualise is what they get, likewise, what they have is a result of what they have visualised.'

Visualisation is a many splendoured thing in that it can be used to attain many things, from building up confidence to perfecting technique to confronting fears. In a documented experiment in America (one of many putting visualisation to the test), two groups of students were given the task of practising basketball penalty shots every day for a month. One group actually physically practised netting the ball whilst the other group lay on a bed or sat in a chair and, using visualisation, mentally practised netting the ball. At the end of the month both groups met up at a basketball court and competed to see which of the two could net the most shots. The group that had practised using visualisation won by a considerable margin.

That isn't to say that you should replace physical practice with visualisation, but certainly use it as a strong supplement. In a self-protection sense I have successfully commissioned the use of visualisation on many occasions, and genuinely believe that almost anything is attainable through its conscientious practice.

Many top martial arts competitors are starting to latch onto visualisation and the benefits it can offer. Chuck Norris, in his competition days, used it before he fought, and said that many times he scored points on his opponents with the exact moves he had beaten them with in his minds eye only minutes before.

Floro Villabrille, the famous unbeaten Filipino martial artist, the victor of countless full contact Escrima and Kali matches, practised visualisation whilst he actually trained. He would always go up to the mountains alone before a match, and in his imagination would fight his opponent over and over again until he felt he couldn't lose. He was quoted as saying 'I can't lose, when I enter the ring nobody can beat me, I already know that man is beaten.'

Before I actually go into the practice methods of visualisation let us first examine what the famous humanistic psychologist, Abraham Moslow, termed the *Jonah Complex* or, in layman's terms, the fear of success:

'You may be surprised to learn that the Jonah Complex stifles the advancement of as many people as the fear of failure.'

Moslow also stated:

'We are generally afraid to become that which we can glimpse in our most perfect moments, under the most perfect conditions, under conditions of greatest courage, we enjoy and even thrill to the God-like possibilities we see in ourselves at such peak moments, and yet, simultaneously, shiver with weakness, awe and fear before the same possibilities'.

Many people would, for instance, enjoy the prestige of representing the K.U.G.B. national squad, but how many of those same people, I wonder, would relish the thought of facing the like of Ronnie 'the Tasmanian Devil' Christopher and others of his ilk at squad meetings once a month. Not so many I think!

METHODS OF PRACTICE

Visual rehearsal, self-actualisation, going to the movies or visualisation, call it what you will, the process is basically the same and really quite a simple way of utilising a little more of your mental muscle.

Initially, the best way of practising visualisation is lying down in a quiet, darkened room. Close your eyes, breathe in and out deeply and relax. Once a relaxed state is acquired try to picture in your mind's eye the goal desired. At first you might find this difficult, but with practice it will get easier and the mental images clearer.

Picture yourself facing your fears or utilising your game plan in a confrontation, again and again, until it is well and truly programmed into your mind. Try to see the desired goal in as much detail as possible. The brain finds it very difficult to discern between what is imagined and what is actual; all it knows is what is programmed into it, so when you come to perform the goal that you've visualised, the brain gets straight into gear. You've rehearsed it so often it thinks it has done it before.

Many people who already practise visualisation only use one of the senses (imagined senses), i.e. sight, out of the possible five. Psychologists talk of the three out of five rule. Using three out of your five senses, they say, will enhance your visualisation practice. Tom 'Mr Legs' Platze, one of the world's greatest body builders says, and I quote:

'If you can use five of your senses in visualisation practice I'm confident that you can triple the results of your visualisation process.'

For instance, if you employ the three out of five rule, and as a hypothetical example your desired goal is to successfully employ your chosen game plan in a self-defence scenario, imagine the feeling of fear within, and you confidently controlling that fear. Imagine the sight and sound of your potential attacker before you, the sound of your voice refusing to baulk at his threats and perhaps as a climax see, hear and feel yourself neutralising him with your well-practised pre-emptive strike, the sound of his body falling, the sound/feel of your feet running away.

The more real and the more detailed you make your imagined performance the better your results will be.

I often practised just before I went out to work as a doorman in the nightclubs, mentally rehearsing techniques that have been successful for me in the past (it's always easier to visualise something that you have done or experienced before). In this sense I have found its practise an invaluable asset.

GOING TO THE MOVIES

As a final note, if you have trouble visualising images try going to the movies. In your mind's eye imagine a huge cinema screen in front of you, and on the screen picture yourself succeeding in your desired goal, confronting the bully, etc. Make the image as vivid as possible, use the three out of five rule and repeat the sequence as often as you can (15 minutes per day) and it will eventually become programmed into your mind. But please remember it is not a substitute but rather an additive to physical training.

Chapter Twenty

Aftermath

'He who wishes to fight must first count the cost.'

Sun Tzu

It took me a week to hunt down the violent criminals that burgled my home, this encompassing many frightening confrontations. Now I was back home, loot in hand, trouble over and peace restored. The aftermath began. It hit me harder than a tax bill. Aftermath, an explosion of emotions, always comes after adversity, after you have taken your body and mind to their physical and mental limits you often experience a partial emotional breakdown (some people experience a total nervous breakdown after being attacked/raped etc.). If you've been exposed to big build ups of adrenalin and it isn't released (the physical act of fighting back/running etc. utilises the adrenalin) as was the case this time, the aftermath is worse, as the body still needs 'release', its natural release being aftermath. Usually I prepare myself for aftermath just by expecting it. When you expect something to happen the impetus of it is lessened. This time, due to the elation of retrieving my loot without even having to fight I forgot my preparation. 'Sharon had gone to visit her nan, I was alone in the house when it started, the depression, the shame, the hate, the worry. I felt like I was dying inside, then the tears gushing out like Niagara floods, then the absolute shame for crying. What a wanker, crying like a baby, but cry I did for half an hour. I sat in to the chair wanting to disappear in to its arms. I was beyond comforting, I jumped out of the chair screaming like a wild animal and punched the wall several times until my hands swelled and bled, then I felt ashamed for damaging myself and cried again. I felt like I was dying. I fell from the chair to my knees and sobbed. This was aftermath.'

Watch My Back

As if the trauma of an attack isn't enough, afterwards follows the aftermath of emotion which can often leave a scar on the psyche that will long outlast any physical scars the victim may have incurred. Some victims of robbery, burglary and rape never emotionally recover. Victims of burglaries are often so incensed by the crime that they cannot bear to live in their house any longer; they sell up and move, then often still live in constant fear of a burglary to their new home, especially older people who have not the will or constitution to fight this corroding emotion. Rape victims, especially the ones who were too frightened to fight back, are often the worst hit by the intangible phenomenon that has driven many to nervous breakdowns, insanity and even suicide. Victims of unsolicited violence are often, as an after effect, too frightened to go out alone and live under the dominion of that fear for many years, some for life.

The stress of the aftermath often takes its toll on the family unit, sometimes, especially in rape cases, causing divorce or separation, then later problems with new spouses and new families. Victims of rape often live with a terrible underlying feeling of guilt and rage (post assault guilt/rage syndrome), believing that perhaps in some perverse way they were at fault. They are also often left with a feeling of low or no self-worth.

Of course, the blame for the sickening crime of rape is never and can never be apportioned to the victim. Much of the guilt stems from the fact that the victim feels as though she did not fight off the attacker with enough zest. The feeling is then re-emphasised when in court (if it ever gets to court – it is said that a third of rape cases are not even reported), the rapist's defending council verbally rips the victim to pieces and attacks her with insulting and insinuating questions, suggesting that she in some way condoned and enjoyed the act and that his client (the rapist) is really the victim. The court case can even be more demanding and damaging for the victim than the rape itself.

EXPECTED SYMPTOMS

Most victims of physical attack, across the board, can expect mild to severe depression and, if capitulation and submission were facets of the attack, post-assault guilt and rage. A severe loss of confidence may be experienced along with temper tantrums, severe mood swings and irrational behaviour. Sometimes prolonged crying spells and spates of depression may occur for no apparent reason. Often there is a feeling of low self-worth and a depressing lack of hope, as though the future is full of doom and gloom.

I have been in many bad situations and have experienced many of these feelings; sometimes they all fuse together and you don't know what it is you're feeling, only that it's bad. Even when you successfully defend yourself you may still get bouts of depression and gloom.

I'm not a medical person, so I would not presume to tell you how to overcome these feelings. I am an empiricist and with me it is, or has been, a way of life; these feelings, as unwelcome as they are, are very common to me. This familiarity loses the feelings' impetus so I can handle them better than most. If you feel like crying, then cry; even deliberately watch a sad film to bring the tears on, as crying can be therapeutic. The tears contain a hormonal release that will make you feel better – it is nature's way of releasing the bad emotions from your body that may otherwise lay trapped. It is said that, in the long term, trapped emotions can have a very detrimental effect, often developing into psychosomatic illnesses, ulcers, irritable bowel syndrome and bad nerves. So do not harbour the tears, let them flow.

The aftermath may be little more than mild depression that you may feel capable of handling. If the symptoms are more severe you should consult you own G.P. or talk to your loved ones: 'A problem shared is a problem halved'.

Another doozy to watch out for post assault is the Black Dog (see earlier). Many I know who have been victims of attack spend weeks, months, years, even the rest of their lives, trying to rationalise their actions and trying to justify the inadequacy of their performance in the attack scenario – or non-performance as the case may be. A perception of failing to protect loved ones in their time of need is another huge cause of depression. As I said before, don't have any of it. In most attack situations flight is not only the right option, it's the only safe and sensible option. But remember to expect the aftermath.

The main aim of this chapter is to enlighten you. Again, 'Forewarned is forearmed'. If you expect the aftermath and prepare yourself mentally, its impetus is greatly lost.

Knowledge is power.

Chapter Twenty-one

Case Histories

In my research for this book I talked to and interviewed many people. I spoke to victims of attack and also to attackers. The following interviews and inserts are typical of all the interviews that I conducted, printed here with kind permission of the interviewees.

There are also extracts and letters taken from the work of my associate, top criminologist and true crime writer Christopher Berry-Dee. I found the interviews enlightening and thought-provoking, and would recommend his work highly.

I have made little comment on the following interviews, preferring you the reader to draw your own conclusions.

I hope you can learn from them as I have.

Gratuitous assault

THE ATTACKER

Nev and Steve are in their early twenties and a part of an infamous gang in Coventry. Some of the details here have been changed, at their request, to protect their identity. They are not reformed characters and are still at large.

Interviewer: Why do you pick fights with people, Steve?

Steve: I like a scrap. 'Specially at the weekend, after the pub.

Nev: [laughs] Or in the pub.

I: Can you give me an example of one incident?

Steve: Yeah, we were going to the chippie after the pub, there was about six of us when we saw this bloke with his woman. She was quite tasty so I shouted, 'Get your tits out.' As you do [laughs]. We all cracked up laughing. The bloke she was with didn't look that happy though. I think he was gonna say something but his missus pulled him away. I knew he was getting heated so I thought I'd wind 'im up a bit more. I might 'ave left it but the lads were geeing me up. So I shouted 'Fucking wimp, your woman fights all your battles for you, does she?' That really got 'im 'cus he shouted 'wot's your problem?' I could tell 'e didn't really want to go [fight], just didn't want to look a twat in front of 'is missus, loads of blokes are like that. Anyway, we all ran over to 'im, 'is missus was trying to pull 'im away but 'e wouldn't 'ave any of it. We all jeered 'im and I said, 'D'you want some then?' He tried to tell me that I was out of order talking to 'is missus like that, I said, 'she's only a fucking slag, anyway.'

He started getting angry again so I shouted, 'COME ON THEN. LET'S DO IT! COME ON!' By this time I was right in 'is face, he looked like 'e was gonna crap 'imself so I shouted right in 'is face, 'YEAH! YEAH, COME ON you fucking wank!' Then I caught 'im smack in the face with the head [head-butt]. As 'e 'it the deck we all laid in to 'im. 'Is missus tried to stop us so one of the boys gave 'er a dig as well. Stupid fucking slapper. I said to 'er 'keep out of the way, you bag of sick.' Then we kicked pieces off 'im. Wanker. 'E deserved every thing 'e got.

I: Why did you choose him as a victim?

Nev: 'E was just there, and 'e fancied 'isself.

Steve: 'E was staring over at us as well, like 'e thought we were shit.

I: What do you mean?

Nev: 'E should 'ave just kept 'is big mouth shut and we wouldn't 'ave bothered.

I: Do you pick fights with everyone that passes you in the street?

Steve: Naw, not everyone, we 'ave to be in the mood.

I: Do you mean you have to have had a drink?

Steve: No, that's not what I said.

I: But you normally have had a drink?

Steve: Yeah, I suppose so.

I: What could he have done to avoid an incident with you?

Nev: [laughs] Lived in a different city. Naw, look, seriously, 'e should 'ave just walked away and kept 'is big mouth shut, and kept 'is eyes to 'imself.

Steve: We wus just 'aving a bit of a laugh, people take everything too seriously. If they don't give any lip then there's a fair chance that we won't give them a good 'iding.

DEAD OR ALIVE

I: What would you do if someone insulted your girlfriend?

Steve & Nev: They wouldn't fucking dare, they know what they'd get.

I: So really you're just bullies?

Steve & Nev: [offended] No way, we'd fight anyone, we don't bully. Look, if you live in Wood End then that's just the way it is, if someone shouts at you or calls your missus you don't say nothing back unless you're prepared to back it up. 'E wasn't, so 'e got some. End of essay! That's the crack. It goes with the territory. If 'e didn't want grief 'e should 'ave swallowed [backed down] and backed off.

I: Tell me about another incident, Steve.

Nev: Tell 'im about the bloke you put in 'ospital. The one that kept staring at you.

Steve: Oh yeah. The dick. I was minding me own business in the bar and this big guy looked at me, I was in a bad mood anyway cus the dole 'ad stopped me money. I looked straight back at 'im and said 'wot you fucking looking at, you bag of puke?' 'E said 'e wasn't looking at me, but 'e said it dead aggressive like so I walked over to 'im and asked 'im again what 'e was staring at. 'E swore at me and said 'e wasn't staring, 'e just thought 'e knew me from somewhere. I said if 'e wanted to go [fight] 'e should step outside, when 'e went to stand up I shoved my glass in 'is face. 'E was out like a light.

Nev: [obviously impressed] 'E was in 'ospital for ages.

Steve: 'Is own fault, shouldn't 'ave fucked.

I: I heard that you stabbed a guy in the same pub, Steve.

Steve: Oh yeah. D'you 'ear about that, then? That was the barman. He grassed on me to the law about the glassing so 'e 'ad to 'ave some as well. I 'eard 'e was a bit of a Karate man so I didn't take any chances. I walked in to the bar first thing in the morning, while it was quiet, less witnesses see. When 'e seen me 'e said I was barred, I said 'Look man, I don't want any grief with you, I know you can motor [fight], I just want to tell you that there is no hard feelings on my part, let's shake on it.' Fucking wanker fell for it. As he grabbed my right hand to shake it I pulled 'im 'ard in to me and stabbed 'im right in the kidneys. 'E went down like a sack of shit. I booted 'im a few times and walked out.

I: Why do you think he fell for it?

Steve: Didn't know the crack, did 'e. Most of these trained fighters are the same. They're all bag punchers.

[both laugh]

I: If you are such a good fighter why didn't you have a fair fight with him?

Steve: It was a fair fight. Where we come from that was fair an' square. Just because we don't follow Queensbury don't mean that what we do ain't fair. You know wot I'm sayin'. The only person at fault was the dick I stabbed, he should 'ave know the rules. I mean, what the fuck's 'e doin' in Wood End and not knowin' the crack. Maybe now he'll learn.

I: How did you conceal the knife?

Steve: I tucked it in the palm of my hand and held it against my leg like this [he demonstrates]. 'E was so pleased that I said I didn't want to fight that 'e wasn't looking for a tool anyway. They all fall for it.

I: You've done this before then?

Steve: Yeah. Loads of times. Not always with a knife, sometimes with a glass or a bottle. They all think it's Queensbury. Fuck Queensbury, 'e's been dead about a hundred years. I don't follow rules, I just do what works.

[both laugh again]

I: What would you do against someone like yourself?

Steve & Nev: [laughing] Run.

Steve: The main thing is, I wouldn't let them get close to me, no one gets close to me. And don't believe anything they say, 'specially if they say they don't want to fight. If they say they don't want it [trouble] and back away, that's all right, but if they say they don't want it and try to get closer then you've got problems. 'Specially the ones who try'n touch you, you know, put their arm around you all pally, pally like. They're the worst ones. Oh and never shake 'ands with any of them. It's the oldest trick in the book but it suckers 'em all. Ben does that [speaking to Nev], shakes their hands and butts them straight in the face. Don't trust anyone.

I: Thanks for your time.

THE VICTIMS

'Noel didn't notice the group of lads stalking his exit from the nightclub, didn't notice that they were watching his every move like a hawk. He had left the nightclub to see if his mate Cam had come back for him [he'd promised to give him a lift home], he was still wearing the black and whites from his earlier stint on the door at the Dog, as far as the barracking lads across the road were concerned he was a B's [the nightclub he'd just left] bouncer. Noel, still busy looking for Cam's car, didn't notice the lads as they crossed over and stood around him. Noel was oblivious to the fact that they had just had an argument with the B's doormen and they thought he was one of them. "You carrying, you got a knife?" the leader asked. Noel didn't notice that the youth proffering the question was concealing one arm behind his right leg. "No," Noel replied evenly. "I don't need one ... "

"'THUD!" Midway through his answer the youth stabbed Noel through the heart, as he fell to the floor, dying, they frenziedly kicked him. Noel died in the ambulance, en route to hospital.'

From the book *Bouncer*

The following interview, though not so serious as the one above, equally demonstrates the dialogue and ritual that often occurs before attack. More than that, it is demonstrative of victims in code white, mentally and especially environmentally. It was conducted one month after the incident, with James McKay from Nuneaton, West Midlands, who was one of three young men attacked in August 1992 by a group of seven men in their late twenties.

James is six foot one tall, weighs 11 stone and attends technical college; he is also a part-time window cleaner.

Matthew is 20 years old, five foot eleven tall and heavily built.

Dominic is 19 years old, five foot eleven tall and of average build.

James is the interviewee.

I: James, would you mind telling me about the night you and your friends were attacked?

James: No, not at all. Me and my friends went out to the local pub on the Saturday night for a bit of a drink at about 9.00 p.m. We met some girls at the pub and were getting on really well with them.

We were having a good night. We left the girls, and the pub, at about 10.45 p.m. to go for the last drink at another pub, further up the road. On the way to the pub we had to walk down a country lane and over a small bridge with steep grass banks either side of us. Seven men, well about seven, aged between twenty-two and thirty, ran up either side of the bank toward us.

I: Where had they come from?

James: We were told after that they followed us from the pub, and they reckoned we were talking to their girlfriends.

I: How come you never noticed them?

James: Well, you don't expect it, do you? We were just talking and having a laugh. I suppose we should have noticed, but, well ... you don't expect it do you?

I: How long did it take them to get up the banks and reach you?

James: About five, ten seconds. It was pitch black and we didn't know what was going on.

I: At this stage did you feel scared?

James: No, not really, we just thought that they were running up to the path. Then one of them punched me in the ribs – that's when I got scared. Looking back, it was obvious what they were going to do, we just didn't think.

I: Did you 'freeze'?

James: Yes, I think so. I got punched in the eye, it wasn't a hard punch, it just shocked me.

I: Did your attacker say anything to you before he attacked.

James: Yeah. Something like 'What you fucking looking at?' I said that I wasn't looking at anything. He said 'do ya wanna fight?' Before I could answer he punched me.

I: What happened then?

James: I was punched a few times, then thrown down one of the banks. I got up and ran home.

I: Why did you run home?

James: I just felt really scared, I didn't want to be there.

I: What happened to your mates?

James: When I got home I rang Dominic and Matthew to see how they were. They both had black eyes and bruised faces. They were more worried about me than themselves, because I was the youngest.

I: How did they feel mentally?

James: They felt alright, just pissed off that they were attacked for nothing.

I: How did you feel?

James: Basically OK I felt a bit of a coward for running. I felt like I'd let my mates, and myself down, and I felt like I'd let my parents down too.

I: Why?

James: Because my dad has always taught me that I should always stick up for myself.

I: And you feel as though you didn't do enough?

James: Yes.

I: In retrospect, what could you have done to avoid the attack?

James: We could have taken a different route to the pub, where we were attacked was really secluded. If we'd have gone a different way it would never have happened.

I: What about the fight itself? What would you have done differently?

James: Well, I didn't really expect the bloke to hit me, I was just going to answer his question when he punched me, he didn't really give me a chance. Looking back, when the blokes ran up the banks we had plenty of chance to run, or even if we didn't run I could have punched one of them in the face. I used to box so I can hit quite hard. I should have hit him before he hit me.

I: What about the fear? How would you overcome the feeling that made you 'freeze'?

James: Last time I wasn't calm, next time I'd try to stay calm and try to hit one of them before I got hit.

CASE HISTORIES

I: How did your parents and friends react to you being attacked?

James: My parents were really worried, but I told them I was alright. My dad said I was lucky, I could have been badly hurt or killed.

I: Did your dad say that you should have fought back?

James: No, no, he understood. He was just glad that I was alright.

I: What about your friends?

James: Some of them called me a puff and a coward because I didn't fight back, but they weren't there, it's not as easy as you think.

I: What are your thoughts on those who called you names?

James: I don't think they'd do any better, in fact when I asked some of them to come and help me get the blokes the next week, they all made excuses why they couldn't make it.

I: They bottled out?

James: Yes.

I: Now it's all behind you, how do you feel?

James: It still bugs me that I didn't fight back. I wouldn't have minded getting beaten up so much if I'd have had a 'go' back. Trouble is it didn't happen how I expected it to. One minute he was talking to me, the next I was being hit.

I: So he suckered you?

James: Yes, I suppose he did.

I: So that still plays on your mind?

James: Yes. It bugs me.

I: Do you know why you were attacked?

James: No. The only thing I can think is that they might have seen us talking to the girls in the pub and not liked it.

I: What steps have you taken to ensure that you are better prepared next time?

James: I'm going back to boxing and I've started weight lifting.

I: What about the mental side?

James: Boxing and weight training are building up my confidence a lot. I feel much stronger mentally.

I: Is there any advice you would like to offer people reading this interview?

James: Only that I hope they learn from my mistakes and take precautions now, before it happens, and not to be ashamed to run away if they have the chance.

Muggers

THE ATTACKERS

'Knowing the enemy enables you to take the offensive.'

Sun Tzu

The two interviewees wished, for obvious reasons, to remain anonymous. They both earned their living from crime, more specifically robbery with violence (mugging), accosting up to eight victims in any one night.

J and P both began their criminal careers at the age of 13. They are now 17, and at the time of this interview serving four years for robbery with violence. Both are six foot two tall with slim to medium build.

I: J., P., why do you commit these offences?

J: For money, and the buzz.

P: It's a good laugh.

I: What time do you instigate your attacks?

J and P: At night.
I: Why not in the day?

J: Too many people about. Too easy to get caught.

I: How do you choose your victims?

J and P: Student types, men carrying umbrellas or wearing glasses, usually aged between twenty and thirty, occasionally older. We also look for people who are well dressed; smart clothes means money.

I: Why those particular types of people?

P: Because they always have money or cards, and they don't give you any hassle.

I: What happens after you have chosen a victim?

P: We follow them, cross the road, walk past them maybe two or three times. Some of them must be thick not to notice what's going on.

I: What is your next move?

J and P: We wait for them to walk into a side street or walk into a park, anywhere quiet. We walk up to them and ask the time, this distracts them while we pull out our knifes. When they look up we say, 'Give us your fucking money!' They usually look blank. Both of us shout at them, 'Get your fucking wallet out', and put the knives closer to their face.

I: Then what?

P: They get their money out and offer you some, but I snatch the lot.

I: What if they have no money?

J and P: We take their jewellery.

I: What if they have no jewellery, either?

J and P: We laugh and say, 'See you later', then run off.

I: What do you do with the money, credit cards and jewellery?

P: I spend the cash on drink, sell the cards for fifty pounds each and the jewellery, unless it's something I like, then I keep it.

I: So you have a drink in between muggings?

P: Yeah!

I: Is there anybody that you would not mug?

P and J: Old women, kids.

I: What do mean, kids?

A: Under twelves.

I: Anybody else?

P and J: We don't like doing drunks.

I: Why, I thought drunks would be easy targets?

P and J: They are, but a lot of them don't take you seriously, they could fall on the knife or something and that could mean a twenty-five stretch [twenty-five years in prison].

I: What would cause you to stop an attack once you've started.

P: If they scream or if they fuck about.

I: What do you mean, 'fuck about'?

J: Start giving you hassle, like pretending to look for their money, taking their time, arguing. There was this old geezer who we were just about to 'do', when he turned into his drive. We stopped him and told him to give us his money, but he just kept on walking to his door. We thought he was deaf, but when he got to his door he turned round and told us to 'fuck off'. That really blew me, man.

I: Does the size of the victim matter?

P and J: No.

I: What would put you off?

P: Build, someone who's stocky or if they look mean, the sound of their voice. If they look wary we don't bother either.

I: What do you mean, wary?

206

P: You know, if they look like they know what we're gonna do.

I: What do you mean when you say 'the sound of their voice'?

P and J: When you ask them the time, if they sound tough.

I: Explain that more.

P: Well, if, when you get close to them they look a bit tough, when you ask them the time if they answer with a rough voice, then we just walk off.

I: How do you feel when you are looking for a victim?

P and J: Nervous, high, on a buzz.

I: How do you feel when your mugging someone?

P: Calm.

J: I'm just laughing to myself.

P: I'm in control, I'm looking around to make sure no one's coming and thinking of getting away.

I: How do you feel after?

P: A great buzz, the more daring it is the more buzz I get. I get round the corner and collapse with laughter. My hands are shaking and my knees are weak, I have to sit down. Then we go and buy some drink.

I: How many people do you mug in one night?

P and J: We have done eight, but most times about six. If we get a lot of money the first or second time we get too drunk to do any more.

I: How much cash do you get in one night?

P: The most is about eighty pounds, but usually less.

I: Can you give me a typical example of one of your attacks?

P: There was this geezer and his missus, outside a telephone box. Their car had the bonnet up, the woman went into the phone box. We walked up to the phone box and pretended to queue for the phone. The geezer looked like he had money, good clothes, smart car. I gave J. the signal by winking at him, I then asked the geezer the time and we both pulled out our knives. When he looked up we told him to hand over his wallet. He said, 'Do you know who I am?' I said, 'I don't care who you are.' He said, 'Do you know who she's on the phone to?', indicating to his wife in the phone box. 'The police.'

This was taking too long I thought to myself. I said, 'I'm going to give you to the count of three, or else', and pushed the knife closer to his throat. He handed over his wallet and we ran off.

All the time this was happening the woman on the phone didn't realise what was going on.

I: *What would you have done if he hadn't have handed over his wallet?*

J and P: Run.

I: *Have you any mates that do the same sort of thing as you?*

P: Most of our mates are into mugging and crime.

I: *Do they all operate the same system?*

J and P: Sort of.

I: *What do you mean?*

J and P: Well, we all learn off each other, some use bats, iron bars or pretend guns, others use knives like us.

I: *Do all of your mates run off if they come up against problems or complications?*

P: Yeah. You can't afford to be caught mugging. Look what happened to us: four years each.

THE VICTIMS

Mary is a middle class, middle-aged woman. She was mugged in broad daylight outside a popular, busy shopping store in London. Her interview is very demonstrative of the four 'D's and of being mentally in code white even though she was environmentally sound. It also demonstrates a dire lack of ritual awareness. Even after the fact, Mary was still unaware of the fact that she was primed by being selected, stalked and approached before attack.

I: Mary, would you please tell us about your incident.

Mary: Yes, surely. I had just finished my usual weekly shopping at H____ [store]. The doorman opened the door for me and I walked outside to call a cab. Two men asked me for the time. I was laden with shopping so I put the bags on the floor to look at my watch. Suddenly I felt an awful wrench on my arm, the next thing I knew these two men had run off with my shopping and my watch.

I: Do you know why they attacked you?

Mary: Well, I can only think that it was because of my watch, having seen that it was expensive, they decided that they would steal it, and then my shopping. I was silly putting it down on the floor.

I: Don't you think that they may have asked you the time to distract you for long enough to be able to steal your belongings?

Mary: Yes, well ... I never really thought of it like that. It does sound a little more logical.

I: Did you see them approach you?

Mary: No, I was too busy trying to hail a cab. I'm not even sure if they approached me or if they were simply walking past at the same time as I left the store. Actually, no, let me think. That's right, the doorman told the police that he had seen the two men hanging around, opposite the store, for several minutes before the attack.

I: Did they both speak to you?

Mary: One did. He said, 'Excuse me, could you tell me the time?' He seemed perfectly reasonable. The other fellow wasn't even looking at me, he was looking the other way. I looked at my watch and ... that was it.

I: Were you not suspicious at all?

Mary: Not in the slightest, I was far too preoccupied with hailing a cab. When I was asked the time I didn't even bother to look at them. I automatically looked at my watch.

I: What have you learned from your ordeal?

Mary: Until now I had learned very little, only to be very wary of giving people the time. In respect to what you have just told me I shall be a lot more wary of everything I do.

I: Thank you for your time, Mary.

Rapists and Murderers

THE ATTACKERS

The following are extracts from interviews and excerpts from newspapers. All are included here to demonstrate attacker ritual and reality.

'A sex attacker who struck in a Southampton park earlier this week may be a dangerous 'stalker' with a vendetta against students.

'His victim fears he has struck before but other women have been too scared to come forward.
'The 25 year old woman, currently studying law at Southampton institute, told this newspaper how the would-be rapist spluttered obscenities about students as he grappled with her in a local park.

"'I have never been so scared," she said, "he really raged about hating students and became very violent. The intensity of his anger made me feel he would really harm me. It was more frightening that anything."
'The mature student, who did not want to be named, described how the smartly dressed man had tried to engage her in conversation before the attack.

"'He said hello so familiarly that I felt that I must know him," she said. "But then he started chatting me up, asking me what I was doing that night, so I just ignored him." At that point the man's behaviour changed. He indecently exposed himself and began grappling with her clothing before trying to push her to the ground.

'Police believe two office workers walking towards the scene just after 5.30pm on Wednesday may have unwittingly forced the attacker to flee.'
The Daily Echo, November 5th 1994

The following is taken from a letter to Christopher Berry-Dee from serial killer Arthur Shawcross, serving 250 years.

'My name is Arthur John Shawcross.

I am labelled a serial killer, if so – so be it. I have been asked, did I kill? To this question I will say [yes], too many times for any one person to do so! I have been a god unto myself, I've been the judge, the jury and the executioner. I, dear people, have murdered, butchered and totally destroyed 53 human beings in my lifetime. I am like a predator, able to hunt, able to wantonly destroy at any given time or moment.

Some of you think that I am a joke, let me assure you that I am not!!

Do you have a choice of when and where you will die?! Stay away from drunk drivers, planes, terrorist, robbers or people somewhat like me!

Can't be done can it?!'

In another letter to my associate, convicted killer Michael Sams talks about his killing of Julie Dart. The letter is self-explanatory.

'It is well documented from the trial that I had intended my first attempt [abduction] to be at Lincoln, my second at Crewe. Had either of these two gone ahead then the captive would not have been allowed to go home. When the 3rd July 1991 at Crewe failed, I have no explanation as why I thought the police would pay a ransom for an unknown, everyday person, but I knew in my mind that they would. And I subsequently found out that they would have done. The actual true events from July 9 to October 1991 are now given.

'I set off from our house at about 7pm, 9 July, Teena thought I was going to Peterborough to decorate her house. I called at an off licence to buy a tin of lager to relax me. I stopped en route to put a false number plate and then went to the 'mucky duck' down the calls in Leeds. There seemed no way that I would pick up a girl without being seen. I had known that Chapeltown was the red light area so I went to have a look. After a bit of searching I found the corner where the health centre was at about 11.15pm. There were three girls on the corner so I parked a little way up the road. Two were coloured girls and one a tall white girl. Shortly after I parked where I could see the three girls, a white, largish, car stopped across the road from the girls. The tall white girl ran across the road to the driver's side, spoke to the driver and then gave him something from her back jeans pocket. At about 11.30 the coloured girls left – so I then went and parked opposite her. She called out "do you want business", I answered yes. She ran across the road passing in front of my car and came to the passenger door and opened it. She told me it was £15 behind the health centre, which I declined, or £20 in the car. I paid her twenty pounds and she got in and directed me to the Thomas Danby car park. She told me her name was June and she was 24.

'When we got to the car park she bent down to take her shoes off. I leant over and grabbed the back of her neck and pressed down. In this doubled up position she couldn't scream. I told her that I would let her up if she didn't scream and kept her eyes closed. I wanted to talk to her, she

agreed, and so I let her sit back. I then slipped a rope I had ready, over her head and secured it around her stomach similar to a seat belt, but one she couldn't undo. When I had done that I said she could open her eyes, which she did, and saw that she was tied and I had a knife. Her hands were tied by her side with the rope so I asked her to pull them out and I tied them together in front of her. I said "right, we're going on a journey." She saw that I had a knife across my knees and so presumed I would use it if she screamed or anything. We went down through the centre of Leeds past the station and on to the M1. At no time when stopping at traffic lights etc., did she try to attract the attention of any other motorists, she just kept talking to me. It was about 2 a.m. when we reached Newark on the A1, I had put a jumper over her face. I said I didn't want her to see what town she was in. She never objected to the jumper over her head. I took her into the workshop with it still over her head, guiding her. Then I tied her to the chair whilst I put the car away.

'When I came back I untied her from the chair and told her to sit on the mattress, she still had her hands tied, and her leg then was also tied by a rope to a bracket, over her jeans. When she saw where she was she said she was not happy about removing her clothes in that cold building. I then told her that she hadn't been kidnapped for photos, but to hold until the police paid a ransom for her release. She actually laughed at this idea. She didn't think that they would pay, and that I had kidnapped the wrong person, her mother had no money.

'She told me that her name was Julie and not June but maintained her age was 24.

'The fact that I was going to kill her in a few hours, in no way showed through to her.

'She asked to be allowed to wash. I untied her hands but not her leg. When she had finished I said I was tying her hands behind her back, so she laid on her tummy and put her hands behind her back. She never had them tied because I hit her with a hammer, I had with me, behind the head to render her unconscious. Then I put a cord round her neck and tightened it.'

THE VICTIMS

Extract from *Ladykiller* by Christopher Berry-Dee and Robin Odell:

'Jean Bradford was 37 years old and married, with a seventeen month old son. She ran a ladies' knitwear shop in Sutton Coldfield. On Friday 6th March 1981, she opened the shop as usual at 9.30 a.m. and served a trickle of customers during the morning. At 12.30 she closed the shop and turned the closed sign round on the door. Her husband collected her and her son and went off to lunch. They returned at about 2.00 p.m. and Mr Bradford left his wife and toddler in the shop.

'At about 2.15 p.m. the women from the shop next door called in for a few minutes' chat and when she departed Jean Bradford was left alone with her son. Half an hour later, about 2.45 p.m., a man entered the shop. He was holding a handkerchief over his face as if to blow his nose. Just at that moment the telephone in the back office rang and Mrs Bradford made her apologies before going to answer it. She came out of the office to make sure that the customer had not left the door open, as she was afraid her young son might wander out in to the street.

Having satisfied herself on this point, she offered further apologies and returned to the phone. The man mumbled something in reply but kept the hand-kerchief up to his nose and mouth.

'With her son by her side Jean Bradford had to hold the line whilst her caller was connected. She put her head round the door of the office and said, "I'm sorry to be long. Can I help you?" The man gave a nervous sort of laugh and walked in to the office. He was holding a knife that he was pointing at her saying that he would cut her unless she kept quiet. Then he threatened to cut the baby and, putting his finger on the telephone rest, disconnected the incoming call. Mrs Bradford picked up her son and held him to her protectively. The man instructed her to go in to the corner of the office and face the wall. Still holding her son and with the intruder's knife at her ribs, she did as she was told. His commands were emphasised with the repeated use of the expletive "fucking". He asked her where the cash was kept. She turned around to show him but he made her face the wall again. She explained that the cash box was behind the curtain which screened the office from the ship. Mrs Bradford's son, sensing her fear, began to scream. "Stop your little girl," the man told her. She explained that it was a little boy and that the child was frightened and asked if she could give him a drink which was on a table in the shop. The man stood close to her, touching the knife to her face and telling her, 'not to fucking move'. He went in to the shop and returned with the child's bottle which he thrust in to Jean Bradford's free hand. After having a drink, the child calmed down.

'The intruder located the cash box and spilled its contents onto the floor where he sorted through the change. He then asked where more money could be found, and she told him there was some in a purse on the shop table. Mrs Bradford found difficulty in articulating her words, all the while being threatened with a knife.

'Suddenly the front door of the premises opened and in walked Mrs Bradford's mother who was her business partner. "Tell them that you are closed," the man instructed, Jean followed his instructions but her mother only laughed and made straight for the office. 'Who's this?' the man asked. "It's my mother," Jean replied. The two women stood close together whilst the intruder asked again about money.

'"Let my daughter go with the baby," requested the older woman. "No," came the reply, accompanied by the threat that he would cut her if she did not keep quiet.

'She persisted in her request and Jean could see that the man was becoming increasingly nervous. She told her mother to shut up and do as she was told.

'He then turned his attentions to Jean and began fiddling with her dress. She asked him what he was doing and he said, "the best way to tie your legs is to get your tights by your feet". So saying, he pulled her tights down by her ankles and lifting up her skirt said "beautiful". He had already told her to put down the child and now instructed her to lower her knickers. She refused but changed her mind when he said, "Well you don't want the baby cut". He then moved behind her and put his left arm around her neck while holding the knife to her face. He whispered that if she didn't want to fucking well get hurt she was to undo his trousers and give him oral sex. "Please don't," she begged but he became more threatening and ordered her to kneel down in front of him. He undid his trousers and told her to take out his penis.

'When she resisted he pointed the knife towards the child and repeated; "You don't want the

baby to get hurt." She complied with his instructions as minimally as possible; "I did as little as I had to," she later told the police in her statement.

'Before fleeing the intruder also raped Mrs Bradford, a crime for which John Cannon was later convicted and received an eight year prison sentence.'

I leave the reader to draw the obvious conclusions.

Chapter Twenty-two

Do's and Don'ts

'He will win who knows how to handle both superior and inferior forces.'

Sun Tzu

In the foregoing chapters we have covered a lot of the things that you should and should not do. Here I'd like to list a few of the more important points to bear in mind.

At the forefront of everything is stay coded up.

1) Don't get too drunk

Alcohol in moderation is fine. If you drink too much, however, you are an easy target for attackers. Alcohol temporarily erodes perceptiveness, balance, distancing, sight, sound – in fact nearly every sense is impaired. You also fail to see danger when drunk and cannot, even if very proficient, expect realistically to see a situation arise or defend yourself whilst under the influence.

2) Don't underestimate or trust an adversary

Confidence is a great attribute, over-confidence is a very weak link. Never allow yourself to underestimate anyone: it is a sure sign, on your part, of over-confidence, and over-confidence begets defeat. If you start feeling too confident about a situation, remind yourself of the possible dangers you are facing. Better to be a little under-confident than over-confident. If faced by a potential attacker, never trust him. The false promise is one of the most common 'terror compliance' techniques used by the attacker.

3) Be basic

If it comes to a physical response, never employ a technique for the sake of dramatic effect. Looking good counts for nothing; many people have lost trying to do so. Use the quickest, most basic and economical technique available to you.

4) Don't delay

Don't hang around. If you can escape do so at the earliest opportunity. The longer you leave it the harder it will become. If you're going to attack a potential attacker, also do so as soon as possible. Any time delay in pre-emptive attack will lessen your chances of success.

5) Be hard

Do not allow sentiment to enter into your mind when dealing with a potential attacker, as he will manipulate and engineer any chink in your mental armour until it is a cavernous opening that he can walk right through. When dealing with bad people you have to be as bad as them if you want to survive, at least for the duration of the attack. Most victims do not even try to defend themselves, believing that any fight-back on their part will only antagonise and thus add to the ferociousness of the attack.

Surveys show that a victim who fights back with vigour usually forces the attacker to abort.

6) Don't be suckered

As you have read throughout this text, deception is the predator's greatest ally.

Understand the rituals and look out for deception. The modern attacker is unlikely to look menacing; rather he may be polite until the moment of his attack.

7) Kill your pride

Pride has no place in good self-protection. If you can run away from a situation or talk your way out of a fight, do it. Survival is all that matters.

8) Don't be squeamish

If sticking your fingers in an adversary's eyes is what you have to do to survive an attack, do it, don't be squeamish or you'll lose.

9) Kill fair play

When an attack on your person is in progress or imminent, there is no such thing as fair play. Do anything and use anything to defend yourself. There is only one rule: there are none.

10) Never do more than is necessary

In defending yourself, it is imperative that you hit and run. Don't hang around trying to finish the job. As soon as you can, run. It is not unheard of for a stunned adversary, even a felled one, to recover and still beat the victim who is close enough to grab

Chapter Twenty-three

First Aid

In the execution of self-defence it is quite likely that you, even if you defend yourself successfully, may pick up minor or serious injuries. You may be with a friend or friends who are injured or you may even wish to treat an attacker who you have injured in the process of defending yourself. The latter is unlikely and not recommended. If your adversary has been neutralised, it is highly dangerous to hang around, though of course the prerogative is entirely yours.

THE PRINCIPLE OF FIRST AID

First aid is the skilled application of accepted methods of treatment on the occurrence of an injury or in the case of sudden illness, using facilities or materials available at the time. It is the approved method of treating a casualty until placed, if necessary, in the care of a doctor or removed to hospital.

First aid treatment is given to sustain life

To prevent a condition from becoming worse

To promote recovery

So, basically, if the injuries are bad, you are looking to do a patch-up job that will suffice until somebody skilled, i.e. a doctor or hospital, can take over. Of course, injuries sustained in physical attacks can be very varied, so we will try to aim at the obvious and potentially life-threatening injuries.

THE SCOPE OF FIRST AID

This consists of four parts:

1. Assessing the situation.

2. Diagnosing what is wrong.

3. Giving immediate and appropriate treatment.

4. Disposing of the casualty to a doctor, hospital or home, according to the seriousness of the situation.

In the attack scenario, from my experience the most common injuries are unconsciousness, face and head wounds and stab wounds to the body.

Unconscious casualty

If the casualty is unconscious, the task of ascertaining his/her injuries is a difficult one because you cannot ask the person where they hurt (well you can, but they are unlikely to answer!). So, a thorough detailed examination of the person is necessary. Note if breathing is present. If absent, immediately commence artificial respiration. Examine over and under the casualty for dampness which might indicate bleeding or incontinence. Stop any serious bleeding before proceeding further with the examination. Bear in mind the possibilities of internal bleeding. Once everything is in order, place the casualty in the recovery position.

The recovery position

If the casualty is lying on his/her back:

1) Kneel beside him/her and place both arms close to the body. Cross the far leg over the near leg. Protect the face with one of your hands. Gently turn the casualty onto their side. This may be done by grasping the casualty's attire at the hip.

2) Draw up the upper arm until it makes a right angle to the body and bend at the elbow.

3) Draw up the upper leg until the thigh makes a right angle to the body and bend the knee.

4) Draw the underneath arm gently backward to extend it slightly behind the back.

5) Bend the undermost knee slightly. The reason for the limbs being placed in this manner is that it provides the necessary stability to keep the casualty comfortable in the recovery position, and stop the casualty from rolling onto his or her back, where there is a danger of choking. If the casualty is very heavy, two hands should be used to grip the clothing. In this instance, you should kneel at the side of the casualty so that when he/she is turned, the face will rest against your knees.

   If bystanders are present, get them to help with the turning. Gently tilt the casualty's head slightly back so as to ensure an open airway.

Artificial respiration

There are many methods of artificial respiration. The most effective is mouth to mouth (mouth to nose), and this method can be used by almost all age groups and in almost all circumstances except when there is severe injury to the face and mouth or when the casualty is vomiting.

1. Ensure the casualty has a good airway by tilting back the head. Support the back of the neck and press the top of the head so that it is tilted backward, simultaneously pressing the chin upward. This will extend the head/neck and lift the tongue forward clear of the airway. This is particularly vital if the casualty is on his/her back, because the tongue may fall to the back of the throat and cause the tongue to be swallowed.

2. Loosen the casualty's clothing at the neck and waist. If the casualty is not breathing, keep the head tilted backward and begin mouth to mouth (mouth to nose) breathing.

3. Open you mouth wide and take a deep breath. Pinch the casualty's nose together using your thumb and forefinger. Seal your lips around the casualty's mouth. Blow into the lungs until the chest rises then remove your mouth and watch the chest fall. Continue these inflations at the natural rate of breathing. Continue until the casualty begins breathing on their own.

   If you can't make a seal around the casualty's mouth, you may try mouth to nose. You may wish to place a handkerchief over the casualty's mouth for hygiene reasons. If the casualty's heart is not beating and his/her colour becomes blue/grey, the pupils are widely dilated and you cannot feel a pulse, put the casualty on their back on a flat surface and strike the chest sharply on the lower part of the breastbone with the edge of the hand. Hopefully this will restart the heart. If not, start external heart compressions whilst at the same time continuing to give artificial respiration.

1) Take up position at the side of the casualty.

2) Find the lower half of the breastbone.

3) Place the heel of your hand on this part of the bone, keeping the palm and the fingers off the chest.

4) Cover this hand with the heel of the other.

5) With the arms straight, rock forward pressing down on the lower half of the

breastbone (about one to one and a half inches in). Adult casualty – repeat the pressure once per second. Make sure the pressure you push with is controlled, as too much pressure may cause damage to the casualty's ribs or internal organs.

6) Check your effectiveness by watching for an improvement in the casualty's colour, noticing the size of the pupils (which should become smaller with effective treatment) and feeling for a progressively stronger pulse.

7) In extreme cases, this method should be continued until help arrives. The rate of lung inflation (mouth to mouth) and heart compressions should be fifteen heart compressions followed by two quick lung inflations, and then repeat until the casualty's heart and breath return or help arrives.

Stab wounds

Potentially a fatal place to be stabbed, a wound in the chest may well allow direct access of air into the chest cavity. When the victim breathes in, the noise of air may be heard. On breathing out, blood or blood-stained bubbles may be expelled from the wound. If the lung is injured, the casualty may also cough up frothy bright red blood. The immediate aim is to seal up the wound and stop air entering the chest cavity. Until a dressing can be applied, place the palm of the hand firmly over the wound, lay the casualty down with head and shoulders raised and the body inclined toward the injured side. If there is first aid equipment available, plug the wound lightly with a dressing, then cover the dressing with a thick layer of cotton wool. Keep it in place by strapping or a bandage. Get hospital help urgently.

Wounds to the stomach (abdominal wall). Place the casualty so that the wound does not gape, preferably on his back with head and shoulders raised and supported with a pillow under his knees. If there are no internal organs protruding, apply a dressing to the wound (if one is available), and bandage it firmly into position. If internal organs are protruding, cover them lightly with a soft, clean towel or a large gauze dressing, secure without undue pressure. If the casualty is coughing or vomiting, be sure to support the abdomen.

Generally speaking, with profuse bleeding from miscellaneous body parts, apply firm pressure with a towel or gauze and try to elevate the body part that is bleeding – leg, arm, etc. – and keep the pressure fixed until the bleeding stops or professional help arrives. If the bleeding cannot be controlled by the application of pressure on the wound, or when it is impossible to apply direct pressure, it is sometimes possible to apply indirect pressure at the appropriate pressure point between the heart and the wound.

A pressure point is where an important artery can be compressed against an underlying bone to prevent the flow of blood beyond that point. Such pressure may be applied while dressing, pad and bandage are being prepared for application, but not for longer than 15 minutes at a time.

Brachial pressure point

The brachial artery runs along the inner side of the muscle of the upper arm, its course being roughly indicated by the inner seam of a coat sleeve. To apply pressure, pass your fingers under the casualty's upper arm and compress the artery against the bone.

Femoral pressure point

The femoral artery passes into the lower limb at a point corresponding to the fold of the groin. To apply pressure behind the casualty's knee, grasp his thigh with both hands and press directly and firmly downward in the centre of the groin with both thumbs, one on top of the other against the brim of the pelvis.

Bleeding from the nose

Sit the casualty down with the head slightly forward and tell him or her to breath through the mouth. Pinch the soft part of the nose firmly for about 8-10 minutes. Loosen clothing about the neck and chest and warn against trying to blow the nose.

All the former treatments you may easily apply to yourself as well as any other casualty occurring from the attack by following the instructions laid out. In serious cases, or if in doubt, always get hospital treatment.

Chapter Twenty-four

Self-Defence and the Law

- THE SECOND ENEMY -

Before I delve into the histrionics of the law and how you the victim stand within it, I must say this. As important as the law may be, you would be foolish to contemplate legal implications when an assault on your person is imminent. To think of such things will cause indecision, which begets defeat. One second of indecision can mean the difference between defending yourself successfully and getting battered, raped, robbed or murdered.

I call the law the second enemy: this is not meant to be derogatory to the police. I am very pro-police, and believe that on the whole they do a very good job, though often thankless. Having been on the wrong side of the law a few times in my capacity as a nightclub doorman, I feel it my duty to warn you of the inherent dangers of dealing with what can be a sticky judicial system, post assault.

Many people are convicted not for what they have done but for what they have said. You are judged on your statement as opposed to the incident itself. So, what does this mean in English? Basically you could defend yourself within the law and yet still be convicted and sent to jail because you did not quote the law correctly when giving a statement. Many of my friends have been sent to jail because they did not understand the law. So if self-defence is your aim and you are serious about it then you had better get to grips with the law that governs your land. I'd rather be punched in the eye by a mugger than shafted by an antiquated and often unsympathetic judicial system. Know the law, know your rights and get a good understanding of how you are going to stand after the fact.

What is not commonly known is that, post-assault, you probably will be suffering from adrenal-induced tachypsychia. This causes time distortion, memory loss and memory distortion, and many other side effects of the adrenal syndrome that can affect your ability to make an accurate statement if the police become involved. When you make a statement to the police it is hardly likely to be accurate taking these things into account. Six months down the line when you turn up in court to defend your actions, everything will hang upon that statement, even though your head might have been out there with Pluto when you wrote it. Next thing you know you are being convicted for what you have said and not for what you have done.

So when you make the statement make sure that you are clear about how you stand in the law and what you can and cannot say. If you cannot think clearly, insist on waiting until the next day before making a statement. If you are not sure of how you stand within the law then insist on a duty solicitor to give you advice. Don't put pen to paper until you feel right. A police cell can be a very lonely and intimidating place when you do not understand the law, and the police can often be guilty of rushing, even pressuring you for a quick statement. This pressure can be very subtle and effective: being left alone for long periods of time, being told that you might be looking at prison if you do not cooperate, 'good cop-bad cop' (yes, they really do try that old trick). Many a tough guy has come out of the police cells with tears in his eyes and a written testimony saying that he did things he did not do because he 'just wanted to go home'.

Part of learning self-defence entails gaining an understanding of the law, because if you defend yourself successfully and eclipse the attacker you will have to answer to a higher authority. 'Better to be judged by twelve, than carried by six'.

The law is even negligent of its own officers:

'Police watchdogs are demanding a hard-line court crackdown on drunken street yobs behind the rising tide of attacks on beat bobbies.

'They want an end to so-called plea bargaining between lawyers, which leads to thugs facing 'watered down' charges.

'The plea for action from Warwickshire police authority is a direct reaction to the 50 percent surge in the number of attacks on officers last year.

'A total of 377 days were lost through sickness as 169 male, 26 female and 16 special police officers reported too badly hurt to work.

'Chief Constable Peter Joslin admitted officers were left frustrated and annoyed when cases of assault against them were dropped in exchange for guilty pleas to other more or less serious charges.

'He said: "Most of the attacks are alcohol related. Only last weekend an officer was assaulted twice in one night, once with a billiard ball in a sock.

"'We are seen more and more as fair game, but it is as much a problem with society as anything else."'

Coventry Evening Telegraph, January 13, 1995

For your information here a few things it might help to know about the law and how you stand within.

When asked what advice he would give to women who were worried about being arrested for hurting a man who was attacking them, George Boyle, Superintendent with the Metropolitan Police for thirty five years before his retirement, said, 'Don't even consider it [the law]. Defend yourself if you are being attacked. Women should always fight back and defend themselves. If they scream they should scream the word 'Rape!' It is more likely to attract attention and make people react. A woman under attack should not swear abusively as people in hearing range might think that they are just another pair of roughnecks who have been drinking too much.'

Talk to any policeman or read any text on law, and from the myriad paragraphs and sub-paragraphs swims, again and again, one word: 'reasonable'. An assault upon a person who is attacking or even about to attack you must show 'reasonable' force if it is to be deemed lawful. The dictionary definition of reasonable is, 'In accordance with reason. Not extreme or excessive'. Section 3 of the Criminal Law Act (1967) states: 'A person may use such force as is 'reasonable' in the circumstances, in the prevention of crime.'

'A man who bit a chunk off another man's nose walked free from the crown court after a jury decided he had acted in self-defence.'
March 1993, Wakefield, West Yorkshire

In actuality, reasonable force is dictated by you, the victim. You determine what is reasonable force. If you think that only a very severe blow will stop your assailant then that is reasonable force. If you think that the attacker needs to be unconscious before you are safe then that is also reasonable force. However, if it is to be deemed as reasonable in the eyes of the law then you need to know which are the right words to say in a statement to make the judicial magic work. These words are only two in number: 'honest belief'. If you make your pre-emptive attack on your potential attacker, then you need to say that you had the honest belief that you were about to be attacked so attacked first in self-defence. If you stuck your attacker with a hatpin that force can be justified by saying that you honestly believed that any less force would have been too little and got you badly injured or maybe even killed by your assailant.

If the policeman taking the statement says of your pre-emptive attack, 'surely you can't be 100 percent sure that he was going to attack you', you might be wise to say that you were 'as sure as I can be' that he was about to attack, that's why you attacked first. If at any time you feel lost or unsure wait for official representation and demand you rights.

Even a serious wounding upon an adversary may be excusable if it is occasioned reasonable in the circumstances, and all the more justifiable in court (though not essential) if the person claiming self-defence demonstrates that at the time of the assault/attempted assault he did not want to fight. As coincidence would have it, this ties in nicely with my theories on fence work and verbal, mental disarmament, i.e. telling your antagonist that you do not want to fight in order to mentally disarm him before you strike. Even the pre-emptive strike is tolerated in law, if the person claiming self-defence can again show that he was in imminent danger of assault and so made a pre-emptive attack to stop the said assault.

This may be demonstrated in law by the person claiming self-defence telling the police or courts (if they become involved), for example, that the antagonist shouted profanities at him and then moved aggressively toward him, forcing him to attack first. Again it helps if you can demonstrate that at the time you did not want to fight. Of course, the pre-emptive strike must be justified. If your antagonist/ potential antagonist has his hands in his pockets at the time of your pre-emptive strike, your actions would, no doubt, be seen as unlawful. If you stepped forward to deliver your pre-emptive strike, it may also be construed as unlawful because you moved toward him rather than he toward you. If you knock the person to the ground using reasonable force, to all intents and purposes, a further strike to the said person would be classed as unreasonable force, and therefore as being unlawful. This also ties in nicely with my recommendation to hit and run. If you do strike when he is down then it was because he was trying to get back up and was therefore still a danger to you.

The use of incidental weapons (as detailed in chapter 4 – 'Attacking Tools') may also be excusable in the law if the former criteria of reasonable force is maintained. For example, a nine stone woman being dragged against her will into bushes by a fifteen stone man whom she stabs in the jugular with a pair of scissors, killing him, would very likely be dealt with leniently by any court in the land. It is likely, however, that she would have to demonstrate that the implied weapon was incidental, and therefore not unlawful. Attacks with such weapons as knuckledusters, flick knives and the like, even in defence, would in most cases be seen as unreasonable, and therefore unlawful.

In brief and to sum up, the defence of property or person are rights in common law (Butterworth – Police Law). Additionally, a person who acts in defence of himself, of another, or of property, is invariably acting in the prevention of crime, in which case he also has the support of the Criminal Law Act 1967, Section 3. For practical purposes, the terms of both the common law and the statutory defences are identical in their requirements.

The issue of self-defence as an excuse for a non-fatal offence against a person has been summarised extremely well by the court of appeal. The court said that it was both good law and good sense that a person who is attacked may defend himself, but that in doing so, he may only do what is reasonably necessary.

The test of whether or not the force is reasonable is an objective one, but it is assessed on the facts as the person concerned believed them to be. It is also important, but not essential, that a person claiming self-defence demonstrates that he did not want to fight.

The law on defence of property or of another, is essentially the same as in self-defence, the essential question being 'was the force used reasonable in the circumstances?' Defence of property does not entitle the owner of property to use force against persons who trespass upon his land without offering force. In such a case the trespasser must be requested to leave before there is any hostile touching. If the trespasser is 'handled' it must amount to no more that is necessary to remove him from the property. If a trespasser offers force, then it may be met by whatever force is necessary to overcome it and remove him. If the owner of the land (house) is severely attacked, even a serious wounding may be excusable if it was occasioned reasonable in the circumstances, but it is always open to the other party to allege that the degree of force was excessive.

For the avoidance of doubt, it must be stated that the mere fact that a person has used force against another was provoked to lose self-control (as opposed to acting in self-defence, etc.), is no excuse in law. Of course, if a person who has used provocative words or conduct then makes some immediately threatening move toward the person to whom his words or conduct are directed, he has carried out an assault, and reasonable resistance to it would amount to self-defence. If no more than provocation is involved, this is relevant in relation to the penalty that the court may award.

Again, I must re-emphasise that too much regard to how you stand within the law could prove detrimental. The time to think about such things is afterwards if the police become involved.

Basically, if you make a pre-emptive attack on an attacker and then make good your escape, which is what I recommend, you should be safe in the eyes of the law.

As a final note: the law differs from country to country, though most recognise the right to 'self-defence'. The foregoing chapter should be used as a rule of thumb and not as actual fact.

For more details contact your local police station.

Epilogue

In the previous chapters we have explored self-protection in its entirety. If the preventative methods herein are conscientiously adhered to, you will undoubtedly reduce not only the chances of victimisation, but also the chances of failing to defend yourself should a situation arise.

Mastery of the techniques prescribed is not necessary, though competence surely is. It is not enough to look at the pictures, read the text and expect competence to automatically come. You must practise, rehearse and act out scenarios. Do not just practise them as dance-like steps, visualise and make them real, put your mind into practice and make-believe you are there. If your chosen partners for practice are giggly and silly, lose them, get yourself partners who want to practise seriously. Make self-protection an everyday part of your life, like eating and drinking. Involve your family, children, spouse: and remember, you don't have to be a victim. Keep coded up and make attack prevention a part of your everyday life.

Appendix:
Drunken style

Maurice (Mo) Teague

As an instructor in self-protection I teach as part of the training syllabus the eight 'A's:

Avoidance
Awareness
Attitude
Anticipation
Action
Aggression
Adrenalin
Alcohol

It is the last, alcohol, which I will discuss in detail, and its relevance to personal protection. If you were to ask me what the single biggest factor in acts of violence was, my answer would be alcohol. As a drinker and a nightclub doorman, I have experience of both sides of the bar, so to speak.

People drink alcohol for many different reasons: the taste, the effect, as a crutch in difficult circumstances, peer pressure (male bonding) or for dependence, but why people drink is not as important as the effects alcohol may have. Alcohol will have an effect on us, an opponent, or both in a confrontational situation. It affects people in different ways – psychologically and physically – and at different times.

Factors
The amount and type of drink – long drinks made with mixers have a faster effect as they enter the blood stream quicker; weight; sex; age; metabolism; personality and drinking experience; social occasion, environment; interval between drinks; mood, mental state; food – absorption is accelerated on an empty stomach; but the important thing to remember is:

Fact
Any amount of alcohol will affect you quickly and wear off slowly.

Fact
Ten minutes after drinking half a pint of ordinary strength beer 50 % of the alcohol will be absorbed into the blood stream. After sixty minutes all the alcohol will have been absorbed.

APPENDIX

Fact
It is impossible to speed up alcohol elimination. A cup of coffee, nor any other method of 'sobering up' will not help. It takes time.

Psychological factor
Alcohol is a depressant.

Awareness
Alcohol affects the way the brain interprets information. For example, is that guy across the bar really staring at you, or was it an innocent, casual glance. While you may have a level of awareness, it will diminish the more you drink.

Judgement
This becomes impaired which is why so many people are genuinely remorseful and shocked at their own behaviour, after reflecting on an act of violence that was totally out of character. This is little comfort to the victim. Alcohol cannot be used as an excuse for battering some innocent to a pulp, the same as a drunk-driver cannot be excused for being the cause of a death on the road. Neither can it be used as an excuse for losing a confrontation: 'He only beat me 'cos I was drunk.' (See Anticipation)

Delusions
'It's OK, I train in [style]. I can handle those ten guys on my own, not only am I well 'ard, I can sing, dance and tell jokes,' which leads me to...

Inhibitions
'Not only am I well 'ard, I can sing, dance and tell jokes, I'm gonna stand on this table and let everyone know. Oi!' (Yes, I've done it too!).

It is obvious to people when a person is drunk by their demeanour and behaviour. By drawing attention to themselves, people can set themselves up as a potential victim. On the other hand, whilst some people become more aggressive under the influence of alcohol, there are others who become romantic, funny, melancholic, relaxed or just fall asleep!

Physical factors
Balance, timing and coordination becomes impaired; reflexes are slowed, both physically and mentally. Vision becomes blurred and sometimes tunnel vision occurs. There is a loss of accuracy and responses are slowed.

Anticipation
During my time in the army when going out in a group for a 'session' (a good drink) we used a method called Shark-Watch. One member of the group would

abstain from alcohol, stay sober and act as look-out for bombs, whilst everyone else could relax. He could also drive us home at the end of the evening!

If you're going out in a group there is usually someone who has to be up early, so employ them as Shark-Watch, not for bombs, but for potential trouble makers and also to keep the group in order.

Considerations

Despite what many people will tell you, drunks can be dangerous. They are not the staggering, sitcom fools trying to put the wrong key in the keyhole of the wrong house door; most acts of domestic violence are carried out by people under the influence of alcohol – ask any battered wife.

Alcohol can numb people to pain-inducing techniques such as locks, holds, restraints and pressure points, thereby rendering the techniques useless.

Many 'fighters' (yobs) are used to fighting under the influence of alcohol and/ or drugs, and as Clint Eastwood might say, 'A man's gotta know his limitations.' It's important if you are a regular drinker that you know and understand the limitations that alcohol places on you.

Training suggestions

If you are an instructor then one idea could be to arrange a 'social' training night, whereby students bring alcoholic drinks of their choice, which are consumed and the effects gauged while training. This is not an excuse for a party, but a controlled exercise, with responsible students aged 18 or over only. Cars must be left at home and the instructor is to remain sober. It is not necessary to get drunk; it should just be to the point whereby students can gauge when they start to become adversely affected during light sparring, drills or grappling, but keep a bucket handy! If on your own, practice Kata or solo training drills.

Ironically many 'real' training classes, whilst striving to recreate as far as possible the reality of a street encounter, are held in a controlled environment with familiar style techniques against fellow students with whom they are familiar. So invite other styles to a cross-training session, exchange ideas and techniques. Introduce role playing, make it unpredictable so that not every encounter is an obvious attack. Someone may approach you on the street and genuinely want to know directions or the time!

In the class use street language and swearing, use dim or even no lighting. Prepare for 'street work' by training outdoors and grappling on concrete.

The only limit is your imagination.

Pubs/clubs

If you're having a drink, chances are you're in a pub or a club, and so we need to consider the drinking environment.

Many people usually frequent their regular pubs/clubs where they are known and they know the other regular clients and staff. People can be territorial about their 'adopted' pub or club and can resent outsiders. If you have a regional accent outside of your home town then this can be enough to draw unwanted attention to yourself. Likewise if you walk into a strange pub and it is full of surly yobs then find another pub quick.

The arena

Pubs and clubs throw together many people of different kinds of beliefs and ideas. Recently in my home town a man was beaten to death after leaving a nightclub apparently in a dispute over football. If you feel strongly about something, it may be better to be discreet at certain times in certain places.

It is unusual for people to drink on their own in pubs/clubs, so if in a confrontational situation be AWARE of the following:

- immediate, multiple attackers, i.e. the protagonists' friends.
- fringe multiple attackers, i.e. people not directly concerned but who will jump in given an opportunity, just for the hell of it.
- girlfriends and neutrals who will interfere with good intent, probably having got the wrong end of the stick about the incident. They may try to restrain you, leaving you unable to defend yourself.

Weapons

Whilst many pubs and clubs employ a search policy on the door, many do not. Concealed weapons, especially knives, must be considered especially in close confines where there is little or no room to manoeuvre. A very good friend of mine was killed with a knife in a club. It happens.

Expedient weapons

It takes no training to pick up a bottle and hit someone over the head with it and the same can be said for many incidental objects found in pubs, including glasses (see Glassing).

Ashtrays, pool and snooker cues and balls can all be used. Many 'theme' pubs have ornamental hangings on the walls and I have even seen swords and hockey sticks within easy grasp. Furniture can also be picked up and utilised. Chairs and stools can be used as clubs or even by pushing people over them.

Likewise stairs and steps, walls and pillars can be used as a cover or for slamming opponents down or into. Basically with a little knowledge and common sense anything can be used as a weapon.

Glassing

It has been estimated that there are 5,500 glassings in the UK each year. Glassings are rarely fatal although, and I draw on personal experience, it has been known.

The scars of glassing, both physical and mental, never properly heal. My theory is that the brain subconsciously 'favours' a hand holding something, and will therefore automatically respond with that hand, using a reflex action, in an encounter. This is not to say that all glassings are not deliberate.

Considerations

Lack of space to manoeuvre must be considered, due to other patrons, furniture etc. Practice training in a confined space now and again. Wing Chun techniques are ideal in close quarters. Expansive moves and kicks may not be.

On the subject of kicks – floors may be wet and slippery with spilt beers and littered with pub debris such as dropped and broken bottles and glasses. Bear this in mind if you end up on the floor – and the chances are that you will. If you end up grappling consider that most pubs and clubs become sweatboxes with people dancing in close confinement. There is every chance that an opponent will literally slip out your grabs and holds.

Toilets

Toilets are a good spot for an ambush. Most men, unlike women, don't go to the toilet in pairs, but actually it is not a bad idea. If you go on your own let your mate know, and always try to use a cubicle.

Bouncers

Do not hesitate to approach bouncers if you anticipate trouble: forewarned is forearmed. Most bouncers are very good, and many local councils require doormen to attend a training course before working.

Leaving

At the end of the night you are just as vulnerable leaving the club and making your way home. You may be on your own, your mates having left; you may be slightly or very drunk and unaware. Consider getting a taxi or a lift from outside the club (difficult, I know) to get you straight home. Try to avoid and limit your vulnerability.

Many people go for something at the end of a night. Burger bars, late night takeaways and taxi ranks become meeting points for crowds of people. Many of these may be 'frustrated' and angry perhaps at having failed to 'pull', and want to vent their frustration and anger on some innocent. Some guy will be provoked into defending his girlfriend from some insult or provocation and get a severe hiding. It happens all the time!

It's easy for me to say, but ignore them, whilst remaining alert: words are just that – words. Try and take refuge in a shop or taxi office; anyway, these focal points are generally well known by the police as trouble spots and they can react quickly if alerted to trouble...but don't count on it!

Summary

If you enjoy the occasional drink and you are serious about self-protection, or you expect your Martial arts to work for you in a self-defence situation, after a few pints it is important that you understand your limitations. Beyond this your training becomes useless. Anticipate whether you will go beyond this point and plan to safeguard yourself and your mates if and when you do. Shark-Watch.

Maurice (Mo) Teague has practised many styles for over 20 years including Judo, Shotokan JKD, Wing Chun, Kali, Thai Boxing et al. He served for many years in the army seeing active service four times. He was a Weapons and Tactics instructor and an Arrest and Restraint instructor. He has taught bodyguards, policemen, prison officers and doormen. He was also a member of the Guardian Angels for a short while. He is the founder member and Chief Instructor of Weymouth Martial arts Centre, teaching 'streetwise', a practical self-protection system. A member of the British Combat Association and a Senior Instructor on the register of Self-protection Instructors.
WMAC, 1A Governors Lane, Weymouth, Dorset, DT4 8BY.

Read on for sample extracts from Geoff Thompson's bestselling autobiography, *Watch My Back.*

Praise for *Watch My Back*:

'A brilliant insight!'
Reggie Kray

'This man is very, very hard. Buy his book if you know what's good for you.'
Maxim

'This is as real as it gets.'
Dave Courtney

'The psyche-outs, the stabbings, glassings, incidents involving the camaraderie of the door . . . Thompson's 300 fights – never losing, not once – are recorded in this excellent book.'
Loaded

'Surviving 300 bloody confrontations and earning the fearsome reputation as a knockout specialist, Thompson takes you as close to real-life street fights as you'll ever want to get.'
Bizarre Magazine

'A compelling insight.'
Arena

'Utterly compelling . . . read it.'
Men's Fitness

'Grabs you by the throat and doesn't put you down.'
Front

'. . . a stimulating read.'
Sky News

Watch My Back is available in hardback and paperback from all good bookshops, or via Geoff Thompson's own website www.geoffthompson.com, or via the Summersdale website, www.summersdale.com.

Preface (From *Watch My Back*)

. . . he'd underestimated me. I would make sure he paid for his mistake. Whenever anyone underestimates me I always know the fight is mine. Their weakness makes them unprepared and gives me a window for the first shot. I train for the first shot – it's all I need. He was still holding the bottle of champagne by the neck. I made a mental note – I didn't want to be wearing it, it just wasn't my colour. We stood close together as I talked, too close really, so I tucked my chin down as a defence against a possible head-butt, forcing me to roll my eyes upwards to see his face. I got right to the point.

'Look, I've never met you before and you come into my club when I'm working and talk to me like I'm a piece of shit. If you do it again we're gonna be fighting.'

He was square on and badly positioned to launch an attack.

'Oh yeah,' he said, lining me up. 'Sure.'

He moved his left leg slightly back and prepared me for the champagne supernova. But he was a fucking amateur and hid his line-up badly. I noticed immediately, it stood out like a hard-on. It might have worked on the part-timers, the lads that liked a fight at the weekend, but I was a veteran in these matters: seven days a week, it was my job to notice when maniacs were trying to hit me with a bottle. I had maybe two seconds in which to make my move before he made his. No decisions to be made, too late for that. Hesitation is the biggest killer in nightclub fighting. The decision had been made for me ten minutes earlier when he told me that I sucked cocks, it was just a matter of putting my game plan into action. Not too detailed a plan, no complications, no equations, no grapple with morality or peer pressure, just bang him. That's it. All this bollocks about karate or kung-fu, about this range or that range, bridging the gap, setting up, weakening them with a kick – there's no need, just hit the fuckers . . . very hard! Time was tight and a single mistake could mean drip-food or worse. I played the game right back and simultaneously moved my right leg, giving myself a small, compact forty-five degree stance, hiding the movement with,

'That's all I'm saying.'

Bang!

A right cross, slightly hooked, hit just above his jawbone as his left hand lifted the champagne bottle towards me. The contact was high so he didn't go right out. Sometimes that's how it works, when the adrenalin is racing, targeting is often off, and you only have to be millimetres out to miss the KO. It did catch him hard though; he reeled back like he'd been run over. His body hit a forty-five degree angle going backwards and for a second I thought he was in sleepsville, but no, he back-peddled rapidly, trying to regain his composure. He was a hardy fucker. Usually when you hit them that hard they have themselves a little hibernation. Not this fella. He tried to stay up and fight but it was too late, he was mine. Like I said, I only need one shot.

I followed with a rapid-fire five-punch combination, slicing open both eyebrows and breaking his nose. Oozes of blood flicked through the air and splattered my white shirt. And me with no condom, too. He covered his bloodied face trying to capture what was left of his nose. As he cowered over I grabbed his white, stained shirt by the shoulders and pulled him face first into the carpet – he was gone. His sugar pedestal melted all around him by the rain of my attack. He kept his face covered, so I axe-kicked his back, many times. Too many. He was a big man to take over, but I had no intentions of letting him back up again, not this night. Kevin, who had been close by watching my back, stepped in and stopped me.

A small crowd of onlookers had gathered. They whispered excitedly. I liked this bit, especially at a new club. Suddenly I was not the soft 'what's he doing here' doorman they all mistook me for. I was a man to be feared. I felt good about the adulation, the back-pats and the line of free Buds on the bar like winner cups. I felt good as the endorphins raced around my blood in a celebratory lap of honour. I felt good that I had survived. The blood on my shirt was my badge; I was proud to wear it for the rest of the night. Deep down though, right in the very bowels of my mind, there was an aching realisation that with every blow I threw in anger and fear I was becoming more and more like the bastard on the floor in front of me swimming in his own blood and snot.

Mr T's girlfriend was running around him like a headless chicken. Collecting her man's blood and what was left of his face in a small cotton hanky that seemed inadequate amidst such mayhem, screaming at me, shouting at the other doorman, wailing for an ambulance and the police: it was all so undignified. I didn't give a monkey's fuck. I was on a high. The worm had turned – control of my fear was my greatest ally, his overconfidence my greatest asset. He'd trodden on a small, insignificant mound of earth and was blown to pieces. It was a fucking landmine. He should have known.

Later, many years on, I shared a beer with the guy. He still had the scars to prove I'd been there and we laughed about our first meeting. He admitted it was his fault and as the second beer passed his tonsils he said, 'I just picked on the wrong guy, that's all'.

Chapter 9 – It's a Knockout
(From *Watch My Back*)

So I was hardening up a little. All the exposure I was getting to violence, dealing with the police and having to face monsters as a way of life was starting to have its effect. At the time I felt good about it. I had learned, mostly through the tuition of John, how to adapt the physical skills of karate so that they worked in the pavement arena. I was no longer scared and could handle just about any situation that came into my life, something I had always struggled to do before the door. I was even starting to take control of situations that, in the beginning, I was happy to let John or the other lads deal with. I had gone from need to being needed. I felt good about the fact that not only was I controlling and looking after myself, but I could also – when needed – control, and look after others. That's the main reason doormen exist, so that they can look after the customers, the property, and not forgetting the staff of course. On one particular occasion it was the cloakroom girl that I came to the aid of.

'What's the problem lads?' My question was direct and hard.

'She won't fucking give us our coats, I've pointed them out to her. They're there, look, there.'

He pointed at two jackets in the middle of a hundred more hanging from coat racks in the tiny cloakroom in the tight reception area of the nightclub. I looked at the girl. Blonde and gorgeous but thicker than a whale omelette.

'They haven't got a ticket, Geoff.' Her voice was scared and I gave her a wink to let her know that I would deal with it. That was my game, what I was paid to do. I felt the ever-so-familiar tingle of adrenalin as it got in place for fight or flight, only in this game there was no flight, you either stayed or you didn't work. Runners got blackballed from every club in the city the very first time they listened to natural instinct and broke the minute mile. Bottling it even once could be a career-ending event, it also crushed hard-earned kudos and self-belief flatter than a shadow; it did for your confidence and reputation what syphilis does for your social standing. They say that you are only as good as your last fight and it's true; you could be the bravest man on earth a hundred times and become a coward by bottling it once. Not fair, methinks, but that, as you might say, is life.

This particular night had been a little slow. I'd just come back from the toilet, where the big nobs hang out, to find these two guys arguing with the cloakroom girl. I have to say that she was a nice little thing, though a bit thick; thought fellatio was an Italian opera, you know the type. The guys arguing with her were in their mid-twenties, scruffy looking, hard-eyed men with barbed attitudes and scowls. They'd come to pick up their jackets from the cloakroom but unfortunately they had both lost their tickets. They couldn't prove that they'd placed jackets in the care of the club. The girl explained that they'd have to wait until the end of the night if they couldn't produce a ticket. That's the club rules, it was nothing personal. The lads were not happy and told the lovely lady that she was 'fucking useless' and intimated that she might get a slap if they didn't get their coats. This is where I came in.

I splayed my arms in front, blocking the gap between the two men and me. This was my fence. Verbal dissuasion – the 'interview' started.

'Lads, you know the crack. You need a ticket. No ticket, no jacket.'

'Yeah, I know, but look,' he pointed at the jackets again, scruffy looking cleaning-chamois leathers, 'they're there.'

'So give me your tickets and you can take them.'

'She fucking told you, didn't she? We've lost the tickets.' He raised

240

his voice challengingly, and moved towards me as he spoke. He was testing me out. It had worked with the young girl, now he was trying it with me. This was a subliminal challenge. As he moved towards me I stopped him with my lead hand fence. I was controlling the play. I picked up the aggression to meet the challenge. It was a game and I was used to playing it.

'Yeah, and she also told you that you don't get the fucking jackets without the fucking tickets. All right?' I deliberately included expletives to raise the play and speak the speak. I stared both of them down as I said it. The bird with the mouth became submissive, my aggression had out-leagued him.

'Come on man, just let us have the jackets. They're ours, honestly.'

I'll be honest, I didn't like the guys – they were big-mouthed bullies. If I hadn't arrived when I did they'd have already taken the jackets and hurt the girl if she'd stepped in their way, I was in no mood to do them any favours.

'No. You'll have to either wait till the end of the night or leave the club and come back for them later.'

They looked at each other hesitantly. Should they go for it or not? They stormed out of the nightclub mumbling something about coming back. The little girl in the cloakroom smiled, I was her hero, I smiled back. To be honest, I never really thought any more about the incident until about 2.30 in the morning when the guys returned. Everyone else had gone home bar John, Simon (the manager) and me.

'What are these two after?' Simon asked, looking at the CCTV screen in the corner of his small, cluttered office. Two men were walking menacingly towards the doors of the club.

'Probably after their jackets, I wouldn't give 'em them earlier because they didn't have a ticket.'

John drew on his cigarette.

'They don't look too happy Geoff.' There was no emotion in his voice.

'Well,' I continued, 'they had a go at the cloakroom girl earlier and they weren't happy when I wouldn't give them their coats.'

The doors to the club banged violently. We watched the lads, on screen, as they kicked and punched the doors. They were unaware that we could see them. At the time the cameras were a secret known only to the club staff.

'Looks like they want some!' John commented.

'Yeah, I think you're right,' I replied, still watching them on screen. A burst of adrenalin hit my belly and ran through my veins. I sniffed heavily, as though I had a cold, to hide the natural inhalation that comes with fight or flight. My legs began their pre-fight shake. I tapped my foot to the sound of an imaginary beat to hide it.

'Well they've certainly come to the right place,' added the manager with a grin. He was our biggest fan. We liked him too. He had stuck with us through thick and thin over the years and had lied to the police, on our account, enough times to warrant an honours degree in perjury.

John and I walked out of the office to the entrance doors. A violent encounter awaited us. It felt no different than going into a sparring session with your mates at the gym. But that was only because our training sessions were more brutal than the real thing – well, we wanted to get it right, no sense in taking the word of some ancient whose last fight, honourable as it might have been, was against a samurai on horseback. The enemy had changed; the environment had changed too, so logically the 'arts' had to change with them. Only, when you try and tell many of today's traditionalists this, they don't hear you because they've got their sycophantic heads stuck up the arse of some Eastern master.

John opened the front doors of the club, the sound of the metal locks echoing into the night. He stood in the doorway, filling the space ominously. He stared at the two men. That should have been enough really, they should have read the 'don't fuck' sign emblazoned across his face like a Christmas banner but they were blind to what was patently obvious to us: they were way out of their league.

'Wot d'ya want?' John was blunt. He frit the shit out of me and I knew him. Someone once said to me, 'What do you reckon you could do against a man like John Anderson, Geoff?' 'Oh' I replied, 'about sixty mile an hour!'

The smaller one got straight to the point. He'd had a long night, he was pissed up and pissed off. He obviously hadn't done his homework on street speak, he didn't know that he was already in quicksand up to his scrawny little neck, otherwise he would have shut his big mouth and called a taxi. 'We've come for our fucking jackets,' said Number One.

'Yeah,' Number Two echoed like a parrot, 'you're fucking out of order.'

I popped my head out of the door over John's shoulder. As soon as they saw me they lit up like luminous nodders, which was appropriate because they were a pair of nobs.

'Yeah, he's the one, he's the wanker that wouldn't give us them earlier on. Out of order.' He stabbed the air aggressively with his finger.

Wanker? Me?

'You didn't get the coats earlier on because you didn't have the tickets and if you don't watch your mouth you won't fucking get them now. All right?'

John grabbed the coats from the cloakroom and held them at arm's length out of the door. As the lads went to take them off him, sure that they had already won because they were getting what they'd come for, he dropped them on the floor at their feet. Grudgingly, amidst a few inaudible mumbles they picked the coats up and dusted them down, like they were polishing a turd. As they walked away, slipping their arms into the leathers, Number One said, hammering the nails into his own coffin,

'We'll be back for you two. You've got a big problem.'

As one, John and myself stepped out of the door towards them.

'Don't bother coming back, do it now!' I challenged.

'Yeah! Yeah! Why not? Lets do it!' Number One said, accepting the challenge. His chest heaved and his arms splayed, his speak became fast and erratic – he was ready to go. Number Two's face dropped like a bollock, his chin nearly hit the floor. He looked at his mate, 'Shouldn't we have talked about this?' he seemed to be saying. He was obviously in no hurry to get his face punched in. He put on his best pleading look, raised his arms submissively and retreated away from us quicker than a video rewind.

It was nearly 3.00 a.m., pitch-black but for the fluorescent lights at the entrance of the club that lit our arena. The air was thick with quiet, less the galloping hearts and frightened bowel movements of our opponents. The manager stood at the doorway, a pugilistic timekeeper about to witness the mismatch of the century. He shook his head knowingly as John and I squared up for the match fight with the two unhappy campers. He had seen John and myself in action more times than he cared to remember and felt sorry for the lads in front of us, one of whom foolishly thought he was in with a fighting chance. He had more chance of getting an elephant through a cat flap.

I must admit, though, that he did have me a little worried – I was scared I might kill him.

John raised his guard like a boxer, mine was at half mast like a karateka. My man raised his own guard high and ready, covering his face in an amateurish boxing guard, heavily exposing his midriff. His stance was short and off balance. His ribs looked mighty suspect.

Adrenal deafness clicked in and tunnel vision locked onto my opponent as he moved in a circle, to my left and around me.

John's opponent took one look at him and lost the fight in Birmingham. He said,

'You're a boxer, aren't you? Fuck that. I don't want to fight you.'

I started to move in for the kill.

Many people lose the fight before it even begins, in Birmingham, as I'm fond of saying, because they mistake the natural feelings associated with combat for sheer terror and allow their inner opponent the run of their head. There is a story of a wonderful old wrestler from London called Bert Asarati. In his day he was a monster of a wrestler with a fearsome reputation for hurting his opponents, even when it was a show match. He was seventeen stone at only five-foot-six and a fearsome fighter. Another wrestler of repute was travelling down by train from Glasgow to fight Mr Asarati in a London arena. All the way down on the train journey the Glaswegian ring fighter kept thinking about the arduous task that lay ahead, and every time the train stopped at a station his inner opponent would tempt him to get off the train and go back to Glasgow. Every time he thought about the forthcoming battle with Mr Asarati, his adrenalin went into overdrive. He was more scared than he could ever remember being. His fear ran riot and started to cause massive self doubt, he began to wonder whether he was even fit to be in the same ring as the great man. Every time the train stopped at a station the self-doubt grew, propagated by his inner opponent who kept telling him to get off the train and go back to Glasgow. At every station the inner opponent got louder and the adrenalin stronger. The wrestler's bottle gradually slipped out of his grasp until, in the end, he could take no more. At Birmingham station he got off and caught the next available train back to Glasgow. He sent a note to Bert Asarati, which read, 'Gone back to Glasgow, you beat me in Birmingham.' His inner opponent had beaten him a hundred miles before he even got to the fight venue.

This is what often happens to people in street situations. This is what happened to John's opponent on this night. He didn't lose the fight to John; he lost it to himself. John, not one to hit a man that didn't want to fight, let him off.

I buried a low roundhouse kick, as an opener to see what my opponent had got, into his ribs. As I had surmised, they were indeed suspect. He doubled over in pain and I swept his feet from under him. He lay on the floor like an upturned turtle. I didn't have the heart to go in for the finish, he was no match at all so I let him back up again and played for a while, shooting kicks to his head – something I would not have tried had the man been a threat. Every time he got back up I swept him back again.

In the end I felt sorry for him and told him to 'fuck off home' before I really did hurt him. He got angry and ran at me, arms flailing. I dropped him with a low sidekick in the belly and followed with a heavy punch to his jaw.

Bang!

He hit the deck heavily and I heard the familiar sickly crack of bone on pavement. He lay before me like an unconscious thing. I wondered whether he was badly hurt. For a second he looked all right, then, to my horror, a huge pool of blood appeared like a purple lake around his head. I thought I'd killed him. The pool got bigger and darker by the second. His face was deathly pale.

He didn't wake.

I felt panic in the pit of my stomach. My life passed before me. John walked over and looked down at the bloodied heap.

'Good punch,' he said, as though I'd just performed a nice technique on the bag in the gym.

I felt terrible. He looked dead and the blood intimated that perhaps I had cracked his skull. I waited for the brains to seep through with the blood, then realised that the guy probably didn't have any. His mate looked on, shaking his head.

'Is he dead?' he asked, adding to my misery. At the word 'dead' my stomach exploded. The adrenalin of aftermath shot through me, I couldn't stay any longer. Thinking that I had killed him was killing me so I wandered back into the club to grab a drink and a bit of calm. This was my worst KO on the door thus far and it scared the shit out of me. At the bar I trembled with fear. I made a promise to God that I would never hit anyone again if only he would let this one live, a promise I made every time some unfortunate with an eye for my title hit the deck, and broke every time they recovered.

Erasmus (no, he didn't work at Buster's) said that 'war is delightful to those who have had no experience of it'. He was right; fighting doesn't look so nice when it's basted in blood.

Outside, John lifted the unconscious man's head out of the blood with his foot to see the extent of the damage. Blood was still pouring out, leaving an explosion transfer across the whole of one paving slab.

'Is he dead?' his mate asked again, almost as though he wanted him to be – something to talk about on a Sunday afternoon in the pub. John gave him one of those looks and he shut his mouth.

Inside the club, already contemplating the big house and life in a cell with a right forearm like Popeye – or a very close cell mate – I made my way to the manager's office and watched the fight on the CCTV recording, just to see how bad I would look should the police get their hands on the tape. My shaky hand pressed Play and I watched the silent re-run on the small screen. It looked bad enough, though it lacked the sounds and smells of what had just occurred. I'm ashamed to say that I almost admired the action as I watched myself battering this non-entity, even using the 'slow mo' to highlight the meaty parts and check out my fighting technique. Sadly I, like most, had become desensitised to screen scraps from a lifetime of watching empty vignettes of violence crafted by screen technicians to stir inspiration. It makes me smile when I see how great directors creatively weave the sow's ear of real violence into the silk purse of celluloid. It would seem that the hypocrisy of people knows no bounds. Millions who abhor brutality, flock to view justified killings and glorious Oscar winning deaths, enacted by handsome thespians with carved features and rehearsed pros. The wowed, entranced audience visualise their finger on the killing trigger.

Someone once said that if they could put smell into cinema every war film ever made would flop at the box office. They were right. The recording did little more in replay than make me smile at how easy it all looked.

I was sickened, and at once enthralled, by what I saw. I quickly rewound the video and scrubbed the tape, then rewound it again and gave it a second scrub, just to be sure. In court, tackle like that could hang a fella. Back up to the bar in the empty club, I helped myself to another drink.

I felt sick with worry. I felt confused by the feelings that ran through my body. I was scared by what I had done and yet, in part, I felt exhilarated by the victory. It was probably due to the fact that, after adversity, the body releases endorphins, a natural morphine, into the blood. These give you a pick-up, a natural high, I guess that's where the confusion begins. Happy and sad at the same time; what a paradox. Years later, after many more KOs, sleepless nights and talks with God, I would develop a tighter control over this panic and learn better to live with fear. For now, I had to contend with the ignorance that came with still being new to it all.

Back outside, my unconscious opponent finally came round, his head in a blood-pillow. He looked like he'd been machine-gunned.

'We thought you were a goner,' his mate smiled.

John shot him another angry glance.

'Well I did.'

John looked on the floor at the three broken teeth lying forlorn on the concrete. They looked a little bizarre without the attachment of gums. He'd obviously landed on his face when he fell; that's where all the blood came from. He followed John's glance to the floor and his eyes squinted as though struggling to focus on the fact that he was looking at his own teeth. It was the first time he had ever seen them out of a mirror. He quickly felt his mouth and the numb, bloodied gap where the same teeth used to reside.

'Your mate's knocked my teeth out,' he said.

'There's no hiding anything from you is there, you fucking genius?'

John found me at the bar looking pale and very worried. I was still thinking about prison and wondering whether this job was really for me. I didn't like the feeling of losing my liberty to a wanker like the one outside collecting his teeth for the tooth fairy. The picture of unconsciousness and a blood splattered pavement stuck in my head like a freeze frame. In that moment of wonderment, Napoleon Bonaparte came to mind – doesn't Napoleon always do that to ya? – when he said (not to me personally of course, the man's been dead for ages) that 'there is nothing like the sight of a battlefield after the fight to inspire princes with a love of peace and a horror of war'. I had just seen the battlefield and felt that inspiration. Unfortunately I was to experience it a lot more, and far worse than this, before I learned the lesson and dumped the door in a transitional leap for a better, less violent existence.

John broke my daydream and ended my agony.

'Don't worry, he's all right, you just knocked his teeth out. Nothing bad.'

A sigh of relief raced through my body, a Death Row reprieve.

'Thank fuck for that!'

I was thanking fuck when I should have been thanking God; sadly, I'm ashamed to say, he had already been forgotten.

'Don't get too complacent, though, Geoff. He's a wanker, he'll go to the police. I know the type.'

'That's OK,' I thought. 'I can live with that. As long as he isn't brown bread.'

We were pretty sure that the police would get involved because it was an 18, a wounding. Broken bones and blood meant a probable charge of GBH with intent, which carries a possible five years in prison. So, as always, me John and Simon got our stories sorted out ready, just in case. The video had already been doctored, twice, so that wasn't a problem either. Simon agreed to say that he had switched the video off at 2.30 a.m. John and I agreed to say that the men did turn up at 2.45

a.m. and that we gave them their coats and sent them on their jolly way. A bit belligerent, but unhurt.

John was right. Within two days of the incident we'd had a visit from plod and were both taken in for a statement. As planned, we recited to our stories like lines from a bad play. 'No. I didn't hit the man, officer. That would be breaking the law. Must have fallen down the stairs' – that sort of scenario. And why not? The police are always covering themselves with accidents and stairs, even when they happen to reside in a station that has no stairs.

'He fell down the stairs m'Lud!'

'What, ten times, officer?'

This was one of the things we always did at Buster's, and did it well; whenever there was an altercation that we thought might attract attention from plod we would immediately work out our story so that, if we were arrested, there would be no confusion or contradiction. Our aim was to get the charges thrown out at station level, if not, next best was to get it thrown out by the CPS (Crown Prosecution Service). If the evidence was 50/50 the CPS had a habit of not proceeding with charges because it would be a waste of taxpayers' money, dragging a case through the courts when there was little chance of a conviction or prosecution. Why waste it on us when they could waste it on so many other things? It was a system that always worked well for us.

Sometimes we would have to tailor our stories so that they fitted a law that is unkind to those whose job it was to stop others from breaking it.

'John, my good man, the story is a little fat and won't fit into this blasted law thing. What I propose we do, me fella, is slim the blighter down with a diet of half truths so that it does fit!'

Genghis Khan said that the British were uncivilised because the law of the land did not protect the people. We made it protect us by lying; it was either that or become a victim of its often archaic precept.

We always kept the story simple, leaving very little to remember.

We never allowed the police, the little devils, to draw anything from us that we didn't want to say. They play the game very deviously, as John and I were about to find out.

As luck would have it, 'Broken Teeth' was hated by plod because he had previous convictions for police assault; they had no intention of doing him any favours. In the old days the lad would definitely have been exposed to the 'accident with stairs' scenario that was almost the perfunctory penalty for 'beating copper', but with things the way they were at that time this was no longer an option, not if an officer valued his pension and wanted to remain in employment.

Robin Williams said that in New York a policeman will shout to a robber, 'Stop or I'll blow your fucking head off!' In Britain, a bobby is more likely to shout, 'Stop . . . or I'll be forced to shout STOP again!'

Thankfully this disease had not yet spread to the door – though it won't be long I think – you hit a doorman and, if the team is worth its salt, you'll pay in blood. That's the unwritten law.

In the interview room the atmosphere was tense, and I practised the 'duck syndrome' to hide the fact that I was experiencing adrenalin. If the plain clothes DC interviewing me could see my fear, she might rightly assume that I was lying through my teeth. I was, of course. I had become a master of the lie.

Let the games begin!

'This guy was a bit of a wanker, wasn't he, Geoff?' WDC was trying to get into my confidence. I wished she was trying to get into my pants – she was gorgeous.

'Absolutely.' I knew the game, I'd played it with better players too, though none so delicious as this one.

'That's why you gave him some pain?'

'Pain? I don't remember giving him any of that.' I was convincing, even I believed me.

'I told you already, Jane,' (we were on first name terms but only because she wanted to hang me), 'I didn't touch him. I had no reason to. He was just a mouthy youth with a fetish for abuse. Nothing more. Probably got dropped by someone less tolerant than me on his way home.'

'Yeah I know, you said. But we both know that you did it. And I don't blame you. He's a pleb, a lemon. Deserved all the pain that you gave him. Off the record Geoff, why did you hit him?'

Ah, the old 'off the record hook', the old 'we don't blame you' trick, the 'let's pretend that we're on his side and then fuck him' ploy. It'll be flattery next, mark my words. I wondered if I might get a cup of coffee and a date out of this?

'Any chance of a cup of coffee, Jane?'

Worth a try.

'Yeah, sure. I'll just fetch one. White with sugar?'

'Thanks.'

Yippee! One down. The coffee was machine-made but welcome. Actually it could have been soup, you can never tell, can you? I thanked her effusively.

'So. You were going to tell me why you hit him.'

I was?

'I just told you, Jane, I didn't hit him.' I was going to tell her that he looked better without teeth but thought better of it.

'You're a bit of a karate man, aren't you Geoff? Was it a karate kick that you hit him with?'

Yawn – flattery! I tried not to smile but I couldn't help myself, a small grin formed on my lips. I felt a belly chuckle rousing down below but held onto it for dear life. This was a serious business.

'I never laid a glove on the guy.'

'Geoff, we know what happened, your mate's already told us. This is off the record. I'm just interested in what happened out there.'

Jane was a beautiful woman, a cracker. I fell in love instantly. She was tall, curvaceous, with dark brown hair and a figure to die for. I liked her a lot. She looked tough in a womanly kind of way, and I couldn't help examining the curves so delicately pronounced through her dark blue skirt and white nylon blouse. There was a faint hint of nipple peeping through, it wasn't cold so I pretentiously surmised that it must have been me. I'd heard of this DC before and by all accounts she was a good girl with loads of bottle. Apparently she could have a fight as well. I liked that in a woman.

As we sat in the tiny interview room at the police station Jane gently questioned me about my statement, trying to trick and trip me. I did my best to answer her as untruthfully as I could. That wasn't too hard.

John wasn't so lucky, all he got was a bald beat cop with a bad attitude and halitosis – his breath could strip paint. His head shone like a polished apple and hair hung out of his nose like spiders' legs. He tried to talk the talk with John but he was swapping speak with the wrong guy. John told him,

'Don't waste your time.'

Damn, back to the drawing board.

As Jane walked me out of the station, after two hours of questioning, she gave it one last go, her parting shot.

'Must have been a really good kick to do that much damage, Geoff. What was it that started it all, anyway?'

I stopped and looked at her. I have to say that I was disappointed. She was insulting my intelligence. I thought she might have had a little more respect.

'What are you trying to say, Jane?' I said in a disappointed tone.

For a second she was silent.

'Nothing,' she said quietly, 'it doesn't matter.'

I made my way out of the station and home. We weren't charged. When I told John that Jane had tried to trick me he laughed his nuts off. In a way everyone was happy, except Broken Teeth who now talks with a whistle. The police were happy because a known police attacker had caught some karma and we were happy because we got away with it, once again. I did get to meet Jane later in a personal capacity: we laughed about the incident and became friends, she was a beautiful woman.